DESCRIPTIVE CATALOGUE
OF THE PHYSIOLOGICAL SERIES
IN THE HUNTERIAN MUSEUM

DESCRIPTIVE CATALOGUE
OF THE PHYSIOLOGICAL SERIES
IN THE HUNTERIAN MUSEUM OF
THE ROYAL COLLEGE OF SURGEONS
OF ENGLAND

PART II

Hunterian specimens demonstrating the
products of generation together with
surviving Hunterian specimens
from other sections

E. & S. LIVINGSTONE
EDINBURGH & LONDON
1971

ISBN 0 443 00777 2

Printed in Great Britain

Foreword

Having already contributed a foreword to the first volume it is now my privilege to record the publication of volume two, produced by the devoted interest of the Curator, Miss Dobson, after a very brief interval.

The Museum itself receives daily praise and its value to students, both junior and senior, is inestimable.

The present work serves to complete the description of all those specimens collected by John Hunter which have survived the impact of two destructive wars; this brings completion to the task, providing a complete record in place of several incomplete catalogues written by Richard Owen and others. A great advantage is the rearrangement of descriptions and the numbering of specimens in accordance with Hunter's own ideas; in this large task the general supervision and interest of Professor Gilbert Causey, the Conservator, has been ever present.

In meeting the considerable expense of publication, the Trustees have found the MacRae Webb-Johnson Fund of immense value, but in paying for more than one catalogue at the same time it has been necessary to call on the funds of the Groves Bequest; a further amount will be required later, if the present intention to publish a fifth catalogue dealing with non-Hunterian specimens is eventually produced.

The sincere thanks of the Board of Trustees are extended to Miss Dobson, who will find very great satisfaction in the completion of this task, and also to Miss Douglas who has acted as Assistant Curator and has been responsible for putting this second volume in shape for the publishers. The Board is also grateful to those of the staff who have ministered to the display and upkeep of the many specimens in the Museum.

VICTOR NEGUS
Chairman of the Board of Trustees

1971

Preface

The main part of this second volume of the Catalogue of the Physiological Series consists of descriptions of specimens demonstrating the Products of Generation and is based on the contents of Volume V of the first (and only previous) complete printed catalogue, edited by Richard Owen, published in 1840. The preparations show how the integrity of the various species is maintained: and this completes Hunter's design to illustrate the 'several links in the chain of varieties displayed in the formation of the different organs in different animals, ascending in a regular progression from the least to the most perfect' (*Phil. Trans.*, vol. 72, 1782, p. 379; and *Works*, vol. iv, p. 293). The section is complete and the arrangement is as Hunter planned it.

Many of the smaller sections here catalogued suffered damage during the war from enemy action and there are no complete series. The items are, however, of considerable interest both historically and intrinsically and as much information about them as is available has been included in the descriptions.

1971

JESSIE DOBSON
Curator

Sources and References

In addition to the volumes noted in Part I of this Catalogue, the following works have been used constantly and thoroughly:

Museum Catalogues:

Fossil Plants. 1855.
Fossil Reptiles and Fishes. 1854.
Fossil Mammals and Birds. 1845.
Human and Comparative Osteology. 1831.
Osteology of Fish, Reptiles, Birds and Mammals. 2 vols. 1853.
Osteology of Mammals. 1884.
Osteology of Birds. 1891.
Osteology of Man. 1879 and 1907.
Natural History in Spirit. 1830 and 1859.
Dried, Vascular and Miscellaneous Preparations. 1831.
Physiological Series, Volume V. 1840.
Histological Series. 2 vols. 1850 and 1855.

Manuscripts relating to the above series.

Contents

I

Products of Generation

INTRODUCTION

In this section is included the extensive collection of preparations which John Hunter designed to illustrate the 'several links in the chain of varieties displayed in the formation of the different organs in different animals, ascending in a regular progression from the least to the most perfect' (*Phil. Trans.*, 1782, vol. lxxii, p. 379).

In the early part of the Series modifications of the impregnated ovarium or 'fruit' of plants are shown, Hunter's selection showing the characters of all the primary classes. There are very few specimens to show the developing germ of the Radiata as most of these require magnification to elucidate the details. Among the Molluscs, Hunter selected one of the species remarkable for its ovo-viviparous generation (Nos. 2942 and 2943) and has displayed several of the singular nidi formed by a secretion of the parent for the protection of the tender ova until the shell of the embryo is sufficiently developed.

The progressive stages of formation of the ovum of the Cephalopods, the development of the embryos and the peculiar place of attachment of the pedicle of the vitelline sac, are illustrated by dissections of these parts in the common Cuttle-fish.

The group that most strikingly illustrates Hunter's unwearied perseverance and determination thoroughly to explore the mysteries of generation is perhaps that which contains his dissections of Insects. Here are preparations to show the development of the ovum and metamorphoses of the Lepidopterous insects; the external and internal peculiarities of their larva, pupa and imago being illustrated by dissections of the Silk-moth. The structure of the cocoon or protecting case of the passive pupa in this species, and the organs of the larva for secreting the valuable material of which it is formed, are shown.

The analogous structures for the protection of the larvae and pupae of the Bee-tribe, due to the industry of individuals having no concern in the generation of the brood for which they labour; the progress of development of the ovum, larva and pupa in the cells thus prepared; and other facts in the singular oeconomy of the Social Hymenoptera are well illustrated. Many of these specimens are described in Hunter's Memoir on the Hive-bee published in the *Philosophical Transactions* in the year 1792. A similar series demonstrates the oeconomy of the Humble-bee, Hunter's observations on which were published for the first time in Volume V of the *Physiological Catalogue*, prepared by Richard Owen in 1840 (p. 38).

The progressive formation and course of the ovum in the internal organs of the Crustacea is well displayed in a dissection of the Lobster (3188).

The section dealing with generation in Fish is particularly fine; Hunter's views on the anatomy of the reproductive organs in the Eel were subsequently confirmed by the researches of the renowned naturalists Jonathon Couch (1789-1870) and William Yarrell (1784-1856).

The circumstances attending the development of the embryo in Reptiles are completely illustrated; most of the external and internal changes accompanying the metamorphoses of the Newt and Frog are displayed in elaborate dissections and entire specimens of the larvae at each gradation of growth. The first appearance of the allantois, as a foetal organ of respiration in the animal kingdom, is displayed by dissections of the embryo of the Snake; and these and other interesting conditions of the vascular system of the foetus of the higher Reptiles are shown in the Tortoise and Crocodile.

The extensive series of preparations illustrating the formation and development of the egg in the Birds commences with the changes produced in the ovarium and oviduct and those which the ovum itself undergoes while in the ovarium and during its passage along the oviducts. The general results of Hunter's prolonged research into this branch of animal development are recorded in the following account which he left in manuscript:

'To understand the progress of incubation, it is necessary we should first understand the anatomy or structure of an egg; and as it is the Bird we are here describing, it is only necessary to understand the structure of the egg of that order of animals.

'The mass of an egg is composed of two parts, the orange-coloured part, called the yolk, and the transparent surrounding part, called the "white" or "albumen": but this term is only applied to its turning white upon coagulation; but as it has all the characters of a mucus called slime, I shall call it the slime. The yolk is a portion of the ovaria, or formed by it; which is what I shall first consider.

'The ovarium in the Bird is in one of two states: one is the quiet or (unexcited) state; the other is the state for impregnation. In the first the ova are small, like millet-seed, composed of a little bag filled with a yolk in miniature. They are formed in a cluster in the loins of the Bird, upon the vena cava, as if formed upon it or growing out from it, so as to be inseparable. These small bodies are of different colours in different birds, and sometimes different in the same bird. As the constitution is changing towards propagation, these little bodies begin to swell, by becoming fuller of the matter of the yolk. Some advance faster than the others, in a kind of regular gradation, forming regular series. As they advance they become attached by a neck, which is small and pretty long in some. Their capsule becomes extremely vascular, more especially the veins, which run from the neck as a centre, and spread in a radiated form on the membrane, and then, as it were, converge on the opposite side. When nearly arrived at full size, an oblong part of the capsule becomes very thin, and the yolk can be seen through it. This gives way and it opens, through which the yolk makes its escape. At this very period we must suppose that the mouth of the oviduct is so placed as to catch it, along which it passes.

'The yolk is in the centre of the slime, seen through it, as it were swimming in it. It is round, and is lighter, in the whole, in weight than the slime, so that it always rises towards the upper side of the egg; but it is not in equal weight in itself through the whole, one side being lighter than the other, which side always keeps uppermost, let the egg be ever so often turned; like the needle to the pole, let the compass be ever so often turned, the point of the needle keeps to the pole. On this side is the cicatricula, in which the chick is formed; therefore it is always nearest the heat of the mother, although the chick is of more condensed materials, and therefore one would suppose it would destroy this quality on this side of the yolk; yet we find it does not, for this side keeps uppermost till the chick almost fills the whole space or shell, and therefore cannot turn, and now it is not necessary it should. It (the yolk) is of the consistence of thick cream, and is coagulable with heat, solutions of alum, alcohol, goulard, &c.

'At each end* of the yolk, towards the long axis of the egg, we may observe a white substance going out, about the size of a white thread, which does not come out at once, but as if its attachment was spread on the yolk, or that it was the membrane of the yolk contracting and sending out the cord. It passes towards the end of the egg, and appears to be increasing in size, more loose in texture, as if gradually dissolving and swelling, and towards its termination it looks like a cloud, or white fumes in the air. These two threads are the axes on which the yolk turns, and keeps its lightest side always uppermost. As the most distinct part or terminations of these threads do not turn with the yolk, the thread, or that end which is nearest to the yolk, must twist when the egg is turned; and if the egg is turned oftener in one way than what the threads can twist, then the yolk must turn round with the egg; but as it is not likely this can ever happen in any natural process, no such inconvenience can ever occur.

'On one side of the yolk is a lighter spot than any of the other, which is

---

* 'I call these "ends" because they are towards the long axis of the egg.'

called the "cicatricula"; in this is the chick formed; but before incubation no traces of the embryo can be discovered, there being no difference between this part that is impregnated, and one not impregnated.

'The "slime" is a secretion from the oviduct,* and is collected by the yolk in its passage along this duct, in its way to the shell-forming part, by which means it surrounds this yolk everywhere, but mostly at the two ends, as the egg is of an elliptical form: and here it appears to adhere to the inner membrane more than anywhere else, probably in some measure connected with the two ends above described. It is transparent, having a slight tinge of a yellow in it. Its attraction of cohesion is such, as allows it to have its figure very much altered, and recovering itself somewhat like an elastic body; therefore not a fluid whose parts can be moved on each other, and always keep the place they are moved into. It coagulates into a white substance, which appears to be lamellated.

'These two parts (the yolk and white) are enclosed in a pretty large opake membrane, which is lamellated, for it can be divided and subdivided into a number of layers; but it would seem to be divided into two, the innermost the thinner. At the great end this membrane is separated into two laminae; the outer, or that next to the shell, continues to line the shell; but the inner passes across, leaving a space between the two of about three-eighths of an inch in diameter, and is concave on that side next to the slime; though not so much as the outer one on the side next the shell. This space is filled with air. Over the whole is the shell, composed of calcareous earth, about half a line in thickness, the outer surface of which has a vast number of indentations on it, as it were, looking porous. It appears to have no regular construction; it does not look like crystallization, as in the enamel of the teeth. The colour of the shell in the common fowl is generally white, but in some it is brown, as in the Chittagong fowl. This shell gives the whole a firmness which defends its contents. It certainly admits air to pass both it and the membrane.

'The egg, which is the produce of the female, or of the female parts in the hermaphrodite, is to be considered in two lights. In one it is to be considered as the uterus, and in the other as the breast. The slime is the uterine part, intended for the support of the chick while in its uterus or egg; and the yolk supports it for some days after being hatched, in place of milk, although for a much shorter time; so that the oviparous animal collects the whole neces-

---

* 'Birds have but one oviduct when grown up, although two are originally formed; but it is the left only that remains. In my maiden Preparation there was one on the right side, but it was a kind of dwarf one. This duct is thrown into considerable convolutions (therefore much longer than what was only necessary for a duct), having a meso-oviduct. It may be said to consist of five parts, which are in some degree different in structure. The first may be called the mouth or fimbria, which is an oblique opening looking (like) a slit.'

sary nourishment, and throws it out at once; while the viviparous retains the rudiments of the young, and furnishes it nourishment as it is wanted.

'We have reason to suppose that the slime comes nearest to the nature of blood of any animal substance we know; and we know it is alive, therefore not necessary to undergo any change to have this effect produced; for it is only the absorption of living parts, therefore is capable of composing the animal without having undergone the act of digestion; and in this alone it undergoes but little alteration, as it composes the whole parts without much loss; for an egg, through the whole process of incubation, only loses . . . grains, and as that would produce a vacuum somewhere in the egg,—more especially as the parts formed are more solid than the parts which composed them,— therefore it is reasonable to suppose they would occupy a smaller space. But it would appear that the cavity at the thick end of the egg, between the two membranes, was intended as a counterpoise for this loss; for as the chick grows, and of course the whole loses in weight, as also in size, this air-bag swells, by a separation of the two membranes, and fills up the space lost. So that this cavity may be said to be in size, in proportion to the loss and condensation of parts which nourished the chick; and this is one of the purposes answered by it.

'As the whole volume of the chick and contents of the egg diminish both in size and weight, it is necessary there should be a provision for the first that the space might be filled: for this there is a provision by means of the air-cell at the thick end, which, in the unincubated egg, is extremely small, but increases as the contents of the egg decrease; and this increase of the air-cell is effected by a separation of the two laminae of which the lining or internal membrane is composed.

'Principles governing the Formation of Animals

'This production of animals out of themselves excites wonder, admiration, and curiosity; and this is commonly the case in effects whose immediate causes are so obscure, more especially when we are ourselves both effects and causes of the same.

'The first process set on foot in the formation of an animal is so small, without that form which it afterwards gradually takes on, and its situation so obscure, that its operation cannot be traced but by taking it up at stated times, when we find a new part either added or come to view, or a degree of perfection having taken place in the part.

'The larger the animal is in any one order, the more perfectly the parts are seen as they rise to view, and, by this, the intermediate steps in them are more within our view.

'If we were capable of following the progress of increase of the number of the parts of the most perfect animal, as they first formed in succession, from the very first to its state of full perfection, we should probably be able to compare it with some one of the incomplete animals themselves, of every order of animals in the Creation, being at no stage different from some of the inferior orders. Or, in other words, if we were to take a series of animals, from the more imperfect to the perfect, we should probably find an imperfect animal, corresponding with some stage of the most perfect. But all our observations can only begin at a visible stage of formation, prior to which we are left to conjecture, which could only lead us back to still fewer parts; but when the first and necessary parts were first formed, as a basis to put the whole succeeding ones into action, so as to increase themselves and form new parts, is not known, nor can it.

'(Magnifying) glasses lead us back far beyond what the naked eye reaches; but these only show us the order of priority in the formation of parts. However, human wisdom can go no further than into the distinction of parts, with their actions and uses when formed.

'The mode of the gradual increase of the parts of an animal may be considered in three views; one, where it may be supposed that the basis of every part of an animal is laid at the very beginning, and that its visible perfection is no more than the parts beginning to grow as they are wanted, but that they were there in embryo. Another, where it may be supposed that at first the parts were formed, but were no more in number than just what were wanted for that state of perfection; and as they came to a degree of perfection, new parts were necessary, and they formed, or formed as they were wanted. And the third is, where the parts were there from the beginning, but that they were altered in form, action, &c. So far as my observations go, I think I can see all the three principles introduced, but probably not in the same animal, nor in the same order of animals.

'According to the first, I can conceive there are, at the very beginning, parts which continue through life, and such is, probably, the *Materia Vitae universalis* and the Absorbing System, which may indeed, according to the third principle, be changed. But according to the second, as the embryo is moving towards perfection, new parts are formed; probably first the brain and heart, with their appendages the nerves and vessels, and so on of all the other parts of the body, which we do not find at first. And we know, according to the third (principle), that many parts are changed in form, adapting their use, arising from that formation, to the addition of parts with the changes in the parts, and this pretty universally.

'Perhaps the flying-insect is the best example of these observations. This insect has three modes of life, and of course three structures of parts. The structure suitable to the first life (ovum) we know little about, but the difference between the second and third we can examine. In the second life (larva) it appears to have no parts but what are of immediate use for the growth of the animal, and some of them very different in form from what they are afterwards, while others remain the same; so that in the insect we have, in the second life, parts that were probably of use in the first; we have, at least in the second, parts that are of use in the third, therefore do not change, such as the brain, nerves, and circulation; but in the third life (pupa), we have new parts entirely, and old ones changed. The new parts formed are, the parts of generation, legs, wings, &c. &c.; parts changed are, the whole of the digestive powers, in some degree the organs of respiration, and probably the organs of sensation. Thus in the progress of growth, in the more perfect animals, we have new parts arising, changes taking place in those already formed, and old parts lost.

'It may be observed, that the more perfect the order of animals is, it comes to a larger size at the first-life than those of an inferior order: thus, a new-born quadruped is nearer to the size of the parents than a bird just hatched, and a bird nearer than a fish, &c. However, there are varieties in this respect in the quadruped, for some have several at a time, which renders them smaller.

'From this account we should suppose that a quadruped would be the first for investigation; but as Nature gives to every order of animals a mode of reproduction peculiar to itself, we are led to examine this process in those where its operations are most easily and certainly come at. This must certainly be the case with some of the oviparous, although not with all, and according to the above position the Bird must be the best, and still more so in those that have fewest young in number and largest in themselves.

'Without this aid our knowledge of this subject would have been very imperfect, and it would almost appear that this mode of propagation was intended for investigation.

'In the investigation of this subject they have commonly had recourse to the common fowl, as being the most familiar; but I found the first appearances so obscure, from want of size in the object, that I had recourse to the progress of the chick in the egg of the goose. I attempted the swan, but it was impossible to procure such numbers as to give me all the necessary varieties. I endeavoured to procure ostrich's eggs, by having them sent to me in spirits; but as the getting such was only a matter of chance, and only one or two in thirty years! nothing could be made out from them. For this purpose, then, I kept a flock of geese for more than fifteen years, and by depriving them of their first brood in my investigations, they commonly bred again the same season.

'As hours make a difference in the first days, it becomes necessary to examine in the night as well as in the day; by which reason, the latter brood in the summer is best adapted, having then short nights.

'Of the different Methods to be taken to examine the Progress of the Chick in incubated Eggs

'The first thing necessary is the breaking and removing part of the shell of the egg, which is to be begun at the upper part. In the breaking of the shell of the egg, when the chick is young, as at twelve, twenty-four, or thirty-six hours, it should not be broken where the chick is, that is, not at the very upper part, but a little way from it, and break it round this most prominent part for the breadth of a shilling: this is with a view to avoid the sharp corner of the shell wounding the membrane and hurting the first rudiments of the chick. Then take off the shell, leaving the lining of the egg on; then remove gradually the membrane from over the chick. This must be done with great care and attention; it should be taken off in layers with a pair of forceps. The egg so prepared should be put into warm water as high as the chick, but not allowed to cover it, as water soon kills it. In this way it may be kept alive some hours. It may be necessary to remark, that, while the heart of the chick acts, the blood keeps red; but as soon as it ceases to act, the blood becomes almost immediately pale, and soon loses its red colour; therefore it is necessary to keep the animal alive as long as possible.* When it is examined sufficiently in this state, then, to see the body of the animal still better, the membrane should be cut all round beyond the foetal circle, and the whole taken off under water; and then have a piece of thin black ivory to slip under it, and put the whole into spirits, which will coagulate the completest formed parts, and bring them to view upon the black ground. In this way I have been able to bring parts distinctly to view that before appeared to be involved in a cloud; also we can bring them under a much larger magnifier, and bring out parts that neither their situation nor glasses could expose.

---

* 'Various were my attempts to effect this, but mostly in vain. I conceived that when I had just exposed the little animal by putting it into water, heated to about 204 degrees, just covering the egg, I might keep it alive by these means, and observe in the same chick the whole progress of growth; but it soon died; therefore I was obliged to have recourse to a succession.'

'When heat is applied to an impregnated egg, the living parts are put into motion, and an expansion of what is called the cicatricula takes place. This very probably begins at the chick as a centre; but it would appear that the whole did not derive its expansion immediately from the chick, for this part would appear to have powers within itself, and the further from the chick these powers are at an early period, the strongest is this expansion of parts; for we find changes taking place in this circle near to the circumference, sooner than near to the chick, which afterwards become distinct vessels, and communicate with the mesenteric artery of the chick. The chick begins to take form to itself in the midst of this expansion, and as it increases, its influence is extended into the surrounding parts.

'In the beginning of the formation of the chick, there is great distinctness of parts, for they gradually take place one after another.

'Of the Membranes of the Chick

'The chick at first, or in its . . . hour, is totally void of membrane, only having over it the external membrane of the yolk, which, when removed (which is easily done), the animal is perfectly bare.

'The first formation or expansion of its membranes are in pretty quick succession, and then go on together, some being sooner completed than others. The first expansion of parts would appear to be the formation of membranes, or changes in membranes naturally belonging to the egg.

'The first membrane that is formed is the membrana vitelli, which forms immediately under the proper membrane of the yolk; so it would appear that at this time the yolk had two membranes (but how far originally so I do not know), the external, a fine transparent one, and the other, more spongy, and having the power of becoming vascular.

'As the parts of the chick begin to form, such as the head and spine, with the medulla spinalis, &c., a proper membrane also begins to form, to cover it. This membrane begins first at the head, and seems to arise from the membrane round the head; and, as it increases, it gradually covers the upper or exposed surface of the head, like a hood; then gradually extends itself along the body, covering more and more of it towards the tail, having always a determined edge: and when got to the tail, it there closes up the animal entirely, on the upper side, and which has only the membrana vitelli upon it, making a circumscribed cavity, in which the chick lies, and which I call the "amnios", as being the immediate covering of the chick, composing a part of the secondines or after-birth.

'This membrana vitelli (germinal membrane) would appear to have formed itself from the intestine; if so, then it was prior to that part being visible; or it might be considered an expansion of, or a process from, the intestine over the yolk, and under its own proper membrane. That part next to the chick appears to divide into several laminae, or has the power of forming several; for we find, by the time the whole has formed such and such parts, that we can separate it into . . . laminae, which are seen in Plates 69, 70, 71.* This membrane is extending itself over the yolk, expanding itself till its edges come beyond the largest diameter, and now, as it expands in length from the chick, it contracts at its edge, and at last encloses the whole yolk, forming on the opposite side something like a cicatrix, to which the last part of the slime adheres.

'From this account of the yolk, and this membrane, it might appear that this membrane was only at first a covering communicating with the belly of the chick, preparatory to, or for, the entrance of the yolk into the abdomen just before hatching. But from its structure it would appear to have some use while under incubation, for it first becomes extremely vascular, and on its inside it is thrown into rugae, as if an increase of inner surface was necessary: wherever this membrane advances, the yolk becomes fluid, beginning at first where the membrane forms, extending itself as the membrane of the yolk extends, by which means the yolk is rendered fit for passing through the duct into the intestine, after the chick is hatched; and it is even not coagulable with heat, so that we may know when an egg has been sat upon, when boiled, for the yolk remains a thin and watery fluid.

'As the chick grows, it presses down the middle of the yolk, first making a deep indent in it; and as it increases in length this indent is increased into a groove, which becomes deeper; and by the time the chick is at its full growth, the yolk is almost divided into two portions, between which lies the chick.

'When the chick is so far advanced as to have most of its parts begun to form, such as the extremities, which is about the (60th) hour, then begins to form the third membrane, in form of a circumscribed bag, which seems to come out from the belly near the anus, full of water. This, by increasing, spreads upon the chick, or over the above membrane, and covers them, and as it increases, it covers the whole albumen that remains; and, as the slime diminishes, it becomes also a covering for the yolk; so the chick, albumen and yolk, are at last enclosed by means of this bag; but as it is a circumscribed bag in itself, these parts are on the outside of its cavity; but, by its forming a circumscribed bag, in its double capacity it may be said to form two circumscribed cavities; and it is therefore to be understood that the chick is

---

* *Catalogue of the Physiological Series*, vol. v, 1840.

only enclosed between this bag and the membrane of the yolk, and is therefore not within its proper cavity, but upon its outside.

'This cavity, originally arising from the rectum, communicates with it by a small duct, and probably is formed upon it, through which passes the urine; whence this cavity should be called "allantois" although the membrane that forms the cavity has various uses; it absorbs the slime as it covers it, and therefore should be called placenta: it comes in contact with the shell, and acts as lungs.*

'The urine in the chick is similar to that of the adult, a white slimy substance; that which is in the allantois is firmer in texture, appearing like strings of coagulated white of an egg, when thrown loose into hot water. The water which it contained at first appears to be absorbed, for none is found towards the last stages of incubation.

'Where the allantois covers the chick it adheres to the amnios, making but one thin membrane between them, but it never becomes attached to the membrana lutei or vitelli. As it extends, it would appear to push from the chick the remaining slime towards the opposite side to that of the chick, as it were clearing the yolk of it more and more, so that the slime becomes smaller, and at last lies like an oblong body close and adhering to the cicatrix of the yolk. So far as these membranes are attached to the membranes of the yolk, they would appear to detach themselves from it by the time it is ready to be absorbed into the cavity of the abdomen; for none of the other membranes are taken in with it, and it has no other attachment to the abdomen in any of this class of animals.

'Of the Use of those Membranes as they arise

'The formation of the chick seems to be but little prior to the formation of the membrana vitelli (germinal membrane), if at all prior; for among the first appearances is a spreading of the cicatricula, and the centre would appear to contain a fluid. That the formation of the chick is considerably prior to the formation of the other membranes is evident; therefore it might be asked, how the chick is nourished, and other functions carried on, till those other membranes are formed? supposing that they absorb the slime. But the membrana lutei (germinal membrane) performs this office, at least at this time, and there was a certain space of the membrana vitelli (germinal membrane) that had the powers of forming vessels and red blood, and which became very vascular. This membrane would appear to answer two

---

* 'In animals that have a (urinary) bladder, this duct forms itself into that cavity. In the crocodile the bladder opens into the gut, but in the quadruped the urachus opens into or forms a passage for itself, called urethra.'

purposes, one for the purpose of the chick, another as a covering to conduct the whole yolk into the abdomen.

'That the membrane which I have called allantois, from its containing urine, answers other important purposes, must appear evident from its extent being far beyond what would answer that purpose. I conceive that the side of this bag, which surrounds and is in contact with the albumen, acts as the chorion or placenta, for it must be by this surface that the albumen is absorbed, and the chick supported. The external part of this bag, which comes in contact with the shell, and as it enlarges lines more and more of it, till at last it lines it everywhere, I conceive to be the lungs, for it is the only part that comes in contact with the air; and on opening an egg pretty far gone, I find that the blood in the veins is scarlet, while it is of the modena colour in the arteries of the bag. Besides, it is much more vascular than any of the other membranes, which is just the reverse of what we should imagine, if it did not answer that purpose.

'Of the Formation of the Parts of the Chick

'As the parts which act in both stages differ very considerably in their structure, the structure of the first not being adapted to the economy of the second, we have an opportunity of investigating those changes which may be said to give us the gradual formation of parts till completed. The heart is the only visible acting part, and the construction of that viscus in the very young is not similar to that of the full-formed. From hence we can have its formation through its various changes.

'The first parts that are visibly formed may be said to be the brain and spinal marrow, although we may conceive the heart and vascular system is also formed, suited to such a state, and that it is co-existing, but not seen, because transparent, while the brain, &c. is opake, and can be rendered much more so; by which means it becomes still more evident; for if the brain, &c. was transparent, the heart would be the first visible object from its motion, and afterwards (from its) becoming reddish.

'The animal would appear to begin at the back, as it contains the spinal marrow, in which is to be included the head, as it contains the brain, and it seems to build forwards, and the new parts are formed in succession; so there appears to be originally no outline of the whole, and the parts to form in it; therefore every part is formed on the outside of the animal: thus we see the heart, then the lungs, the intestines, and over the whole the skin of the abdomen, which is not perfected till the animal is ready to hatch, and sometimes not even then.

'As this only relates to the bird, it may be supposed to belong to it only; but there is reason to believe it is the same in other animals; for in some monsters, in the quadruped, we have no abdominal parietes, only the bowels covered by a thin skin, which leads us to conjecture it possible that they also are formed without any abdominal parietes. This state of deficiency of the parietes of the abdomen has all its degrees, some much more, others less.

'The chick is formed first on its back, and then turns on its left side; and till this period the heart is not seen, or if it exists it must lie before the medulla, which will, from its transparency, render it obscure; for in this side view, we see, as it were, the profile, and from its lying in a transparent fluid, it can be seen moving in it even before there is any red blood.

'Of the Blood's Motion in the Chick

'The circulation of the blood in the foetus of the common viviparous animals may be divided into two parts: the first is that which passes immediately through both sides of the heart with the connexion between the arteries of the right and left side of the heart. The second is that which is connected with the membranes for the foetus's nourishment.

'In the oviparous animals the motion of the blood may be divided into three; first, as above, for instance, its motion immediately through the heart, and the communication between the arteries of the right and left side; the second, as above, viz. the connexion with the membranes for nourishment; and the third (which is probably peculiar to them) is the circulation into the membranes for the influence of air, which membranes may be called the foetal lungs.

'The vessels of the chick are different from the human, more like (those of) the puppy or kitten, although different from them in some of their vessels. The motion of the blood in the chick, in and through the heart, is not different from (that in) the quadruped; that is, the communication between the right side and the left is the same, having a foramen ovale, but the communication between the two arteries is a little different, having two "canales arteriosi" instead of one.

'Of the peculiar Arteries of the Chick

'These arteries are three; the two first, or what may be called a pair, and which answer to the umbilical arteries in the quadruped, arise from the iliacs, and pass by the sides of the bones of the pelvis towards the opening of the abdomen, and when got out of that cavity through this opening, ramify on the three membranes above described. The third is a continuation of the mesenteric artery, and is principally lost on the membrana lutei.

'Of the veins

'There are two venae umbilicales; one (which is the largest) belongs to the amnios, chorion and lungs, and is similar in its termination to the umbilical vein in the quadruped, the trunk of which passes into the abdomen, then upwards to the liver, enters between its lobes, and opens into the vena cava inferior, just as it enters the heart. The other belongs to the membrana lutei, and passes into the abdomen, joins the mesenteric vein, which would appear to divide into two, one forming the vena portarum, the other joins the vena cava inferior between the kidneys, and which communication remains through life.

'In the diastole of the auricles more blood passes into the right than what it can contain, and the overplus passes, as it were, through the right auricle into the left, while at the same time the left is receiving blood from the lungs, so that the left is filled partly from the body, therefore they are equally filled with blood. But the quantity from the lungs is increasing every day in proportion as the lungs increase, for the lungs can hardly be said to be coeval with the heart.

'Of the Brain and Spinal Marrow

'It would appear, upon (examining) the most early of these parts, that they were originally formed in two distinct parts, a right and a left; at least there is a transparent line which runs through their whole length, dividing them to appearance into two; but these parts are too small and too tender to allow of ascertaining this as a certain fact; and indeed this division takes place in some degree in parts in the adult; for we find the cerebrum and cerebellum divided into two, as also the medulla spinalis nearly divided into two, longitudinally. The union in the brain of the chick seems to take place soonest about the basis of the brain, making the anterior end appear as if slit into two, like a pair of pincers.

'Of the Formation of the Intestines, &c.

'The intestines, and probably the liver, spleen, kidneys, &c., are the latest formed; yet the principle upon which they are formed must be begun early, for the mouth is early formed, as also we may suppose the anus, for the bag described as above (allantois) arises from it; therefore there is only the intermediate canal to form, and its communication with the yolk; but as all those parts are only fitted for the second stage of life, it was only necessary they should be perfected by that time. The small intestines which join the yolk are drawn further out of the belly as the chick grows, but before the chick hatches they are gradually pulled in.

'The parietes of the abdomen are the latest in being formed, and when that is effected the animal is completed; but this is much later in some of the oviparous animals than in the quadruped, and the lateness of forming this part is owing to the yolk's being taken into the cavity of the belly at or near hatching; and to effect this purpose we find that from the circumference all round the opening into the belly arises a muscular expansion which enters the yolk (besides its proper membrane), surrounding the whole, which by its contraction draws the yolk towards the opening, and then by its contraction that part of the yolk which is close upon the mouth of the opening is shoved into the belly; and by this action some of the yolk (which is become fluid) is squeezed into the intestine, which by regurgitation in that canal is carried up into the stomach, and is there first coagulated to be afterwards digested.

'As birds have air-bags within the abdomen, I find that at a certain period of growth of the chick they begin to form. They begin at the lower point of the lungs like a small hydatid, and extend further and further into the abdomen, before and on the outside of the kidneys: they are at first full of a fluid; as they extend, they are, as it were, squeezed among the intestines, so as to take on the shape of the intestines of those parts, and at last filling the whole abdomen among them. Soon after others are forming, or other openings communicating with this, and the lungs are also beginning to attach themselves so as to form a communication with other parts, as the ribs, sternum, vertebrae, &c.

'The lungs are, at first, detached bodies, as in the quadruped, but when arrived about the third week (in the goose) they begin to be attached to the ribs, but not so early to the diaphragm.

'Among the latest formed parts of the chick are the eyelids. When gone through one half of their period of incubation, the whole anterior surface of the eye is exposed, and the termination of the common integuments is perfectly round (Fig. 12, pl. 76). But in a day or two more it begins to form itself into an oblong opening (Fig. 16, Pl. 76) which becomes narrower (Fig. 5, Pl. 75) and then the increase of lid becomes more remarkable in the lower lid, becoming first almost straight (Fig. 17, Pl. 76), which afterwards becomes rounded on its edge, almost covering the whole of the lower part of the eye (Fig. 18, Pl. 76), and about a day or two before they are hatched the lower lid has spread upwards so much as almost to cover the whole eye (Pl. 78).

'The membrana nictitans begins earlier to form than the eyelids (Fig. 16, Pl. 76).

'It may also be observed, that at no period could I observe a membrana pupillaris.

'The little horny knob (Figs. 17, 18, Pl. 76) at the end of the beak with which it breaks the shell when arrived at the full time and makes its escape, is also gradually forming into a more regular and determined point, the progress of which is seen from the first figure to the sixth.

'When very young we may observe *two* oviducts, one on each side; they would appear to be behind the kidneys at their first formation, but become more and more forwards as the chick grows, and before hatching the right seems to decay.

'There are two kinds of down on the chick, one long, which comes first, about two or three days before hatching; a second, a fine down, forms at the roots of the other. It is probably the long down that comes off with the feather.

'The chick some time before birth has a kind of mixed action of life, for it breathes, and we can hear it pip and chirp in the egg; and we find that the adult circulation through and out of the heart is formed before birth: yet it is receiving its nourishment from the remaining slime.'

Works, vol. v, pp. 199-216.

The illustrations can be found in the 1840 catalogue.

The specimens prepared by Hunter to demonstrate the development of the Mammalian foetus are equally comprehensive, though in some groups the preparations are designed chiefly to show changes in the external form. The nature and organisation of the corpus luteum are well demonstrated in a series of dissections from different species, in some of which the progressive changes of the impregnated ovisac after the escape of the ovum are shown.

Hunter expressed regret at the want of opportunity to investigate the generation of the Marsupialia which he considered to be the most interesting part of the natural history of animals. In the appendix that he wrote to White's *Journal of a Voyage to New South Wales* published in 1790, he says of the Opossum 'There is something in the mode of propagation in this animal that deviates from all others, and although known in some degree to be extraordinary, yet it has never been attempted, where opportunity offered to complete the investigation. I have often endeavoured to breed them in England; I have bought a great many, and my friends have assisted me by bringing them or sending them alive, yet never could get them to breed; and although possessed of a good many facts respecting them, I do not believe my information is sufficient to complete the system of propagation in this class.' (For further details of this group of animals see *The Mammals of South Australia* by Frederic Wood Jones. Adelaide, 1923.)

After having displayed the progressive development of the germ, the foetal appendages and envelopes, and the modifications of the impregnated oviduct and uterus in the different classes of animals, Hunter next proceeds to show how the young animal in many cases, after its extrication from the foetal coverings, is nourished and sheltered by the parent until it has acquired sufficient powers to provide for its own support. In the first of these series of accessories to the generative function, we find the mammary glands, structures exclusively confined to the highest class of animals and suggestive of the name of the class in modern zoology. This series, however, commences with those well-known preparations from pigeons, which illustrate the temporary alteration of the structure of a common part to fulfil the partial function assigned to a special gland in the Mammalia. These preparations form the subject of Hunter's memoir 'On a Secretion in the Crop of Breeding Pigeons for the nourishment of their young' (*Works*, vol. iv, p. 122).

In the Marsupialia the peculiarities of the mammary gland and nipples are shown in connection with the abdominal cutaneous pouch, which forms a natural nest for the prematurely-born, minute and naked young of this class. The tubular mouth and the grooved tongue, by which the young retain a firm hold on the elongated nipple are shown.

Here also are shown the analogous natural cavities on the exterior of the body for sheltering the young in other classes, as, for example, the dorsal cells of the Surinam Toad, the ventral marsupium of the Sea Horse and Pipe Fish.

The series ends with specimens showing various types of nests constructed by the parents for the protection of the young offspring; these are found in birds, rodents and sometimes in certain fishes.

The first division of the *Physiological Series* illustrates the organs and functions by which the individual is capable of self-support. In this second division is shown the manner in which generation succeeds generation in order to maintain the continuity and integrity of the species.

In Plants

2858 A portion of Sallow (*Salix caprea*), separated by artificial fission from the parent stem, planted in moist earth for a short time, and then uprooted: it exemplifies the effects of the inherent capacity for self-existence in the separated part, which has sent downwards several roots, and put forth from the upper and exposed extremity a leaf-bearing shoot.

2859 A strip of the liber or inner bark from some dicotyledonous plant, most probably a Willow, showing the development therefrom of adventitious roots proceeding from the ligneous body.

2870 The summit of the stem of the Knee-holly (*Ruscus aculeatus*), showing the position of the fruit upon the leaf-like peduncle. The apparent stem in this plant appears to be only a modified floral axis. In *Ruscus androgynus* the peduncle is still more expanded, and presents entirely the aspect and performs the functions of the true leaves, which in this genus are reduced to mere scales: each fruit is enveloped by the withered sepals.

2871   A specimen of the simple fruit or 'utriculus' of the Amaranth or Prince's Feather (*Amaranthus hypochondriacus*). It is one-celled and the pericarp is membranous and dehiscent by a transverse incision.

2873   A portion of the Larkspur (*Delphinium pictum*) exhibiting several of the seed-pods or 'folliculi' developed in groups of three in each flower. Each follicle is one-valved and one-celled, but contains many seeds which are attached along each margin of the suture by which the follicle is dehiscent or splits open to discharge the seeds.

2874   The fruit or 'pericarpium' of the *Nigella damascena*. This consists of a collection of several concrete follicles in a single flower: each of these folliculi, like those of the Larkspur, is one-celled and one-valved. The seeds are numerous and attached in two rows, one to each margin of the suture by which the cell is dehiscent. This genus is one of the few plants of Ranunculaceae with a syncarpous fruit.

2875   A portion of the stem of the yellow Lupin (*Lupinus luteus*) with the 'legumen' or seed-pod, of which one valve has been removed, showing the separate cavities for the seeds formed by septal processes or projections of the placenta; the seeds or ovula have been bisected to show the cavity in each which contains the embryo.

2876   A twig of the Bladder Senna (*Colutaea arborescens*) with two seed-pods or legumens; these are each two-valved, one-celled, many-seeded, superior and dehiscent by a suture along both the anterior and posterior margins. One of the valves has been removed from each legumen to show the numerous ovula or seeds which are attached by long umbilical funiculi to the margin of the inferior or ventral suture.

2877   A portion of the stem with several fruits of *Agrimonia eupatoria*. The ovaria are distinct, inclosed in the persistent tube of the calyx, which is fringed with hooked bristles.

2879   A section of the stem bearing the female spike, consisting of longitudinal series of fruits or 'caryopses' of the Maize (*Zea mays*). The rachis or axis is not dissected, but the number, aggregated and regular positions of the fruits and the stigmata, which are the longest known in the vegetable kingdom, are worthy of notice.

2880   'The stem of the Bladder Alyssum (*Vesicaria utriculata*) with specimens of the fruit attached: a portion of the pericarp has been cut away on each side to show its two-celled structure, and the transparent dissepiment by which the cells are separated.'
       This description no longer applies. The fruits have become detached from the stem and the structure is difficult to determine.

2881   A portion of a twig with two groups of the fruit consisting of five concrete carpels of the Fraxinella (*Dictamnus fraxinella*): one carpel is laid open, showing the thick soft coarsely villous outer coat, and the thin smooth inner coat or endocarp; the seeds are pendulous, and attached to the upper margin of the carpel.

2882   The terminal portion of the stem of *Thlaspi arvense* with several of its flattened, two-celled fruit or 'silicula'. In one of the larger fruits the act of dehiscence has commenced by the two valves beginning to separate from the septum. The seeds, which are not numerous, are attached to two placentae adhering to the septum and opposite to the lobes of the stigma.

2883   A portion of a stem of the Mignonette (*Reseda odorata*), with many of the fruits or 'capsules'. These are dry, many-seeded, unilocular, three-valved and with three parietal placentae, to which the ovules are attached. The ovaria are constantly open at their summits.

2884   The terminal portion of a stem of *Antirrhinum majus* with several of the capsule attached. These are peculiar for their mode of bursting which is by two terminal foramina. The placentae are large and the seeds very numerous and minute.

2885   A specimen of the fruit or capsule of the *Datura stramonium*; the valves of two of the cells have been removed, showing the seeds and their placental attachments.

2886   A longitudinal section of the umbel and fructiferous stem of the Onion (*Allium cepa*).   The flowers are supported on long and slender pedicles, which radiate from the contracted floral axis.

2887   The umbel or floral axis of the Onion, with several of the flowers removed, showing the 'bulbilli' at their base.

2888   The bulbiferous 'umbel' of the Garlic (*Allium sativum*).

2889   Several specimens of the fruit of the Nutmeg (*Myristica moschata*).   Some are entire; from others half of the fleshy and valveless sarcocarp has been removed to show the multipartite 'arillus', commonly called mace, which surrounds the seed, and which is developed as an additional membrane after fertilisation of the ovule.

2891   A specimen of the calyx and fruit of the Blue Nightshade (*Nicandra physaloides*). The fruit is exposed by the reflection of two of the reticulate lobes of the calyx, which increases in size after fecundation; it consists of a thin, indehiscent pericarp, containing numerous seeds.

2892   A similar specimen in which a portion of the calyx and of the dry pericarp have been removed to show the ripe seeds in three of the cells.

2900   A portion of a branch with several fruit or 'pomes' of the dwarf Medlar (*Cotoneaster vulgaris*).   The structure of this fruit agrees with that of the apple.

2901   A section of the fruit of the Melon (*Cucumis melo*).   This fruit, which is technically termed 'peponida' is one-celled, many-seeded, inferior, fleshy and indehiscent. The seeds are attached, at a distance from the axis, by pulpy placentae to the fleshy parietes of the pericarp; and in the present case the cavity of the pericarp is filled with pulp, in which the numerous seeds are imbedded.

2902   A branch with male and female flowers and fruit of the Scotch Fir (*Pinus sylvestris*). The fruit of this and of other species of Pine is principally characterised by modifications of the placentae: the carpella, which are developments of the placentae, are here scale-like, spread open and bear naked seeds.   The flower of the fir is called an amentum or catkin: it is destitute of calyx and corolla, being furnished only with bracts.

2903   A portion of a stem, with several of the fruit or 'sorosis' of the *Broussonetia papyrifera*. This modification of fruit is characterised by the cohesion, in a single mass, of the ovaria and floral envelopes.

2904   A similar specimen.

2910   The embryo of the yellow Lupin (*Lupinus luteus*) in which is shown germination and the development of the plumule.

2911   The seed and embryo of a Pea (*Pisum sativum*) in which germination has pretty far advanced. The wrinkled and partly-collapsed state of the seed indicates the exhaustion of the farinaceous and nutritious contents of the cotyledons consequent upon the development of the radicle and plumule.

2912   The seed and embryo of the common Bean (*Faba vulgaris*): one half of the 'testa' has been removed, exhibiting the exterior of the cotyledon of that side: germination has commenced, and the radicle has protruded through the testa and begun to shoot downwards. Above the radicle may be seen the line of division between the exposed and covered cotyledon.

2913   The seed and embryo of a Bean in which germination is more advanced, the radicle descending, and the plumule ascending, but without any corresponding ascent of the cotyledons, which remain buried in the earth during the whole period of germination, and are therefore called 'hypogeous'. The rootlets, which are about to be developed, are recognisable by their opaque white colour and slight projection from the radicle.

2914   A similar preparation, showing a more advanced stage of germination. The accessory or secondary rootlets now extend from the base of the primary radicle.

2916   A similar preparation, in which the development of the embryo is so far advanced as to be independent of the nutriment afforded by its amylaceous appendages. A section has been removed from the seed to show the change which has taken place in the hypogeous cotyledons during the progress of germination; they now present a dark grey colour, and coarsely-granular, dry texture: the fecula in their cellular tissue having disappeared, and been consumed in the support of the germinating embryo.

2917   The seed of the Chestnut (*Castanea vesca*) containing two embryos, each of which has developed its radicle and plumule. The external coat of the common enveloping membrane or 'testa' is reflected from one side of the seed.

2917A   The seed of a Chestnut, showing the development of the radicle.

The following six preparations were subjects of the experiments instituted by Hunter, to determine the principle upon which the radicle and plumule of the germinating plant take definite and opposite directions in their growth; the one proceeding centripetally or downwards in the soil, the other centrifugally or towards the surface:

'That this is a general principle in vegetation' he observes, 'requires no illustration, but what is the immediate cause is not so easily determined. I conceived it might be the light, not warmth, for the ground is often warmer than the air, or surface, into which vegetables are often growing. To ascertain this, as far as I could, by experiment, I took a tub, about eighteen inches deep, and about two wide, and filled it with fine mould, in which I planted some Beans and Peas; their eyes were placed in various directions, and over the surface was placed a close-meshed net. The mouth of this tub was turned down, was raised about three feet from the ground, and was suspended between two posts. Round the tub, and over its bottom, which was uppermost, were placed wet straw, mats, etc., to take off any influence the sun or air might have upon its contents, and a small hole was bored in its bottom, to which was fixed a small long tube that came through the straw. This was intended for pouring some water, if I found the earth get dry, into the tub. Under the mouth of the tub I placed looking-glasses, in such a way that the light was thrown upon the mouth of the tub, or surface of the earth. The weather was fine, so that through the whole day there was the reflection of the light from the looking-glasses upon the surface of the mould, which was much more powerful than daylight without the direct rays of the sun. This I continued till I conceived that the Beans and Peas had grown some length, but not finding their tops coming down through the surface of the mould, I examined the contents of the tub, and found that they had all grown upwards, towards the bottom of the tub, and that in those whose eyes had been placed downwards the young shoot had turned round to arise up. As one experiment leads to another, I wished to see how a Bean would grow if kept in a constant rotatory motion. For this purpose I put some earth in a basket, having the shape of a cylinder, and about a foot diameter, with the two ends of wood for greater strength, through the centre of which I fixed an axis or spindle; in this earth I planted a Bean, about half-way between the surface and axis, with its eye to the surface. The basket was laid across the mouth of a large tub, with the ends of the spindle resting on the edges of the tub, which were fitted to one another so as to allow of easy motion. Round the basket was rolled some small cord, to the end of which was suspended a box, water-tight; into this was put lead, so as almost to make it sink in water, and which was sufficient to turn the basket round in the open air. This large tub was filled with water, and the box placed upon it, and the spindle with the basket placed across the mouth of the tub; a very small hole was bored at the lower end of the tub, which allowed the water to escape, but very slowly; as the water sunk in the tub the box descended, and as the box descended the basket turned round. This tub took about twelve hours in emptying, and during that time the spindle with the basket only turned about one and a half: the tub was repeatedly filled, and when I conceived that the Bean might have grown some inches, if it had grown at all, I examined it, and found it had grown as much as if it had been planted in the common ground; but it had no particular direction but that of passing in a straight line from the Bean, which was at first towards the circumference, the direction in which it was placed; but in its course it had met with a small stone, which had turned it in the direction of the axis, and it had gone on in a straight line in that direction. Here, as there was no fixed inducement to grow in any one direction, the Bean grew in a straight line, in that direction given it by chance.'

Works, vol. iii, pp. 285-287.

2919   The seed and embryo of a Bean, in which the foramen (micropyle), or place of protrusion of the radicle, was directed upwards or towards the surface of the earth; the growing radicle, as soon as it had extended beyond the resistance to its descent offered by the seed, has become bent downwards; the plumule on the contrary has immediately ascended.

2920   A similar preparation, in which, from a change of position of the seed during germination, the direction of both plumule and radicle has been altered.

2921   A similar preparation, in which, from similar causes, both the plumule and radicle have twice changed the direction of their growth.

2922   A similar preparation.

2923   The seed and embryo of a Bean, in which the radicle, in consequence of some obstruction to its natural course of growth, exhibits a spiral curve. The testa has been removed from the seed, which exhibits the two cotyledons.

2924   A similar specimen, with the testa entire and germination further advanced.

In Polypes

2925   A Sea-pen (*Pennatula phosphorea*). The ova or gemmules are developed chiefly at the back part of the pinnae or lateral processes; many of them can be observed in this situation, where the integument is ruptured.

They appear to be developed, not in a distinct ovarium, but in the common connective, or cellular tissue of the part. It is believed that they are discharged by the mouths of the digestive sacs or polypes.

In Acalephes

2926   A Medusa (*Cyanaea aurita*) showing the 'gemmaria' turgid and opaque, from the number of the ciliated gemmules which they contain; these present a yellow colour from the action of the spirit. The gemmaries are situated in the interspaces of the oral tentacles; and open each by a separate ciliated orifice, on the central or inferior surface of the body.

In Echinoderms

2927   A Star-fish (*Asterias rubens*), with the ventral or inferior parietes of two of the rays dissected off, and the ramified ovarium and alimentary caeca displayed: the latter are *in situ*, and present a deep yellow colour: the opaque and white ovaries are reflected downwards; they are turgid with ova. On the opposite side two other rays are laid open, the digestive caeca displaced, and the ovaria exhibited *in situ*.

2928   A Star-fish (*Comatula solaris*). The ovaria are here much more numerous than in the Asterias, being situated in the pinnate processes of the rays.

In Cirripedes

2929   A specimen of the common Barnacle (*Pentelasmis anatifera*) with the outer horny elastic coat of the pedicle reflected; and the inner tunic slit open to show the ova in the substance of the pedicle.

2930   A specimen of the Vitreous Barnacle (*Pentelasmis vitrea*), with the ova similarly exposed in the substance of the pedicle.

In Annelides

2931   Specimens of the ova of the Earthworm (*Lumbricus terrestris*).

In Molluscs

2932   The ova, or 'spat' of the Oyster (*Oestrea edulis*); they are of extreme minuteness, and appear as a white sediment at the bottom of the bottle.

2933   Several specimens of the ova of a Slug (*Limax ater*).

2934   A portion of the viscera of a Snail (*Helix hortensis*) showing several spherical ova in the terminal portion of the oviduct.

2935   Several ova of the *Helix hortensis* after exclusion from the oviduct.

2936   Several of the ova of a Snail (*Helix*), in which development has so far advanced that the form of the shell may be distinguished through the outer envelope.

2937   Ova of another species of Snail, in a similar stage of development.

2938   Ova of another species of Snail, far advanced in development.

2939   Ova of the *Helix pomatia*, soon after their exclusion from the oviduct.

2940   Similar specimens, with development further advanced, exhibiting the rudiments of the shell.

2941   Young specimens of *Helix pomatia*, soon after their exclusion from the ovum.

2942   A specimen of viviparous fresh-water Snail (*Paludina vivipara*). The soft parts have been removed from their shell; and the large ova may be discerned through the transparent tunics of the oviduct.

2943   Three specimens of the same species of *Paludina*. In the upper one the shell has been removed, and the oviduct laid open and emptied of its contents: in the middle specimen, the embryo *Paludinae*, with their rudimental shells, are exposed *in situ*: in the lower specimen the soft parts are in the shell, from which a portion of the basal whorl has been removed to show the relative position of the uterine portion of the oviduct.

2944   A cluster of the nidamental capsules of the ova of a univalve mollusc (*Buccinum*) They are oval, subcompressed, attached by a short pedicle, and truncate at the opposite or free extremity, on which is situated the transversely elliptical orifice leading to the interior of the nidus.

2945   The float of the Janthina (*Janthina fragilis*) with a cluster of the nidamental sacs of the same mollusc. The float is formed by a secretion of albuminous matter disposed in the form of subcylindrical cells, aggregated together in an oblong mass, and filled with air: it is attached to the posterior part of the foot, being in situation analogous to the operculum of other Univalves, which is wanting in the Janthina. The chief destination of the float is to serve as a basis of attachment for the capsules containing the ova; and when their formation and disposition upon the float are completed, the latter is detached by the parent animal. The ova are thus buoyed upon the surface of the sea, where they are exposed to those influences, as the light and heat of the sun's rays, by which the development of the embryo molluscs is best promoted. The capsules are of a flattened pyriform or ovate shape, and composed of a delicate subreticulate film of albuminous secretion, prepared by a laminated nidamental gland near the termination of the oviduct.

2946   A similar but smaller specimen of the float and nidamental capsules of the Janthina.

2947   The nidamental capsule of a univalve mollusc. It presents a flattened transversely oblong form, consists of a thin, subtransparent, amber-coloured tissue, and contains about thirty embryos with the nucleus and first two whorls of their shells completely formed.

2948   A cluster of the nidamental capusles of the Whelk (*Buccinum undatum*). They are depressed, of an irregular oval figure, with one side convex, and the other flat or concave; they are attached by one or more parts of their margin: their external surface is irregularly striated; their internal surface smooth and formed by a thin and delicate membrane, to which numerous extremely minute ova are attached. Several of the capsules are laid open to expose these.

2949 A portion of Oyster-shell, to which several of the nidamental capsules of the same mollusc are attached. In some of these, which are laid open, the lining membrane is distinctly shown.

2950 A group of eighteen nidamental capsules of a *Turbinella* superimposed and adherent to each other. They are of a flattened subpentagonal form, and each contained between twenty and thirty embryos. From two to three whorls of the shell are completed in each embryo, and some have acquired both their characteristic sculpturing and colour.

2950c Group of egg capsules (dried) of a Mollusc.
This specimen formed part of the Kew collection.*

2951 The remains of an elongate, reticulate, compound nidus of a Gastropod, attached to a fragment of a bivalve shell. Only one of the component capsules is entire; the rest are broken open and the embryos have escaped.

2953 The ovarium of a Cuttle-fish (*Sepia officinalis*), laid open, exposing the reticulate calyces or ovisacs in different stages of development: in a few of the largest and darkest-coloured the ova are mature.

2954 The ovarium, oviduct, oviducal gland and nidamental glands of a Cuttle-fish. The oviduct is distended with numerous mature ova, which have burst their calyces and passed into that tube. A bristle is inserted into the excretory outlet of each of the detached nidamental glands, from one of which a longitudinal section has been removed to expose its compact laminated structure.

The ovum, consisting of the germ, the yolk and the vitelline membrane, is invested by successive layers of inspissated albumen, as it traverses the short and wide oviduct and the cortical membrane or chorion is formed by the terminal gland. After quitting the oviduct, the ovum is closely surrounded by a nidamental investment and provided with the filamentary appendage by which the parent attaches it to the appropriate foreign body.

2955 A cluster of the ova of the Cuttle-fish, attached by the filaments secreted by the

---

* In 1841 70 anatomical specimens were presented to the Royal College of Surgeons when the collection of scientific instruments and curios, formerly housed at the Royal Observatory at Kew, was distributed to various institutions. George III and Queen Charlotte were much interested in natural history and many gifts were made by various persons for the museum established at the Observatory in 1769 and used for the education of the royal children. One of these 'sundry persons' was 'Mr John Hunter, Surgeon'. Of the 70 specimens presented to the College 28 had been prepared by Hunter but only 5 of these have survived (717 A, 723, 3504 A, 3719 A, 2950 c).

nidamental glands to a portion of vegetable substance. The nidamental, cortical, and amniotic membranes have been removed from one of these ova, and the embryo is exposed.

2956 A cluster of the ova of the Cuttle-fish, similarly attached by their nidamental pedicles, which are twined around the stem of a fucus.

2957 A small cluster of the blanched and semi-transparent ova of the Cuttle-fish, in which the embryo, far advanced in development, and with its appended (originally orange-coloured) yolk-bag, may be discerned in each ovum.

2958 Three ova of the Cuttle-fish in a similar condition, exhibiting their contained embryos.

2959 An ovum of a Cuttle-fish, laid open, exposing the embryo and its yolk-bag or vitelline sac. The pedicle of the latter appendage, instead of being attached to the abdominal surface, passes to the head and descends along the anterior part of the mouth and gullet, to communicate with the stomach. This communication is permanently indicated by the anterior caecal pouch of the crop in the Octopus.

2961 The embryo of the Cuttle-fish further advanced, and the diminished vitellarium, with the place of attachment of the vitelline duct exhibited.

2962 The embryo of a Cuttle-fish, at nearly the full period of development from which the ventral parietes of the abdomen have been removed to show the fully developed ink-bag, the branchiae, the infundibular valve, and articular cavities: the lateral fins are also completed.
The above three specimens are mounted together.

In Insects

2963 A specimen of the Flesh-fly (*Musca carnaria*) with the ventral parietes of the abdomen dissected away, to show the ovaria and oviducts *in situ*.

2964 One of the flattened circular packets of ova of the Flesh-fly.

2965 A Flesh-fly, with the abdomen laid open, and two of the packets of ova removed from that cavity, showing the development which they undergo while retained in the oviduct of this larviparous insect.

F<small>IG</small>. I

A drawing, probably by William Bell, of the twig of a fir tree with a gall made by *Aphis abietis*. (Hunterian Drawing Book I, p. 75.) Specimen No. 2972.

2966   A similar specimen, in which the young larvae are exhibited, regularly arranged parallel to one another, and ready to be extruded when a fit nidus has been found by the parent. By virtue of this ovo-viviparous modification of insect-development, the Flesh-fly is enabled to retain her brood longer than most other species, and to deposit them in a condition capacitating them for commencing the destruction of the putrescent substances which they are destined to reorganise, without loss of time.

2967   Several specimens of the larvae of a small Gnat (*Culex sp.*). They pass this stage of their existence in water, and are provided with two fringed branchial appendages.

2968   The pupa of a Gnat.

2969   Several specimens of Mosquito, in the imago state.

2970   A section of the skin of a Reindeer containing the nidi of three Breezeflies (*Oestrus tarandi*). A portion of one of these nidi had been cut off, the better to expose the anterior extremity of the contained larva, which, like that of most dipterous insects, is 'ecapitate', or without a distinct scaly head.

2971   A section of the skin of a Reindeer, showing an empty nidus of the *Oestrus tarandi*.
        The instrument by which the female Oestrus pierces the tough skin of deer and cattle is a horny tube consisting of four pieces, which, like the joints of a telescope, are retractile within each other. The last segment terminates in five points, three of which are longer than the others, and hooked; when united together, they form an instrument like an auger, only, having these points, it can bite with more effect.

2972   Two specimens of the young shoot of a Fir-tree converted, by the irritation of the ova and larvae of the *Aphis abietis*, into a gall, resembling one of the fir-cones, or a miniature pineapple. A longitudinal section has been removed from the upper gall, showing its compact solid structure, and the cavities in it containing the larval aphides.

2973   A twig, with some leaves of the black Poplar, exhibiting galls developed on the leaf-stalks, in consequence of the presence of the ova and brood of the *Aphis bursariae*. These galls present a somewhat angular form.

2974   A leaf of the Willow, with several tubercles developed in its cellular parenchyma, in consequence of the irritation of the ova of some insect.

2975   A twig of the common Wild Rose, from the extremity of which a large tuft of moss-like fibres has shot out, in consequence of the irritation induced by the presence of the ova and larvae of the *Cynips rosae*. A section of this abnormal vegetative growth has been made, by which several of the nidamental cavities are laid open, and their smooth inner surfaces, with the enclosed small white larvae, are exposed to view. The surrounding tuft was called by the older Naturalists 'bedeguar', and was esteemed a valuable medicinal substance.

2978   Impregnated ova of the Silk-worm Moth (*Bombyx mori*), showing different stages of the development of the larva. The larvae have been excluded from some of the ova.
         This was one of three preparations illustrating the experiments by Hunter on the impregnation of ova.   *Works*, vol. iv, p. 461.

2979   Several larvae of the Silk-moth, in different stages of growth, from the period of exclusion until they have attained an inch in length.

2980   A full-grown larva of the Bombyx mori, or Silk-worm.

2981   A full-grown larva, dissected so as to display the principal parts of its anatomical structure. A longitudinal incision has been made immediately above the spiracula or breathing pores of one side, and the integument has been reflected from the dorsal aspect of the body, exposing the straight and wide alimentary canal *in situ*, with the small white secerning tubes attached to the parietes of its posterior part. By the side of the intestine the convoluted tubes which secrete the silk are shown. The longitudinal dorsal vessel, or heart, is attached to the reflected portion of integument.

2982   A full-grown larva, with the integument removed from the right side of the body, showing the silk-gland of that side, the alimentary canal and biliary tubes.

2983   A full-grown larva, dissected to show the alimentary canal *in situ*, and especially the magnitude of the gastric portion or stomach, at the period of the larva's greatest voracity.

2984   A Silk-worm near the close of its larva state, when it has ceased to feed, dissected to show the remarkable diminution of the size of the stomach.

2986 This specimen is mounted with Nos. 2995, 3009, 3010. The letters serve to identify the specimens in the several jars.

A Silk-worm, towards the close of its larval stage, with the abdominal walls dissected from the dorsal and lateral aspects, to show the commencing enlargement and functional activity of the sericteria (the silk gland); the dilated or secerning portions of which are beginning to be distended with the dark albuminous material of the silk. (A)

2995 The thin, dense, compact inner case or chamber of the cocoon, which is laid open to show the larva, about to cast its last skin and pass into the pupa state. (B)

2997 A similar preparation, showing the silk-moth in the pupa state; the last larval skin, or mask, having been thrown off, and lying crumpled up by the side of the pupa. (A)

2998 A similar preparation. (B)

2999 A similar preparation, exhibiting an advanced stage of the transformation of the pupa; the exuvial integument of which has been worked down towards the bottom of the cocoon. (H)

3000 A similar preparation. (L)

3001 A similar preparation, showing the imago in the condition preparatory to commencing its escape from the cocoon. (A)

3002 A cocoon, through the inner case of which the imago has eaten a round hole and has protruded its head. (B)

3003 A similar preparation, with the act of extrication farther advanced. (C)

3004 The imago, with the cocoon from which it has just emerged. (D)

3007 A deserted cocoon of the Silk-moth, laid open to show the exuvial remains of the pupa. (E)

3009 A larva, near the completion of that stage of existence when it is about to cast its skin, which is beginning to open at the back. (C)

3010 A larva about to pass into the pupa state; with its last skin loose and ready to be shed: one-half of it has been removed to show the pupa within.   (D)

3011 The pupa or chrysalis of the Silk-moth, enveloped in its pupal integument or 'puparium'.   (D)

3012 The pupa, with the pupal exuvium shed, but remaining attached to the anal segment.   (F)

3013 The pupa removed from its puparium, to show the commencing development of the wings, and other characteristic external parts of the imago.   (C)

3014 The pupa in the state of ecdysis, with the wings, legs, and antennae of the imago farther advanced in their formation.   (L)
      The seven following preparations show the progressive development of the external organs of the imago, to the perfect formation of the Silk-moth:

3015 A pupa, with the rudimental wings of one side removed.   (E)

3016 A similar specimen, at a more advanced stage of development.   (G)

3017 A similar preparation, with the pupal exuvium removed from one side of the head to show the rudimental antenna, and the disappearance of the horny lateral mandible, which was adapted to cut and tear the leaves on which the voracious larva fed, but has now given place to the suctorious organ termed 'antlia', formed chiefly by the elongated maxillae.   (K)

3018 A male imago.   (F)

3020 A female pupa, with the wings half developed: the ova which distend the abdomen may be seen through the transparent parietes of that cavity.   (M)

3021 A fully developed female Silk-moth, ready for oviposition.   (H)

3022 A similar specimen.   (I)

The nine following preparations exhibit the changes and development of some of the internal organs of the Silk-moth during the pupa state:

3023 The pupa with the ventral parietes removed from the back of the abdomen to show the shortened stomach and the commencing elongation of the slender intestinal canal.   (A)

3024 The right moiety of a longitudinally bisected pupa, showing the elongated intestinal canal, bent in a close fold upon itself.   (B)

3025 A male pupa, with the abdominal cavity longitudinally slit open, showing the alimentary canal and the two testes in the form of small white glandular bodies, situated near the posterior third of the alimentary canal: they are closely approximated to each other in their natural position.   (C)

3026 A male pupa, farther advanced, exhibiting the fusion of the originally distinct testes into a single glandular body.   (D)

3027 A female pupa, with the ventral parietes of the abdomen removed to show the rudimental tubular ovaria.   (E)

3028 A female pupa, somewhat farther advanced, with the ovarian tubes displayed from the dorsal aspect.   (F)

3029 A female pupa, at a more advanced stage, dissected to show the development of the seminal reservoir or 'spermatheca', in addition to the ovarian or essential parts of the productive generative system.   (G)

3030 A female pupa, still more advanced, with the ventral parietes of the abdomen removed to exhibit the increase of length of the ovarian tubes, and the completion of the contained ova.   (H)

3031 A more advanced pupa, with the ovaria and fully formed ova displayed *in situ*.   (I)

The following six preparations show the female generative organs in adult Silk-moths:

3032 A female imago or perfect Silk-moth, with the dorsal parietes of the abdomen removed to show the ovarian tubes and ova *in situ*.   (A)

3033 A similar specimen, with the abdomen laid open from the ventral aspect, and the ovarian tubes turned down.   The generative organs have broken off and perished.   (B)

C.H.M.—D

3034   A female Silk-moth, similarly dissected.   (C)

3035   A female Silk-moth with the ovarian tubes more fully displayed.   (D)

3036   A female Silk-moth, showing the accessory organs of generation.   These are the
       bursa copulatrix or sperm reservoir, and the accessory glands.   The former is a
       large vesicle with thin semi-transparent walls, parts of which have been removed;
       the latter is a small, bilobed, opaque gland situated between the *bursa copulatrix*
       and the expanded rectum.   It probably secretes the eggshell and the substance
       by means of which the eggs adhere to foreign bodies.   This specimen is much
       damaged.   (E)

3037   A female Moth with the ventral walls of the abdomen removed to show the
       ovarian tubes and ova *in situ*.   (F)

3038   A female Puss-moth (*Cerura vinula*), with the ventral walls of the abdomen removed
       and with a great part of the ovaries and intestinal canal dissected away to
       expose more clearly the accessory parts of the reproductive apparatus.

3039   A female of the Small Purple-barred Moth (*Noctua nupta*) with the ovarian tubes
       shown from the right side.   The specimen is much damaged and the ovaries
       are lost.

3040   A female Poplar Hawk-moth (*Smerinthus populi*) with the ventral walls of the
       abdomen removed and the ovarian tubes with the linear series of contained ova
       reflected downwards.   The ovaries have become detached from the body of the
       moth and are somewhat broken, but they still show the ripe ova lodged, like a
       string of beads, in the ovarian tubes, each in a little dilatation.

3041   A female Privet Hawk-moth (*Sphinx ligustri*) with the dorsal walls of the abdomen
       removed and the ovarian tubes displayed, beaded with ripe ova.   The ovaries
       have broken off and are mounted below the moth.

3042   The ovaries of another species of Hawk-moth.
           The organs have been removed from the body, and are somewhat broken,
       but they show towards the anterior extremities of the ovarian tubes unripe eggs
       and towards their more posterior parts (at the upper end of the specimen) ripe
       eggs, each lying within a little dilatation of the tube.

3043 The female of a species of Hawk-moth (*Smerinthus*) with leaves to which she has attached several of her ova.

    The eggs are scattered irregularly upon the under surface of the leaves; this is the most common situation of the ova of Lepidoptera, especially in those species which oviposit in the summer and in which the larvae are excluded before the fall of the leaf.

Eggs of several species of Lepidoptera, showing differing modes of oviposition:

3044 A portion of the stem of a vine with numerous ova of a *Bombyx* or *Sphinx* attached to it in closely aggregated longitudinal rows.

3045 Two pieces of twig with chaplets of the ova of the Lackey Moth (*Lasiocampa neustria*) twined around them in a close spiral.

3046 Two pieces of oak twig, with the ova of the Egger-moth (*Lasiocampa quercus*) similarly arranged and attached to the bark. They are laid in autumn, and are not to be hatched until the spring; so that besides being independent of the fall of the leaf, by this mode of oviposition the eggs derive the benefit of the steady temperature of the living vegetable bodies to which they are attached.

3047 Numerous ova and new-hatched larvae of a Moth (*Bombyx*). The ova have a shining exterior, and are enclosed in a silken covering secreted by the parent moth. The larvae are minute and very hairy.

3049 The capacious alimentary canal of the voracious larva of some large Lepidopterous Insect: the white capillary tubes attached to the side of the stomach, and opening into the small intestine, are the hepatic organs.

3050 The alimentary canal and silk-glands of the larva of a large Moth. The secretory parts of the glands form a dense convoluted mass around the posterior part of the alimentary canal. Their anterior, duct portion, has perished.

    In Lepidoptera each silk gland narrows anteriorly to form a fine duct; near the head the ducts from the two glands unite and open by a short common segment at the apex of a conical papilla or spinneret situated below the mouth.

3052 The hairy larva of the Tussock-moth (*Laria pudibunda*).

3054 The larva of a large exotic *Bombyx*; it is ornamented by numerous spots, which reflect an iridescent lustre.

This specimen shows admirably the external characters of a Lepidotperan larva. The body is worm-like and segmented. Each of the first three segments behind the head bears a pair of jointed legs, which persist and function later as the legs of the imago. The hinder segments are provided with unjointed pseudo-legs, cushion-like and fringed around the margin of their tread with a number of hooks. The hinder pair of these legs projects from the posterior extremity of the body and is known as the claspers. By means of the pseudo-legs the cater-pillar adheres firmly to its food plant, leaving the head and fore-part of the body free for the movements necessary in browsing.

Upon each side of the body upon the first and the fourth to the eleventh segments may be observed the large oval spiracles, through which air is conveyed to the respiratory system of tracheal tubes.

3055   The larva and pupa of the Cabbage Butterfly (*Pieris brassica*).

3056   The pupa of a Butterfly pendent from a leaf by its posterior extremity.

The external surface of the pupa-case reflects rich metallic iridescent tints, whence the name 'chrysalis' popularly given to this type of pupa, and in consequence to pupae in general.

3057   The chrysalis of a Butterfly, through whose transparent pupal skin may be seen, in place of the tissues of the pupa, a number of maggots.

These are parasites introduced probably as eggs into the body of the Cater-pillar; there they live and grow at the expense of their host and ultimately when fully fed, consume the entire soft tissues of the host, leaving only the indigestible cuticular pupa skin.

3058   A lustreless chrysalis of another species of Butterfly.

3059   Part of the branch of a tree enveloped in the web spun by the larvae of the Satin Moth (*Eriogaster lanestris*). The larvae weave the web for their common pro-tection.

Besides the dried larvae, which may be seen clustering upon the web, specimens of the pupa with its cocoon and of the perfect insect are also shown.

3060   The larva of a large Hawk-moth, probably *Acherontia atropos*.

3061   The pupa of a Death's-head Hawk-moth (*Acherontia atropos*), from the right side of which the pupa-case has been dissected off to show the nascent organs of the future imago, upon which the outer case is moulded. The long proboscis, afterwards spirally coiled, is now bent closely upon itself: the long antenna lies, anterior to the wing, in a groove between that margin of the wing and the second pair of legs: the legs are disposed in parallel lines and meet in front of the thorax. The pupae, which are thus enclosed in a simple case, not divided into special compartments for the different members, were termed by Linnaeus 'pupae obtectae'.

3062 A male Death's-head Hawk-moth in the imago state, with the ventral wall of the abdomen removed to show the large single testis, situated behind the coil of intestine.

3063 A female Death's-head Hawk-moth, similarly dissected to show the ovaria *in situ*; only a portion of these tubular organs is thus displayed.

 The sexual characters afforded by the antennae and the anal segment of the abdomen may be noticed by comparing this with the preceding specimen.

3065 Three of the ova of a Beetle belonging to the family *Cerambycidae*.

3066 A female Chafer (*Melolontha solstitialis*) with the dorsal walls of the abdomen removed to show the ovarian tubes and ripe ova *in situ*.

3067 A female Chafer (*Acrida*) from which part of the ovarian apparatus with the contained ova had been removed.

 The preparation is much damaged and of the genital apparatus mentioned in the original description only two ripe ova remain; they are large and of rounded oval form.

3070 A female Rose Beetle (*Cetonia aurata*), with the ventral walls of the abdomen removed, part of the ovarian apparatus displayed, and a group of ripe ova therefrom mounted separately. The ova are spherical and of about the size of large shot.

3072 The larva and its cocoon of a large exotic species of *Cerambyx*.

 The outer wall of the cocoon is formed by portions of twig irregularly attached to each other by silken filaments, and the strong case, thus formed, is lined by a close and thick layer of fine and soft silk.

3073 A longitudinal section of the cocoon of the same larva: it is admirably adapted for strength, warmth, and concealment.

3074   The pupa of the Stag-beetle (*Prionus cervicornis*), showing the rudiments of the thoracic segments and their locomotive appendages.

3075   The pupa of the Stag-beetle exhibiting the characteristic organs of the imago in process of formation.

  The head and thorax with their appendages are clearly defined. Upon the head may be seen the antennae, the great mandibles and the other lesser mouth parts. The three segments of the thorax are still independent, but the lateral parts of the second and third are produced to form rudiments of the wings and wing covers, though at this stage these organs are still quite small. The limbs are fully formed and lie curled up upon the ventral surface of the body. The appendages, unlike those of the pupae of the Lepidoptera, project freely from the general surface of the body, each encased in a tubular sheath formed by a simple extension of the pupal skin.

  Upon the sides of the abdomen may be observed a series of vertically elongated spiracles.

3076   A pupa of the Stag-beetle removed from its pupal integument.

  The several parts characteristic of the adult Beetle are fully formed, except that the wing-cases and wings are still relatively small and curve round the sides of the body leaving the dorsal parts of the abdomen exposed.

3077   The pupa of a Scarabaeus, showing from the ventral aspect the limbs and other appendages, not glued to the body as in Lepidoptera and some other Insects, but projecting freely, each encased in a sheath of the pupal skin.   (A)

3078   The pupa of a Dung Beetle (*Geotrupes stercorarius*) with the dorsal walls of the abdomen removed to show parts of the slender (coiled) alimentary canal.   (B)

3079   A similar pupa, further advanced in development, removed from its pupal skin. Except for the small size of the wings it shows all the external characters of the adult.   (C)

Four specimens illustrating the metamorphosis of the Palm Beetle (*Calandra palmorum*):

3080   A larva, showing its external form. The head is very clearly defined: but the rest of the body is a shapeless, swollen sac, with little sign of segmentation except for the three pairs of jointed limbs attached to its anterior (thoracic) region. Posteriorly it terminates in a short vertically flattened process, which may represent a pair of false legs, similar to the claspers of the Lepidopteran caterpillar.   (A)

3081   A similar larva in longitudinal section, showing parts of the alimentary canal. This, unlike that of the caterpillar, is slender and considerably coiled towards its posterior end.   (B)

3082   A pupa.   The various parts of the adult are roughly indicated, but their somewhat coarse appearance is mainly due to the fact that each appendage is encased in an independent sheath of the pupal skin.   The proboscis, characteristic of the Weevils, is fully formed and bears at its extremity minute tubercles, the rudiments of the reduced mouth parts of the adult.   (C)

3083   An imago.   Compared with that of the pupa, the body is markedly reduced in length and bears no sort of resemblance to that of the larva.   The outer cuticle is hard and deeply pigmented.   (D)

3084   A bundle of cocoons of an Ichneumon (*Microgaster* sp.).
        The ova are deposited in the body of a caterpillar and after passing there the larval state as entozoan parasites, feeding upon the adipose tissue of their victim, they spin cocoons, which are enveloped in the silky substance here shown.   (A)

3085   A cluster of pupa cases of *Microgaster*, together with some specimens of the fly.   (B)

3086   A similar specimen.   (C)

3087   A group of pupa cases of a *Microgaster* allied to *Ichneumon glomeratus*.   A section has been removed from one side of the nidus, showing the closely aggregated cells that contain the individual papae.   (D)

3088   Two groups of pupa cases of a species of *Microgaster* with a specimen of the fly and a dried caterpillar that probably was the host preyed upon by the larvae.   (E)

3089   Several longitudinally ribbed cocoons of a species of *Microgaster* attached to the inner surface of a piece of bark.   (F)

3090   Two elliptical pupa cases of an *Ichneumon* attached by one side to pieces of bark. They are smooth and parchment-like and have been perforated at the upper end by a large round aperture for the escape of the imago.

3091   A portion of the twig of a Rose-tree showing a series of galls containing the cells of a Saw-fly (*Tenthredo sp.*).

Gall formation is apparently due partly to the infection of the plant tissue by a secretion injected into them by the mother fly, partly to the products of the growth of the larva.

The Saw-flies make an incision in the plant by means of a pair of filamentary saw-like appendages of the anal segment that works backwards and forwards alternately.   After the incision is made the saws divaricate sufficiently to allow the passage of the egg into the tissues of the plant.

3092   Two Hymenopterous Insects of the genus *Bombex*, in the imago state.

3093   A fertile female or queen Hornet (*Vespa crabro*) with the dorsal walls of the abdomen removed and the ovarian tubes unravelled and turned down, showing the great number and progressive development of the ova.

When first formed at the distal extremities of the ovarian tubes the ova are spherical, but as they ripen the shape gradually alters to an elongated oval.

3094   A fragment of a Hornet's nest in which most of the cells are occupied by pupae.

Many of the marginal cells have been laid open longitudinally, exposing the pupae within; these lie with the head towards the mouth of the cell and show in their external form the characters of the adult, but are soft, pale and devoid of pigment.

The mouths of the cells occupied by pupae are closed by a projecting dome-shaped cover, through which the head of the contained pupa can be seen.   This cover is the exposed cocoon which is spun by the larva shortly before pupation and forms a complete lining to the papery cell of the comb, projecting beyond its mouth and closing it.

3095   A piece of the comb of a Hornet's nest, showing in surface view numerous pupal cells each closed by the projecting dome-shaped extremity of the cocoon.

Through this transparent cover may be seen the head of the contained pupa, with its antennae and pigmented eyes.   The comb is made of paper, composed of vegetable fibre chewed up by the adult and mixed with the secretions of the mouth.   The combs consist of cells enclosed and protected by an outer case of paper.   Within the cells the larvae undergo their development, and just before pupation spin a silken cocoon, that forms a complete lining to the paper cell and closes its mouth.

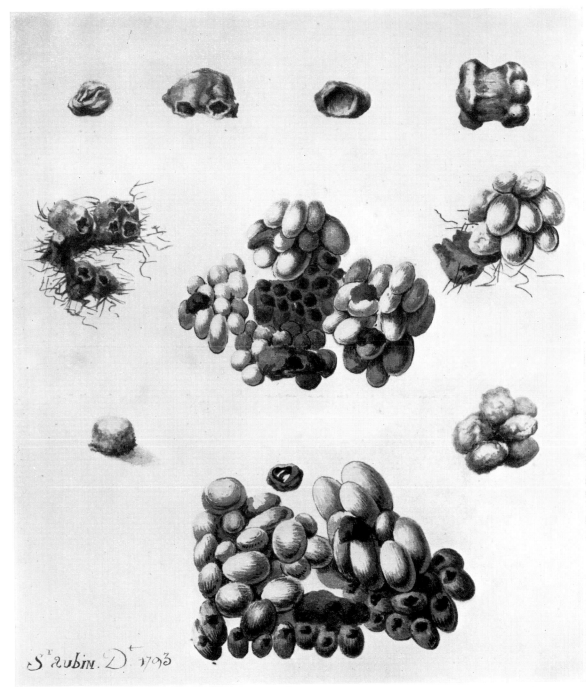

S. Aubin. D.ᵗ 1793

FIG. 2

A drawing by St Aubin showing the structure of the cells of the Humble Bee and the manner in which they are fixed.
(Hunterian Drawing Book I, p. 80.) Specimen No. 3118.

Fig. 3

A piece of Honeycomb showing the 'worker' cells occupied by pupae; and many of the 'drones' by larvae. Specimen No. 3130.

3096   A young larva of a Hornet (*Vespa crabro*), invested with a thin exuvial tunic.

3097   A fully-grown larva with, below it, the remains of the semi-transparent lining of
       the cell within which it lay.   This membrane is a delicate silken cocoon spun
       by the larva shortly before pupation.

3098   A fully-grown larva, within its semi-transparent cocoon.

3099   A pupa with, below it, the remains of the delicate lining of its cell.   The pupa has
       the form characteristic of the adult, with its various appendages fully differ-
       entiated, though somewhat rough-hewn in appearance owing to their encase-
       ment in extensions of the pupal skin.
           The wings at this stage are relatively very small and are directed towards the
       ventral aspect of the body.
           Amongst the debris of the cocoon may be seen a black mass, which consists of
       faecal matter ejected by the larva shortly before pupation.

3102   A common Wasp (*Vespa vulgaris*) in the imago state.

3103   Two portions of the nest of a Hornet, showing numerous cells occupied by pupae.
       On the surface of the comb is mounted an imago.

3104   A fragment of the nest of a social Hymenopterous Insect, which has been suspen-
       ded from a tree.
           Most of the hexagonal cells of the comb are open and the progressive growth
       of the larva, from the small ovum to the pupa in the closed cell, is very clearly
       displayed.
           The egg is glued to the wall of an uncompleted cell by the pole that will
       eventually form the posterior end of the larva.   When the eggs hatch the adult
       workers feed the growing larva and heighten the walls of the cell.   At the close
       of larval life the full-fed larva spins a delicate silken cocoon which completely
       lines the cell and projects beyond its mouth, forming to it a dome-shaped cover.
           A specimen of the adult Insect is attached to the comb.

3105   A similar preparation.

3106   Two Hymenopterans of the genus *Pelopaeus*, one in the pupal, the other in the
       imago state.
           Note, in both, the curiously elongated and narrow waist, and (in the pupa)
       the relative absence of pigment and the undeveloped condition of the wings.

3107 The larvae and imago of a Mason Wasp (*Odynerus parietinus*).

This Insect bores a cylindrical cavity from two to three inches deep in hard sand and, after cementing the detached particles into little oblong pellets, arranges them round the entrance of the hole so as to form a tunnel, which is often not less than two or three inches in length. It is in these artificial subterranean cells that the eggs are laid and the larvae nourished. They may be found in this country in sandy banks exposed to the sun.

3108 A fragment of a Wasp's nest, in which nearly all the hexagonal breeding cells have been deserted.

3109 A similar fragment, in the cells of which are larvae in different stages of growth.

3110 A piece of decayed wood, which has been bored by a Leaf-cutter Bee (*Megachile centuncularis*).

The long cylindrical tunnel has been laid open, showing within it six cells or nests of the Bee; each cell is completely independent of the rest and is formed of large pieces of leaf rolled together.

It is not clear whether the Bee itself bored the tunnel in the wood. Leaf-cutter Bees apparently are in the habit of using any suitable hole or crevice in which to build their cells.

3111 A cell of the Leaf-cutter Bee removed from the burrow and laid open longitudinally to show the contained larva curled up at the bottom of the cell and above it a mass of food material. The cell is thimble-shaped, convex at the end occupied by the larva and truncate at the other, and plugged by a wad of leaf fragments and vegetable debris.

The larva is a maggot-like grub, with a distinct head, but limbless. (A)
Mounted with 3113, 3115, 3116.

3112 The cell of a Leaf-cutter Bee, opened and with the larva removed to show a mass of food material, consisting of a mixture of nectar and pollen, inserted into the cell by the parent.

After the cell has been built, the Bee deposits within it a store of food sufficient to nourish the grub till it is ready to pupate, and then inserts the eggs.

3113 The larva of a Leaf-cutter Bee, removed from its cell. (D)

3115 One of the cells of a Leaf-cutter Bee, laid open to expose the fully-grown larva.

The grub at this stage, having consumed the food material stored in the cell, has much increased in bulk and occupies the entire cell.   (C)

3116   A similar preparation of the cell of a Leaf-cutter Bee, showing the fully-developed imago lying within it.   The head of the Bee is directed towards the truncate end of the cell.   (B)

The following specimens illustrate a Hunterian manuscript on the life history and nesting habits of the Humble Bee.   The manuscript was copied by William Clift and is printed in full in Richard Owen's edition of the *Physiological Series*, vol. v, p. 38 and in the *Works*, vol. v, p. 60.   The substance is as follows:

The young queen emerges from the pupa in the late summer and after copulation hibernates.   In the early spring she seeks a mouse-hole or some other suitable spot in which to build a nest.   In this she first forms a single cell of wax for the storage of honey and then makes a mass of farina upon which she deposits six or more eggs and covers them with more farina.   The eggs hatch and the young larvae feed on the farina, to which more is added from time to time by the queen.

By the time the larvae are ready to pupate each has eaten nearly all the farina surrounding it.   Within the cavity thus formed, it spins a dense silken cocoon, forming with its neighbours an irregular comb of ovoid cells.   The larva then pupates, leaving a mass of excrement and cast larval skin at the bottom of the cell.   Meanwhile the queen has deposited on the edge of the comb a fresh mass of farina and lays on it more eggs.

After the first brood has emerged, the work of adding new masses of farina to each successive comb is delegated to the workers and the queen is solely occupied in laying eggs.   Each comb after it has been vacated by its brood is used for the storage of honey.

The workers and drones emerge from the pupae from June onwards, the queens a month or so later.   The queens only, and of them but a very small percentage, survive the winter.

3117   A fertile female or queen Humble Bee (*Bombus terrestris*) with the ventral walls of the body removed to display the ovarian tubes *in situ*.   (A)

3118   Three groups of the irregular suboval cells of a Humble Bee.   The cells in the upper group have been vacated by the emergence of the perfect insects; at the bottom of each may be seen a mass consisting of the cast skins and faeces of the grubs.

   Those of the central group are occupied by larvae ready to pupate.   In those of the lower group are pupae far advanced in development.   (B)

3119   The larvae and an imago of the Humble Bee.   (C)

3121   Several of the cells of the Humble Bee, some of which are laid open to show within them pupae far advanced in development.   (D)

3122   Four cells of the Humble Bee; one is entire, the others are laid open, so as to expose respectively the dorsal, ventral and lateral aspects of the contained pupae, which are destined to be 'workers'.   (E)

3123   A series of cells of the Humble Bee, showing the progressive development of the pupa to the assumption (in the upper cell) of the imago state.   These pupae (except two workers mounted below) are of larger size than those shown in the previous specimen and are destined to be Queens.   (F)

The next series of specimens illustrate Hunter's memoir 'Observations on Bees', (*Works*, vol. iv, p. 422.)   The following is the substance of Hunter's account of the honey-comb:

The combs of the Honey Bee, unlike those of wasps, are set vertically, and consist of a double series of hexagonal cells projecting horizontally from either face of a median vertical plate.

The central plate is pitted by the bottoms of the cells, but the cells of either side are not directly opposed to one another, the base of a cell of one side forming parts of the bases of three contiguous cells of the other side.

The comb is formed of wax secreted between the ventral abdominal plates of the workers and is composed of cells of several different kinds, some being used for storing honey and pollen (Bee bread), others for the nurture of the young.   The latter are of three types:

1. Small cells adapted to the size of 'workers'.
2. Larger cells, situated towards the lower part of the comb, for the nurture of males, or drones.
3. A few irregular and much larger cells, attached to the margin of the comb, for the development, by special feeding, of fertile females or queens.

The eggs are laid by the Queen at the bottom of the cell and are surrounded by the workers by a drop of nutritive matter or pap composed of bee bread and honey.   After about five days the eggs hatch, giving rise to a small grub which lies coiled up at the bottom of the cell in the droplet of pap.   Upon this pap the grub feeds and as it grows more pap is constantly provided for it by the workers.   When fully fed at the end of about four days the larva occupies nearly the whole cell and alters its position so that it lies at full length with the head directed to the mouth of the cell.   When pupation is near the workers seal the cell with a porous cover of wax and foreign debris. The larva meanwhile has ejected its faeces and cast its last skin, moulding the skin with the addition of a little silk into a cocoon-like lining to the cell.

In less than a fortnight the metamorphosis of the pupa is complete, the pupa skin is cast, and the perfect insect bites its way through the cover of the cell.

The vacated breeding cells are used again and again for the nurture of subsequent broods and in the course of time become much blocked up by the cast larval skins and faeces of their successive occupants, till they are no longer usable.

The production of queens and workers on the one hand and of drones on the other depends on the fertilisation or non-fertilisation of the egg—a fertilised egg giving rise to a female, a non-fertilised egg to a drone. Whether a fertilised egg shall develop into a worker or a queen depends upon the nature of the food supplied to the larva.

3125   A portion of Honeycomb, showing the breeding cells of the workers and the young in different stages of development, from the ovum cemented to the bottom of the open and incomplete cell, to the commencement of the pupa stage, when the cell is closed by the adult workers with a cover of wax and farina. Larvae may be seen at various stages of development curled up at the bottom of the cell.

3126   A similar specimen. The larva at first lies coiled up at the bottom of the cell, but as it nears pupation it changes its position and the axis of its body becomes parallel to that of the cell, which it finally fills, before it is closed up by the workers to undergo the metamorphosis from the pupa to the imago state.

Upon the edge of the specimen many cells are in longitudinal section, showing within them pupae filling the whole cell, with the head close against the cell cover. The specimen is somewhat macerated so that in many cases the wax walls of the cells have disintegrated, exposing a delicate lining consisting mainly of the cast skin of the larvae.

3127   A piece of Honeycomb composed entirely of breeding cells, mostly occupied by larvae nearing the period of pupation. The larvae at this stage occupy the entire cell, lying in it at full length with the head directed towards the cell mouth. In many instances the larvae have ceased feeding and the cells have been sealed by the workers.

3128   A portion of Honeycomb with the pupae of workers or infertile females in the breeding cells.

The cells that contain the pupae are sealed. Here and there amongst them are cells filled with Bee bread, a food-material made from the pollen of flowers and mixed with honey by the workers to form a pap with which to feed the larvae.

3129   A piece of Honeycomb in which the breeding cells are sealed and contain pupae. The cells on the left side of the specimen are larger than the others and project above the general surface of the comb. They are peculiar to the young drones or males.

3130   A similar specimen in which the 'worker' cells are for the most part occupied by pupae, and those of the drones by full-fed larvae, or pupae in the early stages of their metamorphosis.

   Here and there perfect Insects may be observed with their abdomen projecting from the mouth of an open cell, in the position in which they give food to the young.

3131   A portion of Honeycomb of a darker colour and with thicker cell walls. Almost the whole cavity of the cell is filled with solid matter composed apparently of the cast skin and faeces of a succession of grubs.

3132   A similar specimen.

3133   A portion of a single layer of old breeding cells, showing the form of the bottom of the cells which were in apposition to the corresponding extremities of the cells of the opposite layer.

   The base of each cell is concave and is separable into three flat surfaces of quadrangular form. Each quadrangle forms one-third of the floor of one of three contiguous cells of the opposite face of the comb.

   Four preparations of old breeding cells showing the laminated mass of cast larval skins by which they are to a large extent filled:

3134   A longitudinal section of a portion of a double tier of old cells, which shows the number of exuvial coats of the larvae with which they have been successively lined.

   Upon the lateral walls of the cell the cast skins are closely pressed together, but at the base the mass formed by them is more loosely compacted, the exuviae being interlarded with faecal matter. (A)

3135   Three similar old breeding cells in longitudinal section. (B)

3136   Three old breeding cells in longitudinal section.   (D)

3137   A similar preparation, with the several layers of membrane, formed by the exuvial coats of successive broods of larvae, turned down.   (C)

A series of specimens showing the immature and perfect stages in the life of the Hive Bee (*Apis mellifica*):

3139   A larva and pupa of the Hive Bee.   (C)

3140   A series of pupae in different stages of development.   (D)

3141   Two workers or infertile females, in the imago state.   (A)

3142   A fertile female, or Queen Bee, in the imago state.   (B)

3144   The pupa and puparium of an Ant.

3145   An Ant at the period of transition from the pupa to the imago state.

3146   The fertile female of *Termes bellicosus*, with the abdomen expanded to about one third the size which it attains when the ovarian tubes have acquired their full development.   The queen is the only fertile female, and mother of the colony; she is confined with the male within the nest in a royal chamber.
      The abdomen is distended to form a huge oval sac upon the surface of which the sclerites of the several segments appear as a series of narrow dark-coloured bands separated by extensive areas of softer chitin.   In the queen Termite, growth (apart from mere distension) takes place after the metamorphosis is complete, new ovarian tubes being added in great numbers to the genital system.

3147   The abdominal walls and ovaries of a queen Termite, at the time of the full development of the ovarian tubes.
      The details of this preparation have been destroyed owing to the lapse of time, but it still demonstrates the enormous size of the abdomen and the multitude

and compact crowding of the ovarian tubes. The abdomen of the fully developed queen can exceed in size the rest of the body by 1,500-2,000 times.

3148, 3149   Preparations of the ovaries of a queen Termite:
A. A portion or lobe of the ovary showing the close aggregation of the ovarian tubes.
B. A longitudinal section of a lobe of the ovary.

3151   A queen of *Termes mordax*, with the abdomen laid open to show the two immense compact lobes of the ovaries *in situ*.

3152   A leaf of Willow, with many oval excrescences or galls produced by the larva of some insect (? *Cynips*).

3154   Nine larval cases of the Caddis Fly (*Phryganea sp.*).

3155   A female Cicada, showing the ovipositor whereby incisions are made in trees for the reception of her eggs. The ovipositor of the Cicadas consists of three pieces; two lateral, with dentate extremities, and one central, shaped like a stiletto. Their action has not been very satisfactorily explained, but it is probably somewhat as follows: a small puncture is made with the stiletto; into this the lateral pieces are inserted. The stiletto being now pushed down between them like a wedge, the side pieces are forced apart; their teeth grip the sides of the puncture, giving purchase for the inthrust of the stiletto and the puncture is deepened and enlarged. The stiletto is then withdrawn, the side pieces inserted again further down the enlarged puncture, ready to take a grip on its sides when the stiletto is again thrust down between them to further deepen and enlarge the hole. The same process is repeated again and again till the hole is deep enough for the reception of the eggs.

A series of specimens showing some of the stages in the life history of *Cicada australis*:

3156   A. The larva, showing the complete absence of wings and the great development of the first pair of legs in adaptation to an underground fossorial habit.

3157   B. The cast skin or exuvium of a larva.

3158   C. A pupa or nymph near the advent of the imago stage, showing the soft and crumpled condition of the wings.

3159   D. An imago, showing the wings now fully expanded, hard and transparent.

The Cicadas are said to exist as larvae for as long a period as 17 years; they then pupate for a few days and emerge in the perfect or imago state to live a free life for a short time and breed. The larva is purely subterranean in habit, burrowing deeply into the earth and feeding upon roots. It will be noticed in the specimen that its mouth parts are suctorial like those of the perfect Insect.

3159A   An exotic species of Land Bug (*Pentatoma*), with the dorsal walls of the abdomen removed to show the ovarian tubes and a few large ova developing within them.

Prepared by Richard Owen.

3160   A Water Bug (*Belostoma grande*) with one half of the ventral walls of the abdomen removed to show the ovary. Two large ova may be seen towards the anterior end of the abdomen alongside a coil of the intestine.

3161   The pupa of *Belostoma grandis*, exhibiting the commencing development of the wings as flat, scale-like projections from the postero-lateral margins of the second and third thoracic segments.

3162   A female American Cockroach (*Blatta americana*) with the ventral walls of the abdomen removed to show the digestive and generative organs *in situ*. The oviducts terminate in a long stout common segment within which the eggs are encased in a chitinous pod or nidamental capsule. In the specimen this capsule may be seen newly formed, within the oviduct. It is a long cylinder, flattened from side to side and fluted transversely by thirty or more parallel grooves.

3163   A female Common Cockroach (*Blatta orientalis*) with the egg-case protruded from the genital orifice and gripped by the terminal abdominal segments.

    The egg case is shorter and thicker than that of the American Cockroach. Its dorsal margin is marked by a toothed seam, along the line of which the case opens when the young are ready to emerge.

3163A   Two empty egg cases of a Cockroach, attached to the inner surface of a piece of bark.

    The Cockroach carries the egg case till she can find a suitably secluded spot in which to deposit it, there to await the hatching and escape of the young larvae.

Presented by Dr. Leach.

C.H.M.—E

3164 A Cockroach entering upon the imago state, after shedding its pupal or nymph skin.   The wings are still soft and the whole body of a dull white colour.

3165 A Locust (*Pterophylla myrtifolia*) with the ventral and left walls of the abdomen removed to show the large flattened oblong ova in the left ovary.

In the Acrididae the ovarian tubes open into a large lateral chamber or calyx, continuous below with its fellow to form a short oviduct, and prolonged above in a narrow gut-like coil.

In this specimen the position of the ripe eggs is not very clear, but apparently they are mainly contained within this enlarged calyx.   The extremities of the ovarian tubes, beaded by a few quite rudimentary ova, may be seen here and there.

3166 A Grasshopper (*Acrida viridissima*) with the spermatheca and one of the wide oviducts or calyces; some ripe ova are mounted separately.

The anal segment of the abdomen is produced into a long, narrow and straight ensate ovipositor, consisting of two flattened horny plates, which are thrust into the earth and then separated sufficiently to convey the ova into the hole thus prepared for them.   H. Dewitz, *Z. wiss. Zool.*, Bd. 25, 1875, pp. 174-200.

3167 A Locust (*Acrida*) with the right side of the thorax and abdomen removed exposing the whole alimentary canal and the right ovary and oviduct full of ripe ova. The ovary has broken off.   The ovipositor is long and slightly bent or sabre-shaped.

3168 The ovary, oviduct, spermatheca, and one of the blades of the ovipositor of a large species of Locust (*Acrida*).   The ripe ova with which the ovary is packed are long and narrow.

3169 A female Mantis (*Mantis religiosa*) dissected to show the alimentary canal and generative apparatus *in situ*.   The ovarian tubes are numerous, short and simple. The ova are at a very early period of their development.

The details of the ovary are not clearly shown; it is stated to consist in this species of about 40 tubes, joined at their bases in clusters of half a dozen, each cluster opening into a common sinus.   The sinuses are arranged at intervals along a tube that unites posteriorly with its fellow to form a common oviduct.

3170 The alimentary canal, ovaria, and oviducts of a Mantis.   The ova are fully developed.   One of the branched ovaries is *in situ*, the other has been detached and unravelled.

3171   The camerated nidamental capsule of a Mantis, from one side of which a section
has been removed to show the series of cells within which the ova are developed.
The female during oviposition upon a twig discharges from the genital
orifice, together with the eggs, a foam-like material. This substance dries and
while still in a pliable state is moulded into shape by the extremity of the body
and the tips of the elytra. How the inner camerated structure is produced is
not known.

3172   The alimentary system with the oviducts and ovaries of a Stick Insect (*Phasma gigas*). Each ovary consists of a long oviducal passage, to the side of which are
attached at intervals numerous short ovarian tubes. At the base of each ovarian
tube is a single large ripe ovum. The apex is quite rudimentary and contains
a few minute underdeveloped ova.

3173   Specimens described in Owen's *Catalogue* as 'ova of the Chigoe (*Pulex penetrans*), in
different stages of development'. They are apparently the abdomens of impregnated females of this species of Flea, distended with ripening eggs.

In Arachnidans

Five specimens of the eggs, cocoon, and young brood of the Spider:

3174   A. A Spider (*Aranea*) with its silken cocoon and brood. Most of the young
Spiders have been hatched.

3176   B. The ova of a Spider.

3177   C. The cocoon of a Spider, opened to show the young brood.

3178   D. The cocoon of a Spider, bisected, showing the brood.

3180   E. The cocoon of a Spider.
Spiders before laying their eggs spin a cocoon for their protection. The usual
procedure is to spin in the first instance a small sheet of silk. Upon this the
eggs are laid and covered by a second sheet. The two sheets are then joined
together and the whole covered with a layer of silk in a manner peculiar to
each species. The cocoon is in most cases put in some sheltered spot, but may
be attached in an exposed position or (Wolf Spiders) carried about by the
female. When the young are hatched and have reached such a size that they

can get their own food, they escape from the cocoon. Till they can feed themselves they do not eat.

3182   Three new-born young of a Scorpion.
          The ova of the Scorpion are hatched within the oviduct of the parent.

3183   A female parasitic Isopod (*Cymothoë lichtenaultii*) with the oostegites or brood-pouch
          covers partly cut away to show the marsupial chamber. Some ova still remain
          therein, but the greater part have fallen out.
          The oostegites are scale-like plates, that arise late in development from the
          coxopodites or basal joints of the thoracic appendages.
          The eggs are protected in the space between the oostegites and the ventral
          body wall for some weeks.

In Crustaceans

3184   A Shrimp (*Crangon*) with several developing ova attached by cementing threads
          to the pleopods or abdominal appendages.

3185   A Crayfish (*Astacus fluviatilis*) with eggs attached to the abdominal appendages.
          The eggs as they leave the oviducts are encased with a viscid cement which
          draws out into a thread and attaches them to the hairs of the pleopods and to
          one another.
          Fixed in this way the eggs are protected from enemies during their develop-
          ment and by the movements of the pleopods are aerated and kept free from dirt.
          The young remain in the egg throughout the winter, hatching late in the
          spring, and when hatched resemble the parent closely. They remain attached
          to the pleopods by their chelae for some time.
          Thomas Henry Huxley, *The Crayfish: An Introduction to the Study of Zoology*, p. 40, 1879.

3186   The left half of a longitudinally bisected Crayfish showing the excluded ova
          attached to the abdominal appendages.

3187   A Crayfish (*Astacus fluviatilis*) showing the abdominal appendages after the exclusion
          of the young. Still attached to the hairs upon the appendages are the cementing
          threads and ruptured shells of the ova.
          Amongst the appendages may be seen two very young Crayfish: these are
          probably some of the brood that have taken shelter with the mother, as young
          Crayfish frequently do on alarm for some time after they have adopted an
          independent life.

3188 A Lobster (*Homarus vulgaris*) with the ovaries and oviducts displayed *in situ*, in the shrunken condition they assume after the extrusion of the ripe eggs. The oviducts are traced to their openings (marked by black bristles) upon the basal joints of the second pair of walking legs.

The ova have recently been extruded and are attached to the abdominal appendages (as in the Crayfish) by threads of an adhesive secretion.

3189 A cluster of the eggs of a Lobster (*Homarus vulgaris*) in a more advanced stage of development, attached to each other by filaments of adhesive secretion.

3190 A female Hermit Crab (*Pagurus streblonyx*) with oblong bunches of extruded ova attached by cementing threads to the abdominal appendages. In the Hermit Crabs these appendages are more digitiform than in free-swimming Crustacea and are reduced in number and confined to one side of the soft abdomen.

The ova are far smaller than those of species such as the Lobster.

3191 A female Crab (*Cancer sp.*) with the extruded ova situated in a large mass between the wide inflected abdomen and the sternum, attached by cementing threads to the pleopods. The eggs, like those of the Hermit Crab, are small, with comparatively little yolk.

3192 The abdomen of a female Spider Crab (*Maia squinado*), showing the long sickle-shaped pleopods with ova attached to them and held between them and the ventral wall of the body.

3194 A female Crab (*Grapsus sp.*) with the extruded ova collected beneath the broad short abdomen.

3195 Ova of a Crab, dried and attached to the side of the bottle.

In Fish

3196 The trunk of a Fresh-water Lamprey (*Petromyzon fluviatilis*) with the ventral walls of the abdomen removed, to show the ovaries *in situ* charged with mature ova. The ova contain comparatively little yolk and are in consequence of small size, like those of most Teleostean Fishes. They develop upon the surface of a single much-folded peritoneal sheet, that extends the whole length of the body cavity; when ripe they are discharged into the abdominal cavity and escape thence to the exterior through abdominal pores.

3197   A similar specimen.

3198   The ripe ovaries of a Freshwater Lamprey, removed from the body.

3199   The ripe ovary of a Sea Lamprey (*Petromyzon marinus*). The ova, though small, are of larger size than those of the Fresh-water species.

3200   Part of the trunk of a Sea Lamprey (*Petromyzon marinus*) with the ventral walls removed to show the condition of the ovary after the dehiscence of the ovisacs and the escape of the ripe ova. Upon either side of the ovary may be seen one of the kidneys with a large inflated ureter along its free margin. The right ureter has been opened and a bristle has been passed along it into the cloaca; upon the opposite side bristles have been inserted into the ureter and the abdominal pore.

3201   A segment of the trunk of a Fresh-water Lamprey (*Petromyzon fluviatilis*) showing the condition of the ovary after the discharge of the ripe ova.
        Mercury has been injected into the ureters but has for the most part escaped.

3202   The hinder part of the trunk of an Eel (*Anguilla latirostris*) dissected from the right side to show the ovaries, rectum, and genital pore.
        The ova, which in this specimen are quite immature, are developed, as in the Lampreys, upon elaborate folded sheets of peritoneum, from which they are cast when ripe into the body cavity and escape to the exterior through a pore situated behind the anus. The ovaries extend some way beyond the anus into the fleshy substance of the tail. Bristles are passed from the abdominal cavity through the genital pore.

The following are Hunter's observations on the mode of generation of the Eel and Lamprey:

'Generation of the Eel

'The natural history of the mode of propagation in the common eel (*Anguilla latirostris*) has, I believe, never yet been described; and this has probably in some degree arisen from a dissimilarity between their (generative) parts and (those of) fish in common, so as not to enable one to reason from analogy; and, as the mode of propagation in animals can only be known when that operation is going on in them, and (by) following it through most of its stages, it has lain almost unintelligible in the eel from the difficulty of finding them in this state. It was not even known whether they were oviparous or viviparous, and from this state of ignorance Sir John Hill* has declared them viviparous; probably from conceiving it (to be the) most probable (mode), as their mode of propagation was so obscure as not then to have been discovered.

'In my pursuits in comparative anatomy, especially (as to) the mode of propagation in fishes, the eel was not forgotten; and, as I found in this fish parts situated similar to the roes in other fishes, although not similar in the immediate appearance for propagation, yet being such as demanded attention, (this) therefore made me more desirous of knowing both the mode of propagation and the use of these parts in case they might not be intended for such purposes.

'That I might be able to ascertain these facts, I got eels every month in the year from the fishmonger with a view to catch them in the breeding season, as also of every size, but I never could distinguish any difference in these parts in any of the months. However, I was told that this was not a fair trial, the fishmongers often keeping them for months in their troughs, in which time we cannot suppose they are going on with this (the generative) process; and to get eels from the river regularly was not an easy matter.

'The part which I suspected to be the ovarium, when viewed with a magnifier, appeared a little granulated like some fatty membranes; and there being in some of the amphibia, as the lizard, frog, &c., regularly formed bodies composed of fat, I boiled this part to see if any oil could be extracted; but it boiled away to a pulp without yielding any. Having failed in all my examinations on this part of the common eel, and being in the island of Belleisle in the summer of 1761, where there was a vast number of conger eels, I dissected some of them for their anatomy, and observed they had the same parts with the common eel which I had supposed to be the ovarium or roe.

'I then opened many to see if I could discover any spawn, but never succeeded.

'As the lamprey and the lampern have, in some degree, a similarity to the common eel, and as their seasons of propagation are known, I next examined them with the same view when full of spawn, and easily found their parts for propagation, which are somewhat similar to those parts in the common eel, as I had suspected; and, although not exactly so, yet sufficiently to show the analogy.

'So far encouraged I did not give up the pursuit in the common eel, and

---

* John Hill (1716-1775), miscellaneous writer: at one time had an apothecary's shop in Covent Garden and later lived in Golden Square: obtained a diploma in Medicine from St. Andrews University and was awarded the Order of Vasa by the King of Sweden. After this he styled himself 'Sir John Hill, M.D.'. He gained a reputation as a botanist and wrote several works on Natural History.

was still further encouraged by Sir Joseph Banks, mentioning that when young, he had observed in an eel the roe full of eggs or spawn; but as he was then not well acquainted with the anatomy of this fish, and only knew there was an uncertainty respecting the mode of propagation, he therefore only preserved a part, and put it into spirit for further examination; but the spirit evaporating, it dried and was rendered unfit for investigation. Sir Joseph giving me leave to look at some sea-eels caught when on his voyage round the world, in them I found the roe full of eggs, and have since compared them with the common eel, in which I have at last discovered the mode of propagation, which is exactly what I suspected from the structure of the parts.

'On the present occasion it may not be improper to give a short description of the roe in the common roe-fish, with a view to show the difference (between them and the eel) which probably was the cause of its (the mode of propagation in the eel) not being before discovered.

'The roe in fishes in common, or what may be called the "roed-fish", consists of two bags; in some these are long, extending nearly through the whole belly of the animal; in others they are round, &c. They are smooth on the outside; and on the inside are thrown into a number of flakes or folds, increasing the surface greatly for the form and attachment of the eggs or spawn.

'These bags terminate each in a duct near the anus, which ducts join each other, forming one, which enters the anus near the verge, through which the ova pass.

'In both the lamprey and lampern the roes are not bags having the ova attached to the folds on their inside, as in the above described, but are composed of flakes or layers attached at one base along the back, having no cavity. Each flake is composed of two membranes united by cellular membrane, and on the inside of each membrane are the ova as close together as they can well be placed; and they may be seen externally through the membrane composing the flake. When these fishes have spawned the flakes become flaccid, but still the nidi may be seen in little opaque spots. The mode of spawning I shall describe in the common eel.

'In the common eel, and also in the conger, the roe is somewhat similar to the above, although not exactly. Each roe is composed of a membrane attached by one edge to the back of the fish, almost through the whole length of the abdomen, and continued into the tail some way beyond the anus; the other edge is unattached, and is longer than the attached one, so that it hangs like a ruffle. On the sides of this membrane are a number of folds, similar to the inside of roes in common; it is similar to half of a common roe slit up through its whole length, having the smooth membrane on one side and the flakes or folds on the other.

'These roes in the lampern, lamprey, conger, and common eel, have no duct or outlet directly belonging to them; therefore the operation of spawning is uncommon, and probably peculiar to this order of fish. The passage out appears to be by two openings, directly from the cavity of the belly just behind the rectum, which unites into one, and opens into the rectum on the further side of that gut just at the verge of the anus.* From this formation of parts, the question is, how do they spawn? In the common fishes the parts themselves explain this operation, and in the present we must have recourse to the same method.

'In the common fish we must suppose that the ova fall off and get loose into the cavity of the roe or ovarium, and then are protruded out of that cavity through the duct, by the action probably of both the roe and of the abdominal muscles, which forces them externally.

'In the eel, &c., we must suppose them (the ova, to be) forced out at the small opening above mentioned by the same kind of action.

'From the structure of the parts, this method of accounting for the operation of spawning appears to be the only possible one; and although it may be difficult to conceive how the spawn, when loose in the cavity of the abdomen, should all be brought to these small openings, and there make their exit, yet it may not be the less true; and that this is the most probable way, is still strengthened by (my) having seen the eggs in the lampern (*Petromyzon fluviatilis*), whose structure is the same (as in the eel), loose in the cavity of the abdomen, in their season for spawning, and other eggs that were not detached, upon the least handling dropped off from the ovaria.

'This structure, although in some respects appearing calculated for the formation of the spawn, yet as that spawn had not been seen and as there was no visible outlet for the spawn when detached belonging to these parts themselves, as in other fish, it was no wonder that in some minds it remained a doubt whether they were the parts or not. This of having no outlet belonging to the parts themselves is a curious fact.'   *Works*, vol. v, pp. 216-220.

Richard Owen added the following footnote (*ibid*, p. 220):

'It appears that eels, as a general rule, do not breed in fresh water, but that there are regular migrations of those with milts or roes enlarging, from inland waters to the sea or to the estuaries of rivers, at the end of summer; and of

---

* 'All of the ray-kind have two openings from the belly, one on each side, by the fin at the anus.'

"elvers" or young eels, from those situations to the fresh waters in spring. These, having passed gradually from the brackish or salt to fresh water, ascend streams and drains and spread themselves through the inland waters. The eels descend the river Yarrow to spawn in the end of September. The "elvers" ascend the river Connor about the 20th of May, in a slender column about two feet wide, along the edge of the stream. They creep up the wet posts of sluices, and sometimes twist themselves into round balls about four inches in diameter, with their head turned outward.'

It was Francesco Redi who suggested that eels do not originate from earthworms, as was then supposed, but breed in the sea, for he had observed elvers ascending rivers in spring. This was the first step towards the solution of what came to be known as the 'Eel question'. Aristotle had pointed out that these creatures appeared to possess no generative organs and assumed that, like so many other living things, they must be derived out of 'the bowels of the earth' by some form of spontaneous generation—a view that even Izaac Walton favoured. Pliny decided that they must rub themselves against rocks and that the pieces scraped off their bodies came to life. Others believed that they originated from horse hairs that fell into the water and were miraculously endowed with a vital spark.

It was not until 1896 that Professor Grassi of Rome communicated to the Royal Society of London through Ray Lankester the story of the reproduction and metamorphosis of the common eel. Lord Lister, the President of the Society, was in the Chair on the occasion of the partial elucidation of the intricacies in the life history of a creature known since the earliest times. Professor Grassi stated that after four years of intensive research he and his pupil, Dr. Calundruccio, had been able to solve the mystery that had occupied the attention of naturalists from the days of Aristotle. Grassi and Calundruccio did not entirely complete the work for it was not until ten years later that Johannes Schmidt published his findings to this effect in the *Rapports du Conseil International Exploratoires de la Mer*.

3203   The ovaries with a portion of the swin-bladder of a Salmon (*Salmo salar*).

Each ovary consists of a longitudinal fold of peritoneum, reflected mesially along its free border and produced upon its mesial surface and within the concavity of its reflection to form a series of large transverse ovigerous pleats or lamellae. In the preparation these lamellae are crowded with maturing ova.

There are no oviducts, but the ova, as in the Eels, are cast when ripe into the body cavity and escape to the exterior through a pore situated behind the anus.

3205 The body of a Barbel (*Cyprinus barbus*) with the ventral walls and intestine removed to show the ovaries, crowded with maturing ova.

The ovaries, as in most Bony Fishes, are closed peritoneal sacs within which the ova form on folds or lamellae. Posteriorly each ovarian sac is continued as a short oviducal canal which almost immediately unites with its fellow to form a common oviduct by which the ripe ova are conveyed to the exterior.

A rod is inserted into the genital outlet, which is posterior to the anus.

3206 The body of a Carp (*Cyprinus carpio*) with the ovaries, in a state of full development, exposed from the ventral aspect. A longitudinal section has been removed from the right ovary to show the compact arrangement of the ova.

3207 A Gold-fish (*Cyprinus auratus*) with the walls of the right side of the abdomen removed to expose the right ovary, which is loaded with mature ova.

3208 A Gold-fish with the left ovary exposed and its capsule removed to show the ovigerous lamellae packed with mature ova.

3209 A Dace (*Leuciscus vulgaris*) with the ripe ovaries exposed.

3210 One of the ovaries of a Cod (*Gadus morrhua*), laid open, and the ovigerous lamellae with the countless ovisacs and ova displayed. The parts have been injected and in places where the ova have escaped show arborescent vessels branching into the lamellae.

The cod spawns in the month of February and it has been calculated that the number of ova in the roe of one female exceeds nine million; the eggs are small and belong to the light, floating, pelagic type.

3211 The hinder parts of the ovaries of a Goby (*Gobias sp.*). The ovarian sacs are fused together in the mid-line; that of the left side has been opened and the ovigerous lamellae and ova removed from it to show its continuity with the oviduct. Bristles have been placed in the oviducts.

3212 One of the ovaries and both oviducts of a Shad (*Clupea alosa*) from the Severn.

The ovary has been injected and cut open to show the vascularity of the numerous ovigerous lamellae and the nearly contemporaneous development of the very numerous ova therein contained.

The lamellae are very prominent and are disposed irregularly in the transverse plane.

3213 The ovaries and oviducts of a Mackerel (*Scomber scombrus*). One of the ovaries has been cut open longitudinally to show the ovigerous lamellae packed with small mature eggs. The ripe eggs of the Mackerel, like those of most sea fishes, are small, transparent and buoyant.

3214 A similar preparation.

3215 A similar preparation in which both ovaries have been opened. The oviducal section of the ovarian capsule is extremely short.

3216 Part of one of the ovaries of a Pike (*Esox lucius*) cut open to show the ovigerous lamellae crowded with ova.

　All the ova are at the same stage of development and apparently are mature. The preparation has been minutely injected. The eggs of the Pike sink in water and when laid are attached to water weeds and other objects.

3217 A Father-lasher (*Cottus bubalis*) opened from the ventral aspect to show the large sac-like ovaries packed with mature ova.

　This species spawns in January, at which time the ova are of a fine orange colour.

　The eggs of Cottus are heavier than water and are attached by the parent to weeds and other objects.

3218 The anterior extremity of one of the ovaries of an Angler (*Lophius piscatorius*) injected and everted, to show the restricted ribbon-like area of the sac upon which ova are formed. The ova are still very immature and are scattered evenly over the surface of the ovigerous band, which is not produced to form lamellae.

3219 The ovaries and the single wide oviduct of a Wolf-fish (*Anarrichas lupus*), everted to show leaf-like ovigerous lamellae projecting from its surface, studded with eggs in different stages of immaturity.

　The limits between the ovigerous and oviducal regions of the ovaries are very clearly defined.

　The eggs of the Wolf-fish are heavier than water.

3220 The pyriform ovarian sacs with the oviducts and rectum of an Electric Eel (*Gymnotus electricus*).

　One of the ovaries has been opened to show the nodular ovigerous lamellae projecting into its cavity. The lamellae contain numerous maturing ova around each of which may be observed a semi-transparent capsule—the ovisac.

The single oviduct formed by the union of the ovarian sacs is peculiarly long.

Two specimens of the ovary of the Electric Eel (*Gymnotus electricus*) cut open to show the nodular ovigerous lamellae within which are ovisacs containing ova at various stages of development:

3221 A. An ovary cut open. Many of the ova are approaching maturity.

3222 B. A similar preparation.

3223 A female Pipe-fish (*Syngnathus typhle*) with the ventral walls of the abdomen removed to show the long, cylindrical ovaries filled with a small number of comparatively large ripe ova.

   The lips of the genital aperture are produced, forming a short ovipositor for conveying the eggs to the breed chamber of the male.

3224 A female Pipe-fish (*Syngnathus aequoreus*) with the ovaries similarly displayed.

   In this species the ovaries are larger than in *S. typhle* and contain a larger number of ova of smaller size.

3225 Part of the body of a Pipe-fish (*Syngnathus acus*) with the right ovary exposed.

   A portion of the subcaudal integument has been dissected off, probably in quest of some trace of the brood pouch, which since Hunter's day has been discovered to be peculiar to the male.

3226 A male Pipe-fish (*Syngnathus typhle*) with the subcaudal flaps of the integument separated to show the impregnated ova lying in two parallel longitudinal bands within the marsupial recess along the under surface of the tail.

   In the Lophobranchs the eggs are attached by the female to the under surface of the abdomen or tail of the male and are in most cases protected by overlapping flaps of integument (Pipe Fishes) or within an almost completely closed brood sac (Sea Horses).

   After deposition the eggs are fertilised and become enfolded by laminal out-growths of epithelium of the brood pouch. A nutritive fluid is secreted by this epithelium and forms the chief nourishment of the young during the period of their incubation.

   Rudolf Kolster, 'Die Embryotrophe bei den Lophobranchiern', *Anat. Hefte*, Bd. 34, 1907, p. 401.

3227   A male of the same species of Pipe Fish with the brood pouch similarly displayed at the period of the completion of the incubation of the impregnated ova. Some of the young Pipe Fishes still remain in the pouch, though most have escaped. The cellular structure of the roof of the marsupium to which the ova were attached is well shown.

3228   The male of an exotic species of *Syngnathus* in which the brood pouch occupies the whole of the under or ventral surface of the abdomen. The flaps by which it is bordered have been spread apart to show the large number of ova that it contains and their adhesion not only to the roof but to the inner surface of the lateral flaps.

3229   A male Snake Pipe-fish (*Syngnathus ophidion*). In this species the eggs, after extrusion by the female and fertilisation, are attached to the reticulated ventral surface of the abdomen of the male, but are not protected by cutaneous flaps.

     In the specimen a coherent mass of eggs is attached (artificially) to the ventral surface of the body; elsewhere it is possible to see the reticulate character of the abdominal wall to which in nature they adhere.

3230   A male Sea-horse (*Hippocampus guttulatus*) with the brood pouch laid open by the reflexion of its right wall and the contained ova exposed.

     Upon the inner surface of the reflected wall of the pouch may be seen the delicate reticular processes that fit in between the contained ova. The entry to the pouch is a longitudinal slit, situated just behind the anus.

3231   A male Sea-horse with the right wall of the brood pouch removed to show the young fish at nearly the completion of incubation.

3232   A portion of the ovary of a Monk-fish (*Rhina squatina*) with ovaries and ova at different stages of maturity. The ripe ova are heavily laden with yolk and are in consequence of large size, resembling the eggs of Birds; they lie embedded in the stroma of the ovary and do not as a rule project far from the surface.

     The ova in this class of Fishes differ in a marked degree from those of Teleosteans both as regards the amount of yolk they contain and in the fact that a few only reach maturity at the same time.

3233   The ovary, oviducts, and part of the liver of a viviparous cartilaginous Fish. Ova at different stages of development project freely from the surface of the ovary. A few are mature; they present a spherical form and exceed one inch (25 mm.) in diameter.

The common entry to the oviducts is shown above the remains of the liver; and the uterine segment of one oviduct is laid open to show the characteristic wavy parallel folds of its lining membrane.

3234 The glandular segment of the oviduct of a large 'Homelyn' or Spotted Ray (*Raia maculata*) mounted with the posterior end uppermost. A large segment has been removed from one of the lobes of the gland, exposing to view the flattened inner surface of the opposite lobe, upon which may be distinguished three areas: a narrow smooth area below, corresponding with the albumen-producing portion of the gland and giving passage to its secretion; a narrow laminate area upon which open the ducts of the egg-shell-secreting portion of the gland; and an extensive, smooth, mucus-secreting area (uppermost in the specimen) overlying part of the egg-shell gland.

Upon the cut surface of the lobe from which a segment has been removed, may be seen the extent of the albumen gland and the convergence of the coarse tubules of the egg-shell gland to the laminated area of the inner surface.

3235 Two eggs of a large species of Homelyn (*Raia*) each containing a completely developed embryo.

In the lower specimen the egg-shell has been reflected so as to expose the dorsal surface of the embryo and in the other the ventral surface is displayed.

The broad pectoral fins, characteristic of the Rays, are folded upon the back and the tail is curved round to the left side.

The external yolk-sac is a large pyriform bag, projecting from the body close behind the branchial region, at the anterior border of the abdomen.

3236 The impregnated oviducts of a Skate (*Raia batis*). The nidamental glands are laid open to show the areas occupied by the albumen and egg-shell-secreting portions. A fertilised ovum encased in its horny egg-shell may be seen through the thin walls of one of the oviducts; the corresponding portion of the other duct has been laid open and the egg removed.

3237 The egg removed from the oviduct of the previous specimen, with part of the shell reflected to show the white flocculent albumen and the yolk within.

The surface is covered by a soft, stringy material. At the apex of the horn that springs from each corner of the shell may be observed a narrow slit. Through this opening water gains access to the shell, for the respiratory needs of the foetus.

3238   A similar preparation with a small portion of the oviduct attached. This and the preceding specimen show the flattened oblong shape prolonged at either angle in curved horn-like processes, characteristic of the Skate's egg.

3239   The cloaca and one of the oviducts of a Skate, with the nidamentary gland divided longitudinally and the succeeding segment of the duct opened to show, lying within it, a fertilised egg enclosed within its horny egg-shell.

3240   The other oviduct of the same Skate, showing the nidamental gland entire and an egg enclosed in its horny shell lying within the lower part of the duct.

3241   A foetal Ray, injected and dissected to show the heart, with the branchial vessels and cardinal sinuses, together with the alimentary canal and the communication therewith of the external and internal yolk-sacs.
         The external yolk-sac has been opened and the yolk removed to show the two layers of which its wall is composed. The internal yolk-sac is formed by a dilatation of the vitelline duct within the abdomen; it can be distinguished in the preparation by the deep brown colour of its contained yolk. A bristle has been inserted into its opening into the alimentary canal at the head of the valvular intestine.

3242   A young Torpedo (*Torpedo narke*) with the ventral walls of the abdomen removed to show the remains of the internal yolk-sac and its connection with the intestine at the commencement of its valvular segment.

3243   A young Torpedo (*Torpedo narke*) at the period when the external yolk has been absorbed and the yolk-sac wholly drawn in: the abdomen has been opened by a crucial incision.

3244   A Torpedo further advanced in growth, showing the similarity of its external form to that of the adult.
         The abdominal viscera have been removed and the ventral muscles dissected.

3245   The egg-shell of a Shark, from the South Seas. It is of an elliptical form with the extremities truncated and their angles produced into long, contorted tendril-like filaments; but its chief peculiarity is the presence of a regular series of about 15 parallel laminae, extending somewhat obliquely across its anterior and posterior surfaces and terminating at either end in close proximity to the thickened margins of the shell.

3246   The oviducts of a Spotted Dog-fish (*Scyllium canicula*) showing the nidamental glands, by which albumen and a horny egg-shell are secreted around the yolk-laden ovum.

   Anterior to the gland the oviduct is narrow and delicate but posterior to it becomes much enlarged and in this part, as has been shown by opening one oviduct, is lined by a deeply pleated mucous membrane.

3247   The egg of a Spotted Dog-fish showing its elongated quadrangular shape and the long, tangled, horny threads that project from each corner and serve to attach it to any suitable foreign body.   The margin of the egg-shell is thickened and at each corner shows a slit, through which water can percolate into the interior, for the respiratory needs of the embryo.   The surface of the shell is smooth.

   The specimen is mounted with the posterior end uppermost.

3248   The egg-shell of a Spotted Dog-fish, dried.

3249   The egg of a Spotted Dog-fish with the shell opened along one margin to show an embryo at an early stage of development with its large external yolk-sac attached to the abdominal wall by a narrow pedicle.

   The embryo is about an inch (25 mm.) in length and the development of the external branchiae has commenced.   These transitory respiratory organs are not true external branchiae, such as those of the Dipnoi and Amphibia, but are thread-like extensions of the ordinary gill lamellae.

3250   The embryo of a Spotted Dog-fish, about 2 inches (50 mm.) in length, with its large external yolk-sac attached.

   The external gills are fully developed.

3251   The egg of a Spotted Dog-fish with part of the horny shell removed to show the embryo further advanced in development; the external gills have not been absorbed.

3252   Two eggs of a Spotted Dog-fish in the shell of each of which a window has been cut to show the contained embryo, at about the same period of development as in the previous specimen.   In the specimen on the left, black bristles have been inserted into the slits in the egg-shell through which a circulation of water is maintained around the embryo.

   It should be noticed that the position of the embryo differs in each egg.

C.H.M.—F

3253   The egg of a Spotted Dog-fish at a somewhat later stage of development.   The
        embryo is coiled around the yolk-sac with the tail overlying the head.

3254   The egg of a Spotted Dog-fish with the embryo at an advanced stage of develop-
        ment exposed *in situ,* and with the ventral walls of the abdomen removed to
        show the internal yolk-sac developed at the expense of the external one, which
        has nearly disappeared.

3255   The uterine or terminal segment of one of the impregnated oviducts (with the
        cloaca) of a Spiny Dog-fish (*Acanthias vulgaris*) injected and laid open and with
        one of the embryos which it contained exposed *in situ.*
            The embryo is at an early stage of development with the external gills fully
        formed and is about 2 inches (50 mm.) long.   It is attached by a long slender
        vitelline duct to a yolk-sac of relatively great size.
            The embryo and yolk-sac lie free in the uterine cavity and are not (except at
        a very early stage of development) enclosed in an egg-shell.
            The walls of the uterus are highly vascular with the mucous membrane
        produced to form a series of longitudinally exposed pleats, each with a large
        artery in its free margin.
            The openings of the oviducts are sufficiently wide to admit water freely to the
        interior of the uterus.
            Black bristles have been passed through the abdominal pores.

3256   The uterine segments of the oviducts with the cloaca of a pregnant Spiny Dog-fish.
            The right oviduct has been everted to show its laminated vascular lining.
        The left oviduct has also been opened to show within it a number of embryos
        well advanced in development.
            Their yolk-sacs are still of large size; through lapse of time they have become
        considerably damaged.
            The cloaca has been slit open and its walls spread apart; quills are inserted
        into the rectum and urinary papilla.

3258   The uterine segments of the oviducts and the cloaca of a Spiny Dog-fish.
            One of the uteri has been opened, showing a foetus far advanced in develop-
        ment with the external yolk-sac considerably reduced in size.   The sac has been
        ruptured and its contents have escaped.

3259   A foetus of *Acanthias* (probably *vulgaris*) with the vitelline duct injected and the
        right side of the body removed.

3260 The young foetus of a Shark (*Squalus*) with the filamentary external branchiae very fully developed.

The yolk-sac has been removed, leaving its long and slender stalk.

3261 A foetal Shark, far advanced in development. The ventral wall has been removed from the left side of the abdomen and the left lobe of the liver cut away to show the course of the vitelline duct and blood vessels within the body cavity. A bristle has been passed behind the vitelline vein as it curves forward to join the portal vein close to its entry into the liver.

The yolk-sac has been removed, leaving a long segment of its stalk attached to the body close behind the pericardiac diaphragm. At this point of junction with the body, part of the outer covering of the stalk has been removed to show its direct continuity with the body wall and a bristle has been passed beneath this covering along the stalk into the body cavity. Within the outer covering can be seen a core (filled with injection) which near the gut is resolved into three vessels—the vitelline duct and the two vitelline blood vessels.

There is apparently no internal yolk-sac.

3262 The foetus of a Shark with a long slender vitelline duct attached to the abdomen.

The yolk-sac has been removed.

3263 The foetus of a Saw-fish (*Pristis antiquorum*) with a slender vitelline duct attached to the abdomen.

The foetus has the general form of the adult but the rostral teeth present the condition of mere cutaneous papillae.

In Reptiles

3264 The ovaries with the oviducts, rectum, kidney, and cloaca of a Menopome (*Menopoma alleghaniense*). The ovaries consist each of a long, broad, plicated, membranous sac, suspended by a fold of peritoneum. The ova and ovisacs develop within the walls of the sac and as they mature project in bunches from its surface. The ripe ova are spherical and of about the size of a small pea; amongst them may be seen numerous smaller ovisacs at different stages of immaturity.

The oviducts are long sub-compressed canals, disposed in numerous short convolutions. Each commences far forward in the body cavity by a free abdominal aperture.

Bristles have been inserted into the cloacal outlets of the oviducts and into the bladder.

3265 A female Newt (*Triton palustris*) with the ventral body walls removed to show the ovaries crowded with mature ova and ovisacs, and (dorsal to them) the long and tortuous oviducts.

3266 A similar preparation in which may be seen the prominence and tumidity of the lips of the cloaca peculiar to the breeding season.

In Urodeles there is usually partial union of the sexes by the apposition of the tumid lips of the cloaca one to the other.

3267 A female Newt (*Triton cristatus*) with the ventral walls of the abdomen removed, to show the ovaries laden with mature ova.

Anterior to them may be seen the commencement of the oviducts much enlarged and rendered translucent by the abundant secretion prepared by them as the ovaries ripen. The secretion swells up when in contact with water and forms a protective envelope for the eggs by which they are attached singly to some foreign body.

3268 A specimen of the same species of Newt, similarly dissected to show the ovaries after the discharge of the ripe ova.

A bristle is placed in the abdominal aperture of the left oviduct.

3269 The larva of a Newt (*Triton cristatus*) advanced in development, with the last remains of the external branchiae visible as a row of small conical processes projecting from under the gill covers.

The tail has assumed the characters and relative size of that of the adult.

3270 A Frog (*Rana temporaria*) with the ventral walls of the abdomen and the alimentary canal removed to show the left ovary and the oviducts *in situ*.

The ova have advanced about half way towards maturity and the oviducts are considerably enlarged and much convoluted.

A bristle is placed in the abdominal orifice of the right oviduct; the cloaca and termination of the rectum have been laid open and bristles inserted into the outlets of the oviducts and bladder.

3271 A similar preparation, showing the ova at maturity. At one pole of the ovum (the animal pole) the yolk is deeply pigmented.

In this specimen the mucilaginous secretion of the commencement of the oviduct has come into contact with water and has absorbed it in large quantities, swelling up to form a translucent gelatinous mass.

3272 The ovaries and oviducts with the alimentary canal and cloaca of a Frog (*Rana temporaria*), showing the ova at maturity.

3273 Part of the ovary of a Frog with the ova mature and ready to burst from the ovisacs.

The pigmented animal pole of the mature ovum is very distinct.

Prepared by William Clift.

3274 A large species of Toad (*Bufo*) with the ventral walls of the abdomen removed and the ovaries, filled with mature ova, exposed *in situ*. The pigment in the yolk is strongly marked.

3275 A similar, but larger specimen of the same species of Toad, with the mature ovaries and contracted oviducts displayed.

3276 The ovaries of a large Toad, laid open to show the ovisacs containing the mature ova projecting into the cavity of the ovarian sac.

3277 A Surinam Toad (*Pipa monstrosa*) with the ventral walls of the abdomen and the alimentary canal removed to show the ovaries and oviducts *in situ*.

The ovarian ova, which are relatively few in number, are mature, of a spherical form and of about the size of a pea. The oviducts are, as usual in the Anura, of great length and are disposed on each side of the ovaries in numerous convolutions. Above the ovaries can be seen one of the fat bodies. These structures are probably stores of food material of use in supplying the quantity of nutriment necessary in the breeding season for the rapid development of the generative organs.

3278 The ovaries, laden with mature ova and the fat bodies, of a Surinam Toad. The mature ova project from the walls of the ovarian sac, forming pendulous bunches; between them may be observed a few minute ovisacs, either as yet undeveloped or atrophied.

3279 A Frog (*Rana temporaria*) with the ventral walls of the abdomen removed to show the posterior or uterine segments of the oviducts distended with ripe ova, which in their passage along the first segment of the oviducts have become coated with an envelope of mucilaginous secretion. This secretion has been in contact with water and has in consequence swollen up into a gelatinous-looking mass.

3280   The spawn of a Frog (*Rana temporaria*).
This specimen originally showed the eggs embedded in a mass of swollen mucilaginous envelopes, but through lapse of time the envelopes have disintegrated.

3281   A small piece of Frog spawn. The mucilaginous envelopes have become shrunken and coagulated and have lost their natural gelatinous appearance.

3282   A series of the young of the Common Frog (*Rana temporaria*), showing the external changes which occur during the progress of the metamorphosis from the larva or tadpole to the mature state.
At first the only organ of locomotion is a compressed vertical tail, as shown in the lowest specimens; then the hinder pair of extremities and afterwards, when the larva has attained its full size, the fore pair of legs appears. As these terrestrial locomotive organs increase, the tail diminishes and finally disappears.
Branchial respiratory organs, at first external, followed by true gills, are in like manner first developed and then give place to lungs. The body and tail are at first supported by a flexible notochord, upon the anterior parts of which are developed at a later stage osseous vertebrae.
A horny beak is exchanged for a wide mouth with teeth; and a complex elongated alimentary canal, adapted for a vegetable diet in the voracious larva, is much simplified and shortened before the mature state is acquired.
The metamorphosis of the tadpole to the adult occupies about three months. The larva leaves the egg after about a week, the hind legs appear about two months later; in a further ten days the fore-legs burst through the opercular membrane under cover of which the first stages of their development have taken place. From this stage in its metamorphosis the larva decreases in size, the tail shortens and the young Frog leaves the water. Ultimately the tail completely disappears.
H. Fischer-Sigwart, 'Das Uberwintern der Lurche im Larvenzustande', *Zool. Gart.*, 1885, p. 299.

3283   Four larvae of the Common Frog (*Rana temporaria*).
The two lower specimens exhibit the first appearance of the hind limbs as minute buds at the root of the tail. The two upper specimens show the final disappearance of the tail.

3284 The larva of a large species of Frog, with both the anterior and posterior extremities developed, but with the tail still of considerable length.

The tail is thick and almost cylindrical, with a narrow integumentary fin-fold along its dorsal and ventral borders. Along either side can be clearly seen the segmental arrangement of the caudal muscles, similar to that characteristic of the body muscles of Fish.

3285 A larva of the same species of Frog, with the limbs further advanced in development and with the tail proportionally reduced in size. In comparison with the previous specimen the tail has shrunk by at least two-thirds of its length. Its fin-fold has disappeared.

3286 The larva of a Jackie or Fish-frog (*Pseudis paradoxa*) about an inch and a half (38 mm.) in length.

No locomotive organs are developed, excepting the tail; the whole body is invested in a thin, smooth, and semi-transparent integument, a broad duplicature of which extends both above and below the caudal prolongation, forming extensive dorsal and ventral fins to increase the locomotive power of the tail. The mouth is small and is provided above and below with thin horny jaws.

There is no trace of external gills, but the situation of the future single branchial outlet is indicated by a sub-circular line, resembling a cicatrix, on the left side of the head a little below the eye and behind it.

The spiral coils of the intestine are visible through the semi-transparent walls of the abdomen.

3287 A similar specimen of larger size, showing an increased number of coils of the intestine; the nostrils are conspicuous upon the upper lip in the form of minute circular apertures; the cicatrix-like indication of the branchial aperture on the left side of the head has become very conspicuous; and the muscular parts of the tail have increased in bulk.

3288 The larva of the same species of Frog prior to the development of the paired limbs. The abdominal cavity has been laid open to show the spiral coils of the enormously developed intestine.

3289 The intestinal canal, with part of the liver, pancreas, and spleen of the full-sized larva of *Pseudis paradoxa*.

3290   The larva of the same species of Frog, after the protrusion of the anterior ex-
        tremities, with the abdominal cavity laid open to show the diminution in the
        size of the intestinal convolutions towards the later period of the metamorphosis.
          One side of the tail has been dissected to show its cartilaginous axis, or
        notochord, and the membranous intermuscular septa in process of absorption.

3291   The larva of a Bull-Frog (*Rana catesbiana*), just before the forelimbs begin to pro-
        trude, showing on the right side the thinning of the skin by absorption for that
        purpose and on the left side the cutaneous (branchial) cavity containing the
        rudimentary fore-leg.
          The branchiae of this side are also exposed and a bristle is passed from the
        branchial cavity through its exhalent orifice or spiracle, which is situated as in
        Pseudis, on the left side of the head.
          The lungs are exposed in the abdominal cavity; they present the form of
        narrow fusiform sacs, their posterior extremities not quite reaching to the hinder
        end of the body cavity.
          The heart is shown within the pericardium; the flattened kidneys are well
        contrasted against the Wolffian bodies situated external to them.

3292   The liver and alimentary canal of the larva of a Bull-Frog at about the same
        period of development, showing its flat spiral coil.

3293   A female Surinam Toad (*Pipa monstrosa*) with the abdominal cavity laid open and
        the alimentary canal and liver removed to show the shrivelled ovaries and the
        collapsed convoluted oviducts, into the abdominal apertures of which bristles
        are inserted.
          The ova have been impregnated and expelled and placed upon the surface
        of the back. Here, by the growth of the integument, they have been enclosed
        in cells, each covered by a semi-transparent lid. Some of the cells have been
        laid open and others apparently ruptured by the young in their efforts to escape:
        these have reached the completion of their metamorphosis, the legs have been
        completely developed and the tail absorbed.

3294   A female Surinam Toad in vertical section, showing the structure of the cutaneous
        dorsal incubating cells. Many of these, having been deserted, are in process of
        obliteration by the thickening and adhesion of their original walls.

3295   A young Surinam Toad at the completion of its metamorphosis.

3296 A female Spotted Salamander (*Salamandra maculosa*), with the abdomen opened from the left side to show the left oviduct during pregnancy.

The terminal or uterine portion of the oviduct is much dilated and contains numerous foetal Salamanders, each about an inch (25 mm.) in length. They lie loose within it, coiled upon themselves and disposed for the most part transversely to the long axis of the canal.

3297 A female Spotted Salamander with the ventral walls of the abdomen removed and the ovaries and impregnated oviducts displayed *in situ*. The left uterus has been laid open and several of the embryos removed and mounted separately below. The anterior portion of each uterus is sharply folded back upon itself.

The separate embryos are coiled and show distinctly their delicate fringed external branchia, the dilatation of the abdomen due to a large yolk-sac contained within it and the vertical flattening of the tail, similar to that characteristic of free living larvae, but unlike the condition in the adult.

3298 The abdominal viscera of a pregnant female Spotted Salamander. In this specimen the division of the oviduct into a narrow convoluted anterior segment, followed by a dilated uterus, is distinctly shown. The narrow portion of the duct passes backwards alongside the ovary and is then reflected forwards to open into the bluntly conical extremity of the uterus.

The latter is strongly dilated, with thin and semi-transparent walls. From its commencement it runs at first forwards and is then, at the level of the anterior end of the ovary, reflected backwards to reach the cloaca.

Each uterus contains between twenty and thirty foetuses. Some of these have been removed on the right side.

3299 A portion of the uterus and two embryos of a Spotted Salamander.

One of the embryos is still enveloped by the delicate walls of the uterus; the other has been isolated and mounted above.

In the latter specimen the walls of the abdomen have been removed to show, attached to the intestine, the large rounded yolk-sac, which affords sustenance to the growing larva.

3300 A section of the yolk-sac of a younger foetal Salamander.

3301 A Snake (*Coluber sp.*) with the ventral walls of the abdomen laid open to show the mature ovaries *in situ*. They contain a chain of closely-packed ova ripe for impregnation and retained by an extremely delicate and attenuated capsule.

A few small, ill-developed ovisacs lie in the interspaces between the mature ovarian ova.

3302   Part of the trunk of a Common Grass Snake (*Tropidonotus natrix*) with the ventral walls of the abdomen removed to show the impregnated oviducts *in situ*.

The abdominal aperture of each oviduct has the form of a wide slit with ample membranous lips which are wrinkled but not fimbriated at the margin; that of the right side is situated six inches (152 mm.) anterior to the one on the left. The oviduct is at first narrow and disposed in short transverse folds; further down it is distended with fertilised ova, which are arranged in a single series somewhat obliquely with respect to each other.

Each ovum is separated from the next in the series by a short segment of narrow undistended oviduct. The ova in this species are laid before the development of the embryo has begun.

Dorsal to the oviducts can be seen a portion of the intestine and the two ovaries emptied of the ripe ova and in consequence shrunken and crumpled.

3303   The ovaries, kidneys, rectum, and portions of the oviducts (in one of which are two ova) of a smaller Snake.

Within the ovaries may be seen a number of immature ova of oval shape similar to the two impregnated eggs in the oviduct, but far smaller.

The impregnated ova lie in dilatations of the oviduct separated from one another by a considerable stretch of undilated duct.

3304   Several eggs of a Grass Snake (*Tropidonotus natrix*) soon after their exclusion, showing their large size, oval form, and leathery protective covering or egg-shell.

3305   A small cluster of eggs of a Grass Snake.

3306   Two ova of another species of Snake, in which the dark-grey parchment-like chorion is strengthened by the deposition of a thin layer of white calcareous matter.

3307   Several eggs of a Snake, of a narrow elliptical form and having the shell marked by fine and slightly waved longitudinal rugae.

3308   A longitudinal section of the leathery outer protective covering or shell of the egg of a Snake, demonstrating the two distinct layers of which it is composed.

3309 The posterior part of the trunk of a Viper (*Pelias berus*) with the ventral walls of the abdomen removed to show the ovaries *in situ*.

These bodies lie one behind the other, on either side of the mid-line and are divided by furrows into nine saccular compartments or ovisacs, each occupied by a large ripe ovum, ready to escape and be received into the oviducts.

3310 The posterior half of a Viper with the ventral walls of the abdomen removed to show the ovaries and oviducts *in situ*; the right oviduct contains five, the left three, impregnated ova. Development has commenced and the embryos (surrounded by their membranes) can be seen through the thin semi-transparent oviduct coiled up like watch-springs and partly embedded in the yolk with which the ova are plentifully stored.

3311 The ovaries, kidneys, and impregnated oviducts of a Viper.

The area of germination upon the eggs contained within the oviducts can be distinguished as a circular dark spot. Development has not proceeded so far as in the preceding specimen.

Two specimens of the impregnated eggs of a Serpent:

3312 A. An egg in longitudinal section. The protective shell has contracted upon some irregular masses of yolk.

3313 B. Two eggs in longitudinal section. The embryos have been removed from the egg-shells and lie below them.

3314 The posterior half of a Rattle-Snake (*Crotalus horridus*) dissected to show the ovaries and oviducts *in situ*.

A few of the ova in each ovary have acquired a considerable size and the ovisacs are apparently ripe for dehiscence.

The external capsule of the ovary is distended by the ripening ovisacs and extremely thin, and the stroma is scanty and of a semi-fluid consistency. The whole course of both oviducts is shown and the terminal dilatation of the one on the right side is laid open.

3315 A portion of the ovary of a Rattle-Snake with several ova fully formed and ripe for impregnation.

3316 The ovum of a Rattle-Snake with half the shell removed to show the embryo snake disposed in three and a half spiral coils in a cavity on one side of the yolk-sac.

3317 The ovum of a Snake, from one-half of which the shell has been removed to show the embryo far advanced in development, embedded in a cavity of the yolk-sac and enclosed with the yolk-sac in a duplicature of the allantois.
The latter has been torn opposite the head of the embryo.

3318 A foetal Snake with the yolk-sac and a portion of the allantois attached to it by the trunks of the allantoic blood-vessels.

3319 A foetal Snake, further advanced in its development, and with the yolk-sac proportionally reduced in size and now appended to the side of the coiled-up embryo.

3320 The egg of a Snake, from which half of the shell has been removed to show the young Snake at the completion of its development.

Four embryo Snakes showing the yolk-sac and its mode of attachment to the body:
3321 A. The yolk-sac has become detached from its duct, which is slender and of some considerable length; it enters the abdomen at about the commencement of the posterior third. The intromittent organs are everted.

3322 B. An embryo of about the same age as 'A'. The yolk-sac is detached but shows its involuted form and the passage of the vitelline duct through the cavity. The body of the snake has been opened to show the viscera *in situ*.

3323 C. A female embryo of about the same age, showing the cup-shaped yolk-sac within which the young snake lies spirally coiled during the progress of its development.

3324 D. An embryo Snake, somewhat older than the preceding, showing the connection of its umbilical cord with the yolk-sac.

3325 A Slow-worm (*Anguis fragilis*) with the ventral walls of the abdomen removed and the viscera displayed in their natural relative position; the parts more particularly intended to be shown are the impregnated oviducts, which are symmetrically situated with respect to each other. Each contains seven or eight ova arranged in linear series and, as in Snakes, each lies within a separate dilatation of the oviduct.

3326 A similar preparation in which the development of the young Slow-worms in the impregnated oviducts is nearly completed. Three of the embryos have been removed from the oviduct and mounted separately.

The development of the young of the Slow-worm, as of viviparous Snakes, takes place without any placental formation or adhesion between the foetal membranes and the oviduct, the large quantity of yolk within the egg sufficing for the nutriment of the embryo during its development.

3327   A Chameleon (*Chamaeleon senegalensis*) with the ventral walls of the abdomen removed and the viscera exposed *in situ*, principally to show the ovaries and oviducts. The ovarian ova are of equal size with a diameter of from 8-10 mm. and are closely impacted in alternate linear series.

The capsule of the ovary is thin and transparent; the stroma scanty and of an extremely delicate consistence.

The oviducts lie on either side of the ovaries and are disposed in irregularly compressed folds.

3328   The ovaries and oviducts with the kidneys and liver of a Chameleon.

The ovaries are laden with mature ova, closely similar in number, form, and size to those of the preceding specimen, but somewhat less regularly arranged.

3329   One of the ovaries of a Chameleon with ova ripe for impregnation.

3330   One of the ovaries, with a portion of the corresponding oviduct, of an Iguana.

Most of the ovarian ova have attained a diameter of from 8-12 mm. They are impacted within the ovary in an irregular manner, with smaller ovisacs and ova in their interspaces. A bristle is inserted into the elongated narrow abdominal aperture of the oviduct.

3331   The ovary of a Lizard in which about 30 ova are in progress of maturation.

They are of spherical form and have attained a diameter of 4 mm.

3332   A Gecko (*Thecadactylus laevis*) with the ventral walls of the abdomen and most of the viscera removed.

In this Lizard two ova only appear to be impregnated and developed at each season of generation; one of these ova is shown *in situ*, the other has been removed from the dilated portion of the oviduct in which it was situated.

Bristles are inserted into the cloacal aperture of each oviduct.

3333   Another specimen of *Thecadactylus laevis* with the abdominal viscera exposed *in situ*, more especially to show the ovum on the left side and a section of that on the right. There is no trace of embryonic development visible in either of the specimens.

3334   A Lizard (*Anolius sp.*) with the ventral walls of the abdomen removed to show the viscera *in situ*, and more especially the oviducts, each of which contains a single large elliptical ovum.

3335   A similar specimen in which a longitudinal section has been made of one oviduct and its contained ovum, showing the large amount of yolk contained in the latter.

3336   Two specimens of *Anolius*, similarly dissected to show the oviducts, one of which, in each specimen, contains a single large ovum.

3337   A Lizard (*Ameiva lemniscata*) with the abdomen laid open to expose the oviducts, each of which contains two large elliptical ova.

3338   An allied species of *Ameiva*, with the abdomen laid open, and a single large ovum exposed, part of which has been dissected away to show the abundant granular yolk.

3339   A Skink (*Tiliqua sp.*) with the ventral walls of the abdomen removed to expose the impregnated oviducts.
      Each oviduct contains from six to eight ova of an elliptical form, 18 mm. in the long diameter. Development of the embryo has commenced in each ovum, as is evinced by the large size of the transparent germinal area on the surface of the yolk. Most of the ova contained in the left oviduct have been removed and are mounted below.

3340   A specimen of the same species of Skink, in which the right oviduct is laid open showing two of the young completely developed. Those contained in the opposite oviduct appear to have been excluded.

3341   A Lizard (*Lacerta bilineata*) dissected to display the female organs of generation, and especially the ovaries, in which are to be seen ova ripe for dehiscence and impregnation. The ova are subspherical and closely packed together within the distended capsule of the ovary.

3342 A similar specimen.

3343 A Lizard (*Lacerta quadrilineata*) dissected to display the ovaries and oviducts *in situ*. Several of the ovarian ova have reached their mature development; the oviducts present a corresponding enlargement and are disposed in numerous short transverse folds.

3344 A similar specimen, with many of the ovarian ova ripe for impregnation.

3345 A Lizard (*Tropidolepis undulatus*) with part of the ventral walls of the abdomen removed to show the ripe ovarian ova in their natural relation to the rest of the viscera, impacted among the coils of the intestine.

3346 A viviparous Lizard (*Podarcis muralis*) with the ventral walls of the abdomen removed to expose the impregnated oviducts.

The right oviduct is *in situ* and contains three ova, in each of which the development of the embryo has considerably advanced. The left oviduct has been displaced and turned forwards; one ovum has been removed to show the extreme delicacy of the wall of the distended segment of the oviduct in which it lay.

3347 Another specimen of *Podarcis muralis*.

3348 The egg of a Lizard, laid open to show the embryo far advanced in development and, mounted above it, an embryo at a similar stage of development removed from another ovum.

The ovum has the general form of the adult, with the limbs and tail fully formed. The head is disproportionately large with narrow, beak-shaped face and great, prominent eyes.

Within the cranium may be observed the brain, with the cerebral hemispheres and optic lobes of equal size.

In the centre of the abdomen is a short pedicle formed by the stalk of the yolk-sac.

3349 The embryo of a Lizard, far advanced in development, showing the long, convoluted umbilical cord and yolk-sac. The latter has been laid open and its contents removed; there is no appearance of the vascular absorbent plicae on its inner surface analogous to the 'so-called "vasa lutea"' shown in the Bird (3432) and the Snake.

3350   A Lizard removed from the egg at near the completion of foetal development.

3351   The right ovary and oviduct with the corresponding kidney and ureter and the urinary bladder and cloaca of a Turtle (*Chelone mydas*).

   The ovary is quite immature and presents the form of a thin ribbon-shaped plicated fold of membrane, with its surface minutely granulated by the commencing development of the ova and ovisacs.

   In correspondence with the immature state of the ovary, the oviduct is a simple narrow tube running in its suspensory fold direct and without plications to the cloaca. Its anterior extremity is marked by a bristle, and the urogenital sinus has been opened to show the prominent papilla through which it communicates with this chamber. A rod has been passed from the cloaca through the anal opening.

3352   A portion of the ovary of a Turtle, injected, with a few of the ova advanced considerably in development and projecting freely from its margin pendant in extensions of the ovarian capsule.

3353   A similar preparation, showing well the broad vascular membrane by which the ovary is suspended and the loose extensions of the ovarian capsule within which lie the ovisacs and ova pendant from the margin of the ovary.

3354   A portion of the oviduct of a Turtle, containing two impregnated ova. Each ovum is contained within a dilated segment of the oviduct separated from similar egg-containing segments by a short stretch of narrow unaltered duct.

   Part of the oviduct has been reflected from the lower egg to show the extreme tenuity of the wall of the duct in the region of dilatation.

3355   Two of the spherical eggs of a Turtle, after extrusion. The egg is protected by a thin white calcareous shell.

3356   Two turtle eggs, preserved dry, showing more clearly than in the previous specimen the finely granular surface of the shell.

3358   A young Turtle, with the ventral walls of the abdomen removed to show the small remains of the yolk-sac, attached to one of the coils of the small intestine.

3359   The heart, lungs, and principal blood vessels of a young Turtle, prepared to show the short communicating vessels between the left pulmonary artery and the left

FIG. 4

Drawing by St Aubin of Specimen No. 3365. (Hunterian Drawing Book II, p. 140.)

FIG. 5

Specimen No. 3376A, showing the single ovary and oviduct of a Cuckoo
(*Cuculus canorus*).

descending aorta and between the right pulmonary artery and the right descending aorta. These connections, comparable to the ductus arteriosus in Man, are subsequently obliterated.

3360 The stomach and intestines of a young Turtle, exhibiting the remains of the two great foetal appendages, viz: the nutritive yolk-sac, which communicates with the small intestine at about one-fourth of the length of the intestinal tube (measuring from the stomach), and the respiratory allantois connected with the termination of the rectum.

3361 Part of the ovary of a Tortoise (*Testudo*) injected, with several nearly mature globular ova in position.

Some of the ova have fallen out of their ovisacs and are mounted separately.

3362 One of the spherical eggs of a Tortoise, removed from the terminal segment of the oviduct, and showing the commencing deposition of calcareous matter on the membranous inner layers of the shell.

3363 Three young Tortoises of different ages, showing the progressive obliteration of the external umbilical aperture.

This orifice is seen in the upper and smallest specimen at the convergence of the anal, pre-anal and abdominal plates of the plastron.

In the lower and largest specimen it is reduced to a narrow longitudinal fissure between the pre-anal plates.

3364 Two eggs of a Crocodile.

The eggs are of large size and oval in shape. In the lower one, part of the superficial calcareous layer of the shell has been removed to expose the deeper membranous layer of 'putamen'.

In the upper specimen half the egg-shell has been cut away to show the young Crocodile, at about the completion of its development, closely coiled up within it.

3365 A young Crocodile removed from the egg, but still attached to it by the umbilical cord and allantoic vessels.

A portion of the ventral wall of the abdomen has been turned aside to show that a portion of the yolk-sac has been taken into the abdominal cavity through the wide umbilical aperture.

3366 The trunk and tail of a young Crocodile, dissected to show the condition of the yolk-sac and allantois at the close of foetal development.

The yolk-sac presents an irregular lobulated form and its short and narrow duct communicates with a loop of the small intestine a short way below the duodenum.

The allantois communicates with the lower part of the rectum by means of a long and very slender duct corresponding with the urachus, but no part of which is dilated to form a urinary bladder in the adult.

The allantoic arteries and veins are also shown.

3367 A young Crocodile with the ventral walls of the abdomen removed to show the remains of the yolk-sac in the abdominal cavity. The pericardium is laid open and a longitudinal section removed from the right ventricle. The cavity of the latter is extremely small as compared with the thickness of its muscular walls.

3368 The viscera of a foetal Crocodile, prepared to show the heart with its principal vessels, especially the two long 'ductus arteriosi' that connect the pulmonary arteries with the two aortae. A black bristle is placed between the ductus and aorta on the right side.

The yolk-sac is shown in section.

3369 The stomach and intestines of a young Crocodile, together with that part of the abdominal wall which surrounds the umbilical aperture, showing the transit of the yolk-sac into the abdomen. One half of the sac has passed through the wide aperture.

3370 The stomach and intestinal canal of a young Crocodile at a later period of development, with the yolk-sac wholly taken into the abdominal cavity and much reduced by absorption of its contents. A section has been removed from it to show the hard coagulated and fibrous character of the remaining yolk.

3371 A similar specimen with the contracted yolk-sac which has, through lapse of time, become a good deal broken.

3372 The thoracic and abdominal viscera of a foetal Crocodile with the yolk-sac and its contents in great part removed and the aperture leading to the vitelline duct displayed and a bristle inserted into it. A number of fine vascular folds radiate from this aperture upon the inner surface of the duct, representing the 'vasa lutea' in the yolk-sac of the Fowl.

A bristle is inserted into the still open duct of the allantois.

3373 The heart with part of the oesophagus and the right lung of a foetal Crocodile.

The auricles are laid open and the septum between them exposed, showing the still patent foramen ovale.

In Birds

3375 A female House Sparrow (*Passer domesticus*) with the ventral walls of the abdomen and all the viscera, excepting the generative and urinary organs, removed.

The single functional ovary, which here, as in other Birds, is the one on the left side of the body, presents a racemose figure in consequence of the small quantity of stroma around the ovisacs and the great accumulation of yolk within the developing ova.

The ovary has, however, only begun to respond to the stimulus of sexual development. The single oviduct is proportionally small.

3376 A female House Sparrow similarly prepared, showing the organs of generation in a state of full development and functional activity.

The large size of the ovary is due to the great development of a few of the ova; of these, two were probably destined for dehiscence and two have already escaped from their ovisacs. One of these latter is contained within the oviduct and has traversed about one-fourth of the distance to the cloaca. The oviduct has been reflected downwards and a bristle inserted into its abdominal aperture.

3376A The posterior half of a hen Cuckoo (*Cuculus canorus*), showing the single left ovary and oviduct at the period of full functional activity.

Two of the ovisacs are of such size that they probably are destined for dehiscence: one presenting a diameter of about 6 lines (12·5 mm.) the other of about 3.

One ovum has already been shed from the ovary and has reached the terminal or uterine segment of the oviduct within which it is coated by the calcareous egg-shell. Part of the wall of this region of the duct has been cut away to expose the egg, from which a small portion of the calcareous egg-shell has been removed to show the putamen or parchment-like membrane that envelops the egg between the calcareous shell and the white.

Prepared for Hunter by Edward Jenner

3376B A similar preparation of a hen Cuckoo, showing the generative organs soon after the close of their functional activity.

Four ova have been matured, shed from the ovary and impregnated; their empty ovisacs may be observed upon the ovary. The oviduct is still of large size and is disposed in broad, irregular, transverse folds.

Also prepared by Edward Jenner.

See 'Observations on the Natural History of the Cuckoo', by Edward Jenner. *Phil. Trans.*, vol. 78, 1788, pp. 219-237.

3377 The egg of a Cuckoo, towards the close of its parasitic incubation, with part of the shell broken away to expose the contained embryo.

3378 The left ovary of a Hen (*Gallus domesticus*) showing the ovisacs at different stages of development.

A few are emptied and collapsed after the escape of the ovum; in one the wide rent through which the ovum passed is shown with great clearness.

3379 The left ovary of a Hen, with contiguous portions of the vena cava inferior and aorta, together with two empty and collapsed ovisacs.

3380 The generative organs, with the rectum and cloaca of a Hen.

The ovary exhibits the ovisacs and ova in different stages of formation, one of the ova being nearly ripe for dehiscence. Different parts of the large plicated oviduct are laid open, showing that the lining of this duct, except for a short distance at its commencement, is deeply folded longitudinally. In the terminal oruterine part of the duct, within which the calcareous egg-shell is formed, the longitudinal plications are deeper, more delicate and more numerous than elsewhere, and are further extended by a regular transverse folding of the lining membrane.

The oviduct is attached on one side to the body wall by a fold of peritoneum, which also extends beyond the free edge of the duct, forming a ligament within which is a considerable development of smooth muscle.

The opening of the oviduct into the urodaeal segment of the cloaca and its relation to the anal orifice is also shown.

3381 The trunk of a Hen, with the ventral walls of the chest and abdomen cut away and the viscera removed to display the organs of generation *in situ*.

The ovary shows three empty ovisacs, which, it may be observed, present no formation of tissue comparable to the corpus luteum of the Mammal. The rent by which the ripe ovum has escaped is in the form of a long fissure with thin but not everted margins; the ovisacs having performed their function, are afterwards disposed of by progressive absorption. The other ovisacs, as usual, contain ova in different stages of formation.

The parts have been minutely injected, so that the non-vascular line or 'stigma' towards which the vessels of the ovisac converge and at which dehiscence takes place, is very clearly displayed. This line is particularly plain upon two ovisacs situated towards the left side of the ovary.

A bristle has been inserted into the wide abdominal mouth of the oviduct, which forms a spreading membranous funnel with delicate non-fimbriated lips of a size proportioned to the magnitude of the ripe ovum which it is destined to receive.

An ovum has passed into the uterine or shell-secreting terminal dilatation of the oviduct and is there exposed by the reflection of a portion of the wall of the duct. The lining membrane of this region is marked by close-set, complex, wavy folds and is highly vascular.

3382 The impregnated oviduct of a Hen, with an egg exposed within the uterine or egg-shell-secreting segment.

The radiating bundles of smooth muscle tissue within the suspensory membrane of the duct are very clearly shown.

3383 The uterine or calcifying segment of the oviduct of a Duck (*Anas boscas*) with an egg exposed within it by the reflection of part of its wall.

The deposition of the calcified shell has not progressed far. Particles of shelly material are beginning to be deposited upon the membrana putaminis.

3384 The ovary and oviduct of a Goose (*Anser ferus*) with the kidneys and cloaca, minutely injected.

The ovisacs and ova are in various stages of development, showing very clearly the structure of the vacated ovisacs and the stigma or line of future dehiscence in those that contain ova approaching maturity.

The terminal uterine or calcifying segment of the oviduct has been laid open by a crucial incision and a piece of quill is passed from it through the contracted aperture that leads to the narrow portion of the tube known as the 'isthmus' by which the membrana putaminis is secreted upon the albumen that has been deposited around the egg in the more anterior portions of the duct.

The surface of the inner lining of the uterine segment is increased by close-set leaf-like laminae arranged in rows set more or less circumferentially.

3385 The ovary of an Ostrich (*Struthio camelus*) in the breeding season, showing ovisacs and ova in very different stages of formation.

The ovisacs are peculiarly dense and those of the riper ova are remarkable for the great length and tenuity of the pedicles by which they are connected with the body of the ovary.

3386   The egg of a Goose (*Anser ferus*) broken transversely and the contents removed, showing the calcareous shell and the parchment-like membrane (membrana putaminis) by which it is closely lined.

3387   A transverse section through the large end of the egg of a Goose, showing the natural separation of the layers of the membrana putaminis, forming the 'vesica aeris'.   The gas contained within this chamber is of importance for the respiration of the embryo shortly before hatching; it contains a larger proportion of oxygen than air.

3388   Another section of the egg of a Goose, showing one half of the vesica aeris.   The layer of the putamen that forms the internal wall of this cavity is thinner than the outer layer.   The two can be separated from one another through the whole extent of the egg.

3389   A Hen's egg, from which a longitudinal section has been removed, to show two unequal-sized yolks, which, having passed at or near the same time into the oviduct, have become surrounded by a common investment of albumen secreted in the upper parts of the duct, and finally in the lower parts by a common putamen and calcareous shell.

The following fifteen (originally sixteen) preparations exhibit the earlier stages in the development of the Goose.   There are original drawings in the Library of some of these specimens or of embryos at analogous stages of development, but the specimens themselves have deteriorated so much that it is impossible to see many of the features described in detail in Owen's *Catalogue of the Physiological Series*, published in 1840.

3390-3399   A series of preparations of very early stages in the development of the Goose (*Anser ferus*).

Most of these specimens have so deteriorated that they are only of historic interest.

The fourth and fifth specimens (*D and E*—3393 and 3394) were at a stage of development similar to that of a chick at the 20th hour of incubation.   The embryo lies in the middle of the area pellucida of the blastoderm and presents the appearance of a narrow opaque streak of thickening.   Around the area pellucida is the area opaca.

F and G (3395 and 3396) are two embryos at a slightly later stage of development. The head of the embryo is considerably enlarged and although still lying in the same line as the trunk, is cut off from the underlying blastoderm by a recess, which gives rise to the head fold. The area pellucida has assumed a pear-shaped outline, with the head of the embryo in the centre of its broader end.

H and I (3397 and 3398). In these preparations the blastoderm has become much crumpled. Parts of the embryo can, however, be seen. In H, the head end shows the commencement of flexure and torsion. In I, this is more marked, the axis of the head and neck being strongly bent ventrally and the head twisted so as to lie upon its left side.

J (3399) is an embryo and blastoderm at a somewhat later stage of development and originally showed the flexure of the head and neck; the enlargement of the head owing to the growth of the brain vesicles; the rudiment of the heart wedged in between the deflected anterior end of the head and the trunk; the rudiment of the eye; and the prominent caudal extremity.

3400 A blastoderm and embryo at a more advanced stage of development, seen from the dorsal aspect.

The head is pinched off the surface of the blastoderm, strongly flexed and turned to the right. The trunk is linear and shows at either end slight swellings, from which later the limbs will be developed.

The stage presented by this specimen is similar to that shown by the developing Chick towards the end of the third day of incubation.

3401 A blastoderm and embryo at a somewhat later stage of development, seen from the ventral aspect.

This preparation shows well the general external appearance of the embryo and area vasculosa of the blastoderm at a stage corresponding with the fourth day of incubation of the Chick.

Upon the blastoderm may be observed the slender branching vitelline arteries passing from the trunk of the embryo across the area pellucida to the area vasculosa, and accompanying them the two lateral vitelline veins proceeding to the heart, which lies within the concavity formed by the strong cephalic flexure of the embryo.

3402 A slightly older embryo. The membranes are considerably crumpled and broken. The embryo originally showed very clearly the external form characteristic of this stage of development: the strong flexure and torsion of the head and forepart of the body; the swollen cerebral vesicles, with the great prominence of the mid-brain; the cup-shaped rudiment of the eye; the ear capsule close behind it; the rudimentary visceral arches; the cervical swelling caused by the heart; and the limb bud swellings upon the margin of the trunk.

3403   An embryo at a later stage of development corresponding with that of a chick at the fourth day of incubation.

In this specimen the growing allantois was formerly visible as a small and delicate bladder, about the size of a pea, protruding towards the right side beyond the margin of the body wall opposite the bud of the hind limb, but the details are no longer obvious.

The various parts noted in previous specimens were here more strongly marked. Particularly to be noticed are the protuberant brain vesicles; the eye with a clearly defined lens within the optic cup; the heart forming a protuberant mass in the recess formed by the cervical and cranial flexure, the prominent limb buds and the coiled caudal extremity.

The hinder part of the embryo is now lying upon its side instead of being prone as at earlier stages.

3405   An embryo further advanced in development, corresponding with the stage reached by the Chick embryo on the sixth day of incubation.

The ventral body wall has closed in, except for a comparatively narrow umbilical aperture, through which pass the stalks of the yolk-sac and allantois and the umbilical vessels.

The head has now assumed a shape suggestive of the adult and shows clearly the great optic vesicle with its enclosed lens.

Posterior to the eye may be seen a small pit from which later the auditory organ will develop.

The limbs are beginning to show definite segmentation into shaft and extremities.

Parts of the foetal membranes have been retained, but their condition is too fragmentary to demonstrate their relations.

A series of Hunterian preparations illustrating the development of the external form and the foetal membranes of the Chick. Although these have deteriorated considerably, most of the features mentioned in the following descriptions can still be identified.

3410   A. The blastoderm of an embryo Chick of 10 somites.

3411   B. A similar specimen of the blastoderm of an embryo of 15 somites, or about

36 hours' incubation. The blastoderm shows clearly the central area pellucida with the area vasculosa surrounding it, bordered by the sinus terminalis and anterior vitelline veins.

The embryo appears as an opaque streak in the centre of the area pellucida and is slightly thickened at one end owing to commencing development of the brain.

3412 C. A blastoderm and embryo further advanced in development, at about 60 hours' incubation. The head has now become pinched off from the surface of the blastoderm and is turned to the right. The area vasculosa and sinus terminalis are more clearly defined and the passage of the vitelline vessels across the area pellucida to the body of the embryo more readily visible.

3413 D. A blastoderm and embryo of about the same age as the preceding, or slightly younger.

3414 E. A blastoderm and embryo towards the end of the third day of incubation. This preparation has at some time been allowed to dry and in consequence shows very little.

3416 F. A blastoderm and embryo at a later stage of development. The cephalic flexure has become very marked and now includes the commencement of the flexure of the neck region. In the concavity of this flexure may be observed a swelling due to the increased development of the heart. The area pellucida is becoming indistinguishable from the area vasculosa and the vitelline vessels have increased considerably in size.

3417 G. A blastoderm and embryo at a later stage of development. In this preparation the enclosure of the embryo in a membranous amniotic sac may be clearly seen. The cephalic and cervical flexures have now become very strongly marked and upon the reverse of the specimen can be seen the small budding allantoic vesicle projecting from the hinder part of the body into the concave space behind the heart embraced by the cephalic and caudal flexures of the body. At either end of the body the limbs are beginning to sprout forth as small oval prominences; between them on either side may be observed a linear swelling parallel to the umbilical fissure; this is the rudiment of the embryonic kidney or Wolffian body.

3418 H. An embryo, with its blastoderm, of somewhat larger size, but exhibiting practically the same stage of development as the preceding specimen. In this preparation the allantois and vitelline vessels are very clearly displayed.

3419   I. An embryo, with a portion of the blastoderm at about the sixth day of incuba-
       tion, showing the progressive enlargement of the allantois which now protrudes
       into the extra-embryonic coelom beyond the borders of the umbilical fissure.
       The head of the embryo shows clearly the optic vesicle and lens and in the neck
       may be observed rudimentary gill arches with indentations or gill-clefts between
       them. The heart has considerably increased in size and forms a marked pro-
       tuberance behind the chin. The limb buds are much enlarged though not yet
       separated into their several segments.

3420   K. An embryo, with parts of its foetal membranes, at a considerably more ad-
       vanced stage of development. The general form of the adult is now plainly
       recognisable. The head, with its incipient beak and large prominent eyes is
       separated from the trunk by a long and slender neck. At the inner corner of
       the eye may be seen a minute rudiment of the nictitating membrane. The
       limbs have assumed a characteristically avian form.

       The above preparations are part of an original series of fourteen. The
       earlier ones, 3406-3409 and 3415, have perished through lapse of time.

   A series of preparations on the viscera of embryo Goslings (*Anser ferus*):

3421   A. This preparation originally showed parts of the thoracic and abdominal
       viscera: the liver, lungs, gizzard and large Wolffian bodies or transitory kidneys,
       from a Gosling at a stage of development corresponding with that of a Chick at
       the end of the seventh month of incubation, but of these structures nothing now
       remains.

3422   B. The viscera of an embryo Gosling at a more advanced stage of development.
       The heart has the form characteristic of the adult, with the apex of the left
       ventricle projecting considerably beyond that of the right. The rest of the
       viscera, with the exception of the gizzard, are considerably damaged. A small
       part of the allantois is retained.

3423   C. The viscera of a Gosling further advanced in development. A section has been
       removed from the right lung to show its capacious cavity and thick spongy wall.
       Hanging from the alimentary canal are portions of the allantois and yolk-sac.
       The walls of the latter display well-developed absorptive folds.

3424   D. A similar preparation of the viscera of an older embryo Gosling. Below each
       lung may be observed a large abdominal air-sac, freely suspended in the ab-

dominal cavity. The junction of the omphalo-mesenteric vein with the vena cava inferior in the interspace of the kidneys is well shown, as also is the connection between the yolk-sac and the intestines.

3425 E. The heart, liver and part of the intestinal canal of an older Gosling. The large umbilical or allantoic vein is shown passing above the fissure of the liver to join the short common trunk of the hepatic veins; one of the allantoic arteries is likewise preserved. The omphalo-mesenteric vein may be seen joining the vena cava beneath the liver; the omphalo-mesenteric artery is likewise shown. The stomach and intestinal canal have been removed, together with the lungs and the left lobe of the liver.

3426 A foetal Gosling towards the conclusion of incubation, with the body cavity exposed from the right side to show the course of the allantoic or umbilical vein.

The vein had been filled with a red injection which has partly escaped but the vessel can be seen passing from the umbilicus along the right side of the gizzard between the two lobes of the liver and anterior to the isthmus that joins them, to the short and wide trunk of the inferior vena cava, where it receives the hepatic veins.

The right lobe of the liver has been removed; and the right auricle has been laid open. The coils of the intestine, the loops of the small intestine to which the yolk-sac is attached, and the omphalo-mesenteric vein are likewise displayed.

3427 A foetal Gosling near the conclusion of incubation, injected by the umbilical or allantoic vein.

The yolk-sac, which has become detached and now mounted separately, is laid open near the slender pedicle of 'ductus vitello-intestinalis' by which it is attached to the intestine. It is stated that (in the chick) this duct remains always patent, and that the yolk does not pass through it into the intestine but is absorbed directly by the vitelline blood vessels.

The termination of the rectum is laid open to show the connection of the allantois with this part of the intestinal canal. A bristle is inserted into the passage of communication.

3428 A foetal Gosling with the yolk-sac and allantois minutely injected. The yolk-sac is laid open and shows admirably the absorptive vascular folds that project into its interior. At the fundus of the yolk-sac may be seen the 'yolk-sac umbilicus' or communication between the yolk-sac and the albumen sac. The latter, which is formed by an overlapping of the chorion, encloses the remains of the 'white' of the egg, which is gradually absorbed into the yolk through the umbilicus. Hanging below the albumen sac is a considerable part of the allantois richly injected. This vascular membrane forms the chief respiratory organ of the foetus.

3429 An embryo Duck (*Anas boscas*) at the latter half of incubation, showing the diminished part of the albumen adherent to the margins of the 'yolk-sac' umbilicus.

The yolk-sac is opened and shows well the wavy absorbent folds that radiate in its interior from the margins of the umbilicus.

3430 A portion of the wall of the yolk-sac of a Duck, showing the absorptive folds upon its inner surface converging upon the umbilicus of the albumen sac.

3431 A similar yolk-sac cut open to show the absorptive folds.

3432 Part of the wall of the yolk-sac and of the membrane enclosing the remains of the albumen.

The absorptive folds due to a pleating of the inner endodermal wall of the yolk-sac are well shown; between this area and the sinus terminalis the absorptive layer has been reflected to show the thin transparent vascular layer. Above the sinus terminalis is a fragment of the chorionic membrane that encloses the albumen.

3433 The stomach and intestinal canal with the umbilicus and anus and a portion of the yolk-sac included within the abdomen, of a young Gosling.

The slender, short and now ligamentous vitelline duct is shown; the urachus or pedicle of the allantois which passes from the anterior part of the rectum to the umbilicus, is also much reduced.

The large proportional size of the 'bursa Fabricii' attached to the cloaca is worthy of notice. This caecal appendage is larger in the young than in the adult.

3434 The umbilicus of a young Gosling, with the yolk-sac, which has been included within the abdomen, minutely injected. This specimen, now much deteriorated, showed a portion of the small intestine with the ductus vitello-intestinalis preserved and a bristle passed through the latter tube.

The retraction of the yolk-sac into the abdomen is stated (in the Chick) to be mainly due to the contraction of the muscle fibres in the inner wall of the

allantois and of the part of the amnion attached to the umbilicus. These
membranes closely invest the yolk-stalk and yolk-sac and by their contractions
squeeze the yolk-sac into the abdomen.

3435   A young Duck (*Anas boscas*) towards the close of incubation, at the period when
the yolk-sac is about to be included within the abdomen.

3436   The trunk of a young Duck at the conclusion of incubation showing the umbilicus
after the passage of the yolk-sac into the abdomen.

3437   The stomach of a young Gosling towards the conclusion of incubation, laid open
to show a coagulated mass in its interior. This is stated in Owen's Catalogue to
be nutrient material which has been transmitted to the stomach by the small
intestine from the vitelline duct. In the later stages of incubation it is doubtful
whether yolk-material passes through the vitelline duct, the whole absorption of
food material being apparently effected by the blood vessels and specialised
epithelial lining of the yolk-sac.

3438   The stomach and duodenum of a Gosling, at the close of incubation, laid open to
show a coagulum contained within it.

3439   A Chicken soon after hatching, with the ventral walls of the abdomen removed to
show the remains of the yolk-sac within the cavity, adhering to the internal
border of the umbilicus.

3440   A similar preparation, in which the short, plicated, umbilical pedicle of the included yolk-sac and the form of the recently closed umbilicus are well displayed.

3441   A similar preparation in which the included yolk-sac is laid open and its contents
removed to show the wavy vascular and absorptive folds of its lining membrane.

3442   Part of the ventral wall of the abdomen including the recently closed umbilicus of
a Chick, a few days older than the previous specimen, showing the diminished
yolk-sac adhering to the inner surface of the umbilicus and connected by means
of the vitelline duct, now reduced to a long and slender filament, to the small
intestine, of which a loop is preserved.

3443   A Hen's egg towards the close of incubation, from which a portion of the attenuated
shell has been removed to show the change which takes place in the membranous

lining of the shell (membrana putaminis) during incubation; it now resembles a layer of thin parchment.   Part of it has been removed to show the vascular surface of the allantois.

3444   A Hen's egg towards the close of incubation from which a portion of the shell has been removed so as to exhibit the vascular allantois and the vesica aeris; the latter is larger than at earlier stages.   It is ruptured by the Chick on the nineteenth day of incubation when the lungs begin to perform their functions by means of the gas which this vessel contains.

3445   The contents of the egg of a Goose, when two-thirds of the period of incubation have been completed; showing the position of the embryo at that period.
        It is bent upon itself and sunk into a deep cleft in the substance of the yolk-sac. The chorion and vascular outer wall of the allantois have been thrown down and are suspended by the umbilical vessels and by the duplicature of the chorion which was pushed before the allantois around the albumen.

3446   The egg of a Goose at a similar period of incubation, laid open and its contents removed, excepting the vascular layer of the allantois, which is closely applied to the inner surface of the putamen or egg-shell membrane.
        The allantoic vessels are in many parts minutely injected; they are ramified so as to submit the blood of the chick in a state of extremely minute subdivision to the air which gains access to it through the pores of the shell and membrana putaminis.

3447   The young of a species of Penguin at the close of incubation, with part of the egg-shell removed.
        The young Bird is disposed so as to form a shape adapted to that of the cavity in which it was developed; the head is twisted obliquely to the right and covered with the right wing and foot.   From the nearly closed umbilicus hangs the remains of one of the vessels of the allantois; the body is covered with a short and fine dark-coloured down.
        Upon the upper side of the apex of the beak is a horny prominence—a temporary structure used in breaking the shell.

3449   The heart of a Gosling near the close of incubation, showing the very deep 'fossa ovalis' in the right auricle and the small foramen of communication between the two auricles.
        The ventricles are laid open, showing the integrity of their septum and their

valves; a fine tendinous cord is here seen to be attached to the free margins of the large muscular valve of the right ventricle.

3450   The principal thoracic and abdominal viscera of a Gosling towards the close of incubation, minutely injected.

The auricles and the right ventricle of the heart have been cut open. In the left auricle can be seen the elliptical form and valvular projection of the foramen ovale. The two arteriae innominatae are also laid open to show the thickness of their walls.

The stomach has been removed to expose the spleen; the cut ends of the vitelline and allantoic veins are displayed; their corresponding arteries are indicated by pieces of black thread tied around them.

3452   A Partridge (*Perdix cinerea*) near the close of incubation, showing the well-developed beak and legs and the plumage of down tufts by which it is covered.

The advanced condition of the young Bird at hatching is associated with the power to follow the parent bird and procure its own sustenance as soon as it has chipped the shell. This precocious development is common to Gallinaceous and certain other groups of Birds and led to their being at one time classed together as 'Aves praecoces'.

3453   A young Passerine Bird after the completion of incubation, showing, in contrast with the preceding specimen, the helpless condition in which it is hatched, viz. naked and blind, or with the eye-balls closed.

The quill-feathers are just beginning to protrude through the skin.

3456   A series of six heads of young Goslings at different stages of growth, previous to hatching, showing the progressive development of the eye-lids, of the margins of the anterior nares, and of the horny knob or egg-tooth formed temporarily at the extremity of the beak for the purpose of breaking the egg-shell in the process of hatching. The first protective fold of the eye-ball to appear is a low ring of integument within which at the inner canthus of the eye, is formed a semilunar fold which subsequently forms the nictitating membrane. Later the horizontal eye-lids are differentiated from the circular fold by an increased growth of its dorsal and ventral parts—and particularly of the latter which throughout life forms the more important of the two horizontal lids.

It will be noticed that in none of these specimens are the eye-lids fused together.

The external nostrils are at first merely slits; gradually their margins protrude, forming finally a short, almost tube-like projection.

3457   The head of a young Gosling at the close of incubation, showing the condition of the eye-lids, the external nostrils and the horny egg-tooth at the point of the upper beak, with which the shell is broken in the act of exclusion from the egg.

3458   A similar specimen of the head of a Gosling, injected, and with the lower jaw removed, to show the posterior nares opening into the mouth through a single elliptical aperture.

Behind this opening can be seen the similar common termination of the Eustachian tubes or internal passages of the middle ear.

3459, 3460   Two heads of Chicks at the close of incubation, showing the sharp-pointed egg-tooth at the extremity of the beak.

Sir Arthur Keith, in an article in the *Annals of the Royal College of Surgeons* (vol. 8, p. 166, 1951) makes the following comment:

'Hunter investigated the development of the chick at two periods of his life; in one passage of his writings he tells us "that about the year 1755 or 1756, when I was making drawings of the growth of the chick in the process of incubation, I then observed . . ." At this time Hunter being about 28 years of age, was still assistant to his brother William. Our specimen (3459) may have come from this early period, but more likely it belongs to a later period—that in which he had established a research station at Earl's Court (1764-1793). At Earl's Court he kept a flock of geese to provide him with incubating eggs. From the volume of the catalogue just cited, we learn why he preferred geese to the common fowl for this purpose (see this volume, p. 7). . . .

'Hence it came about that the Hunterian specimens which illustrate the development of the "shell-breaking knob" on the shelves of our Museum, are from the goose not from the chick. There is a series of six, showing all stages in the development of the knob in the goose (3456). . . .

He goes on to say:

'My interest in this Hunterian specimen was reawakened by an investigation recently published in the Transactions of the Zoological Society of London (xxvi, 503, 1950) by my friends Professors J. P. Hill and G. R. de Beer, the last named being now Director of the Natural History Museum, South Kensington. The title which they give to their publication is:— "The

3456

Fig. 6

Drawing by St Aubin (Hunterian Drawing Book II, p. 158); and
photograph of Specimen No. 3456.

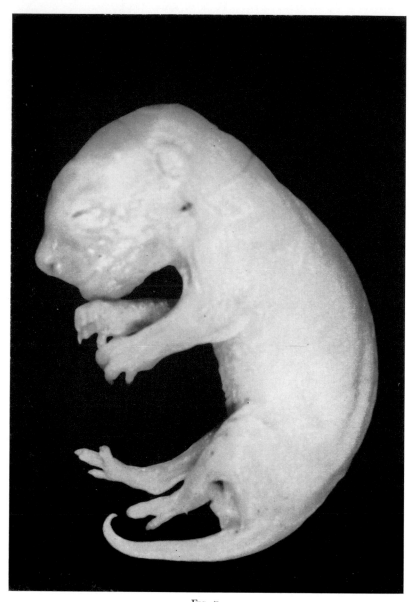

FIG. 7

Specimen No. 3461: a Kangaroo, three weeks after birth.

Development and Structure of the Egg-Tooth and Caruncle in the Mono-tremes, and on the Ocurrence of Vestiges of the Egg-Tooth in Marsupials". From them I learned that Hunter's description of the shell-breaking knob was the first recorded in England. The actual passage claiming priority for Hunter reads:— "Although Aldrovandus (1597) may have been the first to describe it, John Hunter is the first English observer known to us to take notice of the caruncle (horny knob) of the chick" (p. 534). Hunter's observation is as follows:

'The little horny knob at the end of the beak with which it breaks the shell when arrived at the full time and makes its escape, is also gradually forming into a more regular and determined point, the progress of which is seen from the first figure to the sixth'. (See above, p. 16).

Another specimen showing this structure is that of a Penguin (3447).

In Mammals

3461 The young or mammary foetus of a Kangaroo, removed from the nipple and pouch of the mother within three weeks after birth.

The foetus is perfectly naked, with the eye lids and external auditory meatuses closed. The nostrils are wide open to allow of the passage of air when the foetus is permanently attached to the teat.

The mouth, unlike that of the uterine foetus, is reduced by the fusion of the lateral parts of the lips to a small round hole adapted to the size of the teat. The entire length of the foetus does not exceed one and a half inches.

3462 A pregnant Water-rat (*Arvicola amphibia*) with the walls of the abdomen removed to show the uteri and their contained foetuses.

The walls of the uteri are thin and semi-transparent and through them can be seen the foetuses, nearing the completion of their development. So far as can be observed successive foetuses lie head to head, and tail to tail.

3463 A portion of the uterus, with two foetuses, of a Water-rat.

The uterus has been slit open to expose the foetuses; one of these is enclosed in the inner wall of the yolk-sac and is attached to the uterus by means of a small circular button-shaped allantoic placenta.

This body is convex towards the uterus and presents a flat surface to the chorion, which is attached to the centre of the disc and overlapped by its margins. Beyond the placental area the chorion is absent, its place being taken by the inner wall of the yolk-sac.

C.H.M.—H

The other foetus is extruded from the ruptured yolk-sac and amnion and hangs suspended by the umbilical cord, which contains the ducts and blood vessels of the yolk-sac and allantois.

3464   A foetal Water-rat near the completion of its development, with its placenta and a small piece of the wall of the uterus.

The foetus is connected with the placenta by a long, slender umbilical cord. Around the point of entry of the cord to the central parts of the placenta can be seen portions of the amnion and yolk-sac.

3465   A foetus of a Water-rat with its membranes and placenta.

The inner wall of the yolk-sac (which in Rodents occupies the position appropriate to the non-placental chorion) and the amnion have been opened and reflected from the foetus. The placenta is circular, convex externally, and flat towards the foetus.

3466   The trunk of a Rat (*Mus decumanus*) with the walls of the abdomen and most of the viscera removed to show the uteri in the early stages of pregnancy.

In each uterus are a number of embryos, each occupying a globular dilatation protruding from one side of the uterine tube.

Successive dilatations are separated by a narrow segment of the uterus.

3467   The lower ends of the gravid uteri with part of the vagina of a Rat (*Mus decumanus*).

In one of the uteri a dilatation containing an embryo is left entire. Two corresponding dilatations of the other uterus have been opened and one of the contained foetuses extracted and mounted separately; the other foetus is not shown.

In the posterior of the two opened dilatations the material portion of the placenta is shown. This forms a cup-shaped thickening of the uterine wall, into the concavity of which fits a small convex process in the centre of the button-shaped disc of the foetal placenta.

From the margins of the maternal placenta radiate a few deep folds of the uterine mucosa.

The foetus extracted from the second uterine dilatation was originally left suspended from the maternal placenta. It has now become detached with the maternal placenta and a small portion of the surrounding wall of the uterus.

It shows the button-like form of the foetal placenta and the separation of its margins by a deep groove from the general surface of the chorion-like yolk-sac wall.

Near the margin of the placenta the wall of the yolk-sac is produced to form four bunches of delicate arborescent villi.

3468 The late foetus of a Rat with the wall of the yolk-sac and the amnion slit open and turned down to show the long slender umbilical cord and the form of the placenta.

The latter is button-shaped, with a small circular prominence in the middle of its external surface. This prominence fits into the concavity of the maternal placenta shown in the previous specimen.

3469 A pregnant Mouse (*Mus musculus*) with the abdomen laid open to show the impregnated uteri near the conclusion of gestation.

3470 The urogenital canal, vagina and uteri, of a pregnant Squirrel (*Sciurus vulgaris*), showing in each uterus three foetigerous dilatations.

As in the Rat (3466) these dilatations protrude from the free margin of the uterine tube and are separated from one another by narrow segments of some considerable length.

Two of the dilated segments have been opened; in one (that nearest the vagina) the chorion and yolk-sac are left entire and the bush of delicate filamentary villous processes projecting from that part of the outer surface of the chorion which is to form the seat of the placental attachment to the uterus, are beautifully shown; in the other the yolk-sac and amnion have been opened to expose the foetus, which is not sufficiently advanced to show separate digits. The umbilical cord is short and wide and contains a loop of the intestine.

3471 The vaginal extremities of the two uteri of a pregnant Rabbit (*Lepus cuniculus*) minutely injected.

One uterus has been slit open to show the vascularity of the mucous membrane; in the other is a foetus far advanced in development. A window has been cut through the uterine wall opposite the placenta and the maternal part of this organ removed, showing the circular form of the foetal part and the delicate transparent yolk-sac wall by which it is surrounded.

The head end of the embryo protrudes through the cut end of the uterus; it is covered by the amnion, from above which the yolk-sac has been removed.

In this preparation the arrangement of the longitudinal muscles of the uterus is very clearly demonstrated.

3472 The ovary, Fallopian tube, and contiguous parts of one of the uteri of a Rabbit with a foetus and its membranes near the close of uterine gestation.

The blood vessels of both the uterus and the embryo have been injected. The yolk-sac and amnion have been opened and the foetus extracted and partly dissected to show the course of the main placental blood vessels. Of these, the allantoic vessels are the most conspicuous; the hypogastric artery running along the stalk of the allantois towards the pelvic basin and the corresponding vein passing to the ventral aspect of the liver. The two vitelline vessels may be seen emerging from behind the stomach and passing towards the cord beneath the liver.

The placenta presents a subcompressed oblong shape and is lobulated.

3473   A young Rodent, soon after birth. It is covered with fur but its eyes and ears are still closed by epithelial concrescence.

3474   A foetal Agouti (*Dasyprocta agouti*).

In Owen's Catalogue this specimen is described as being 'near the close of uterine gestation' but from the closed condition of the umbilicus it would appear that the foetus had been born.

The skin is entirely devoid of hair, except for silky vibrissae on the upper lips, above the eyes and in front of the ears. The eyes and ears are closed by epithelial suture.

3475   The foetus of a Cavy (apparently a Guinea-pig) (*Cavia porcellus*).

The body is covered with fine short hair, and the vibrissae of the lips, with a swollen pad from which they spring, are well developed.

The eyes are still closed, but the ear passages are patent.

A process resembling a rudimentary nipple may be observed on the inner side of each thigh near the knee joint.

3476   The foetus of a Porcupine (*Hystrix cristata*) at the termination of its uterine development.

The eyes are open and the body is covered with fine, soft hair. The situations where the principal quills are to be developed are indicated by a wrinkled modification of the external surface of the skin, but as yet there is no sign of the actual quills.

The claws are fully formed, long, pointed, and powerful.

See R. I. Pocock, 'On the external characters of Hystricomorph Rodents', *Proc. Zool. Soc.*, 1922, p. 365.

3477   A foetus of a Cape Anteater or Aard-vark (*Orycteropus capensis*), about four inches in length (102 mm.).

FIG. 8

A foetal Pangolin (*Manis brachyura*).   Specimen No. 3478.

The body is completely hairless and there are no indications of vibrissae around the mouth or upon the head.

The general form is similar to that of the adult, though the tail is relatively short. The eyes are closed. The digits show slight indications of claws, which are capped by soft, disc-like pads.

3478 A foetal Pangolin (*Manis brachyura*) about six inches (153 mm.) in length.

The lozenge-shaped tegumentary scutae, which will develop into the horny scales of the adult, are marked out and each is bordered by a swollen rim.

Strong claws are developed on the toes and present the features characteristic of those of the adult. The eye-lids and ears are still closed. From the mouth protrudes the long vermiform tongue.

The umbilical cord is relatively short and gradually expands as it recedes from the foetus. Part of the amnion and fragments of the other membranes have been preserved.

3479 A foetal Armadillo (*Tatusia*) with its umbilical cord, near the close of uterine gestation.

At this stage the foetus has all the features of the adult, with the characteristic divisions of the tegumentary armour clearly displayed. The eye-lids are not fused together.

3480 A foetal Sloth (*Bradypus tridactylus*) at the latter period of uterine gestation. The pectoral situation of the mammae and the rudiment of a thumb, deserve notice in this preparation.

The body is hairless, but upon the lips and chin are a number of short papilliform processes.

The foetus resembles the adult in the length and slenderness of the neck and in the great disproportion in length of the fore and hind limbs.

Some of the following eleven preparations (3481-3491) are probably those described by Hunter in a MS., of which a transcript was made by Clift. This note (which is printed in full in Owen's *Catalogue of the Physiological Series*, vol. v, p. 120) is entitled 'Experiments on the Impregnation of Ewes'.

The condition of the genitalia is described in nine Ewes which were killed at periods varying from 24 hours to 8 complete days after having taken the Ram. In no case was Hunter able to find an ovum, but this was no doubt due (as Owen observes) to the fact that the ovum of the Sheep is 'pellucid, colourless, and much more minute than Hunter had evidently anticipated'.

In his notes Hunter pays special attention to the condition of the vacated ovisac and corpus luteum and to the contents of the genital tract. It is probable that some, if not all, of the following specimens were made from the material used in the above experiments; the condition of the parts shown suggests that Nos. 3483, 3485, 3486, 3489, and 3490 certainly were.

3481   The reproductive organs of a Ewe (*Ovis aries*).

Each ovary has been bisected; an old corpus luteum in process of degeneration is present in both. A black bristle has been inserted into the abdominal aperture of each Fallopian tube. The right horn of the uterus is laid open to show the longitudinal series of cotyledonary burrs; these are formed by local thickening of the connective tissues of the mucosa and during pregnancy are the seat of placental attachment of the foetus.

The cervix uteri and the beginning of the vagina have also been opened to show a series of vulvular processes directed towards the vagina and progressively increasing in size as they approach that canal.

3482   The reproductive organs of a Ewe at the period of sexual excitement, injected. The left ovary has been divided. Near the margin a large empty ovisac is exposed, which contained an ovum ripe for impregnation. The passage through which the ovum escaped is marked by a black bristle. The inner surface of the sac is plicated. At the base of the ovary is a plexus of vessels. A small section has been removed from the opposite ovary and the corresponding Fallopian tube and uterine horn have been slit open. A part of the cavity of the opposite uterine horn and of the cervix uteri is exposed. The summits of the cotyledonary burrs in the uterine horn are slightly depressed as if preparatory for the reception of the capillaries of the foetal cotyledons.

In the sheep during the first stages of the period of sexual excitement (pro-oestrum) the uterine mucosa increases in thickness and its blood vessels become congested, with slight extravasation into the cavity of the uterus and some destruction of epithelium. During the succeeding period (oestrus) when ovulation and copulation take place, these symptoms disappear; the epithelium is renewed and the mucosa resumes its normal thickness.

3483   The reproductive organs of a Ewe a short time after impregnation. Each ovary presents an orifice supported upon a nipple-like prominence, from which the ripe ovum has escaped; a section of the left ovary has been made by the side of this perforated prominence and the cavity of the vacated ovisac is exposed. The lining of the sac is plicated by the ingrowth of the epithelial and fibrous tissue of its tunics. The Fallopian tube and uterine horn of the same side have been laid open through their whole extent; the cavity of the cervix uteri and that of the beginning of the vagina are likewise exposed. The summits of the cotyledons in the uterine horn are more deeply depressed than in the previous specimen. A black bristle is inserted into the mouth of the right Fallopian tube and another through the passage that traverses the several valvular folds in the cervix uteri.

This specimen is apparently from the Ewe No. 2 that Hunter killed and examined 24 hours after she had taken the Ram.

In this animal he observed that the fimbria of each Fallopian funnel was spread over the corresponding ovary and stuck to it. 'Each ovary had a pouting nipple upon it, one of which seemed to have burst.' No ovum was observed. (At this period it would be passing down the Fallopian tube.)

3484 A similar preparation of the reproductive organs of a Ewe. The left ovary has been divided to show the vacated ovisac and the ease with which it can be separated from the surrounding stroma. Bristles are placed in the abdominal orifice of the right Fallopian tube, through the valvular septa in the cervis uteri and from the cervix into the right uterine horn.

This specimen corresponds with the condition observed by Hunter in the Ewe which he killed on the third day after she had taken the ram. In this individual the genital tract was slit throughout its length; it contained mucus.

3485 The reproductive organs of a Ewe killed four days after having taken the ram. This corresponds with the condition shown in Hunter's Ewe No. 5. In this individual he observed the fimbria of the Fallopian tubes closely adherent to the corresponding ovaries. Both ovaries presented nipple-like prominences; of these, the left was the largest and was described as being extremely red in its projecting part; in the centre of each of these nipples appeared an opening. In the specimen both ovaries have been divided close alongside the above-mentioned nipples; on the left the cavity of the ovisac was large, but much restricted by the infolding of its walls; on the right no cavity was apparent. The Fallopian tube, uterus and vagina are cut open. The cervix uteri contained abundant mucus, in the cornua there was little, if any, except near the Fallopian tube; in the Fallopian tube was nothing but mucus.

3486 The reproductive organs of a Ewe, minutely injected. The appearances presented by this preparation are described by Hunter under the head of 'the 6th Ewe', which he killed five days after she had taken the ram.

The left Fallopian tube and uterine horn have been opened, as have also part of the right horn and the cervix uteri and head of the vagina. The left ovary is in section, with a bristle passed through the opening by which the ripe ovum escaped.

The depressed or flat surface of the uterine burrs shows a richly vascular and fine villosity.

In the sixth Ewe, Hunter observed that one ovary only showed signs of ovulation. This one he divided, and noted that the corpus luteum was easily separable from the surrounding tissue, that its cavity was much encroached upon by plication of its walls and was without contents.

Upon slitting up the uterus he found within the horn of the impregnated side a loose red body which appeared to be attached to each uterine cotyledon and extended into the horn of the unimpregnated side.

The description of this body suggests an early stage of attachment of the blastocyst, but it is difficult to reconcile this with more recent investigations which show that in the Sheep the impregnated ovum reaches the uterus on the fourth or fifth day after coitus, but that the blastocyst remains free till the seventeenth day and that its attachment is not complete till the thirtieth day. It is possible that this body may have been uterine secretion mixed with red injection exuded from the cotyledonary villous areas.

3487   A portion of the coloured substance removed from the preceding specimen.

3488   The ovary and Fallopian tube of a Ewe killed six days after having taken the ram.
The ovary is bisected, showing the ovisac from which the ripe ovum has escaped, completely obliterated by the development of its tunica and thus replaced by a fully formed corpus luteum. This body is separated by a layer of loose vascular connective tissue from the surrounding stroma of the ovary.

3489   A similar preparation of the ovary and Fallopian tube of a Ewe, presenting the appearances described by Hunter under the head of 'Experiment 7th. Repeated.'
The experiment took place in October 1792, the Ewe being killed six days after coitus. The corpus luteum was very large and prominent.

3490   The ovary, Fallopian tube, and part of the horn of the uterus of a Ewe killed eight days after taking the Ram.
The ovary, which contained two corpora lutea, has been divided and subsequently a section has been made of the cut surface of one of the corpora lutea to show the remnant of the ovarian follicle represented by a linear trace leading from the centre to the circumference (this trace is no longer apparent).

The appearance in this specimen corresponds with that described by Hunter in the 8th Ewe which was killed 192 hours after having taken the Ram. On slitting open the Fallopian tube and uterus he found only cream-like mucus 'with some white (substance) almost like curd in some of the interstices of the cotyledons'. This substance was without much doubt the secretion of the uterine glands.

3492 A vertical section through the uterine cotyledonary burr of a Ewe killed four days after taking the Ram.

The preparation has been minutely injected, dried and preserved in oil of turpentine.

3493 Two young embryos with their membranes, of a Sheep.

The embryos are about 8 lines (16·8 mm.) in length with the limb buds just appearing. The chorion and amnion surrounding one of the embryos has been opened and the embryo laid bare and the yolk-sac displayed. The allantois has vascularised the chorion but no development of the foetal cotyledons has yet taken place. The blastocyst in the Sheep remains unattached to the uterine wall until about the 17th day after conception and during this period the yolk sac is functional for the nutrition of the growing embryo.

3494 A portion of one of the horns of a pregnant uterus of a Ewe, from which the foetus and its membranes and cotyledons have been removed.

Several of the cotyledons of different sizes are shown. These are hemispherical in shape, with a central cavity bordered by a sharp margin beset by delicate villous processes. One cotyledon is in section; it is completely hollowed out by a spacious cavity which, in the natural state, was filled by the foetal cotyledon, and is lined by a soft honey-combed membrane.

3495 The extremity of one of the horns of the uterus of a pregnant Ewe, with a portion of the chorion of the embryo.

The uterine cotyledons are greatly enlarged and present the form of a bee-hive, with the base, in some cases, constricted to form a broad pedicle of attachment.

The cavity within each uterine cotyledon is occupied by the foetal cotyledon, which enters it at its apex through a restricted aperture; surrounding the aperture is a collar of foetal villi, but up to this point the chorion is simple.

3496 A portion of the uterus of a pregnant Ewe, including one of the cotyledons and the corresponding foetal membranes.   The entire cotyledon has been bisected showing the size and form of the cup-shaped cavity of the uterine component and the mass of foetal villi occupying its interior.   This mass consists of two elements: the chorionic villi, composed of extensions of the trophoblast supported by mesenchyme cores which carry branches of the allantoic vessels; and extensions of the sub-epithelial tissues of the uterus which form the vascular walls of crypts in which lie the chorionic villi.

3497   A segment of the uterus of a pregnant Ewe, including four cotyledons with the corresponding part of the foetal membranes.

On one side of the specimen the wall of the uterus has been removed from two of the cotyledons, showing the villous mass of chorionic and maternal tissue that occupies the cavity of the uterine cotyledon.

Upon the other side two cotyledons are in section showing the mesenchyme base of the foetal cotyledon, from the convex surface of which the chorionic villi spring.

The tissues upon the section surface have to some extent been teased, so that it is possible to distinguish the delicate, branched extremities of many of the chorionic villi, floating free of the crypts in which they were lodged.

3498   The placental cotyledon of a Ewe, bisected, showing as in the previous specimen the combined mass of chorionic villi and intercrypt septa that occupy the concavity of the uterine cotyledon.

3499   A small portion of the chorion and allantois, injected, of an embryo calf (*Bos taurus*) stated to have been about four inches long.

The section has been removed from near the blind extremity of the chorionic sac.   Upon it may be seen several rudimentary cotyledons.   Each is a circular villous patch, measuring about 5 mm. in diameter.

3500   The blind extremity of the blastocyst of the same embryo, showing the commencement of the formation of the foetal cotyledons by the development of groups of minute, branching villi in particular places upon the surface of the chorion.

At the upper end of the specimen the chorion has been dissected from the vascular wall of the allantois which forms its deeper layer of endochorion.   This latter membrane consists of two layers—a sheet of soft flocculent mesenchyme carrying the allantoic vessels and a smooth lining membrane of hypoblast (the inner wall of the allantois).

3501 A piece of the same injected chorion and allantois as that shown in 3499, removed from near the place of attachment of the embryo. It includes two foetal cotyledons, each of which is a flat sub-circular group of branched villous processes.

The high vascularity of the villi is obvious from the deep colour imparted to them by the red injection mass.

3502 A small piece of the wall of the uterus of a Cow, at a more advanced period of gestation, including one of the uterine cotyledons, minutely injected.

The cotyledon is a prominent, rounded mass of soft tissue attached by a restricted pedicle to the wall of the uterus. Its convex surface is deeply pitted by a honey-comb of crypts within which, in the natural state, are lodged the branching villi of the complementary foetal cotyledon.

The wall of the uterus between the cotyledons is highly glandular.

3503 An entire placental cotyledon of a Cow with the surrounding parts of the chorion.

The maternal cotyledon has been severed from its connection with the rest of the uterine wall by the section of its pedicle of attachment and is seen from the uterine aspect.

Its pedicle is narrow and for a small area around it the surface of the cotyledon is smooth, but with this exception the surface is honey-combed with crypts for the reception of the villi of the foetal cotyledon.

Along the margin of the cotyledon the foetal villi have been withdrawn from the maternal crypts, thus showing their feathery branching form and the loose connection there is between them and the crypts within which they are lodged.

Upon the reverse of the specimen can be seen the smooth and comparatively non-vascular wall of the allantois by which the chorion is lined.

3504 Part of the maternal cotyledon of the placenta of a Cow, minutely injected.

3504A A foetal cotyledon (probably) of a Cow, with parts of the surrounding chorion minutely injected.

In this preparation the contrast between the great vascularity of the foetal villi and the comparative bloodlessness of the simple chorion between the cotyledons is very strikingly shown. The foetal villi decrease in size towards the periphery of the cotyledon. Their tufted, feathery form is well displayed.

This specimen is from the Kew Collection (see above, p. 27).

3505 A portion of the chorionic sac of a Cow, including four of the foetal cotyledons, minutely injected; the arteries red and the veins white.

Each cotyledon consists of a sub-circular group of elongated, branching, conical, highly vascular villi. Those in the centre of the cotyledon are larger than those close to its margins.

Upon the reverse of the specimen can be seen the smooth inner layer of the chorion, formed by the epithelial wall of the allantois. In places this membrane has been torn, to expose the soft stratum of mesenchyme interposed between it and the trophoblast layer which forms the outermost part of the chorion.

3506 A similar preparation of part of the chorionic sac of a Cow, including four cotyledons.

The arteries have been injected red and the veins (less minutely) white.

3507 A similar specimen of the foetal cotyledon of a Cow, with parts of the surrounding chorion, injected.

Along one side, the cut made in separating the specimen passes through the cotyledon. Upon this cut edge are shown, in succession, the large vascular villi of the trophoblast, the vascular allantoic vessels in section and the non-vascular epithelial wall of the allantois.

3508 A single large foetal cotyledon of a Cow, minutely injected.

The wall of the allantois has been stripped from the inner surface of the chorion, showing the network of allantoic vessels ramifying in the mesenchyme interposed between the epithelial wall of the allantois and the trophoblast of the chorion.

3509 A small piece of a foetal cotyledon of a Cow, injected to show the vascularity of the villi.

3510 A placental cotyledon of a Cow, in section.

The uterine vessels have been filled with white injection, and the foetal ones with red. At the upper end of the specimen some of the foetal villi have been withdrawn from the crypts in the maternal cotyledon. Upon the rest of the section surface the distinction of the foetal and maternal constituents of the placenta is clearly indicated by the difference in colour of their respective injections. Upon the cut edge of the foetal cotyledon can be seen the several layers of the chorion—a smooth transparent membrane constituting the epithelial wall of the allantoic sac; a gelatinous intermediate layer of mesenchyme permeated by the allantoic vessels and their branches; and a richly vascular villous trophoblastic layer.

Where a villus has been cut along its axis it can be seen that its central part or core is composed of mesenchyme.

3511 A similar section through the placental cotyledon of a Cow.

This apparently is the other half of the cotyledon shown in the previous specimen.

3512 A similar preparation of the placenta of a Cow in which the maternal blood vessels have been injected red and the combined maternal and foetal cotyledons divided centrally, perpendicular to their surface, from the inner side of the chorion to the centre of the pedicle of attachment of the uterine cotyledon.

The pedicle consists of fibrous tissue within which may be seen numerous blood vessels in section. At the line of junction of the pedicle with the placenta, these vessels branch and run between the crypts mainly at right angles to the surface.

3513 The placental cotyledon of a Cow, in horizontal section.

The section has been taken through the centre of the cotyledon and includes the distal parts of its central core of fibrous tissue. The maternal blood vessels are injected red. The radial disposition of the terminal branches of these vessels in the walls of the placental crypts is clearly shown.

3514 A similar section in which the surface of the cotyledon has also been sliced off.

In the centre of this tangential section numerous crypts are apparent as small cavities, interspersed with them are minute maternal blood vessels cut transversely; towards the outer parts both crypts and blood vessels owing to their radiating disposition are cut more nearly parallel to their axis.

The other section surface is similar to that shown in the previous specimen.

3515 A foetal Calf, three and a half inches (89·2 mm.) in length, enclosed within its amnion and suspended by the umbilical cord, to which a small portion of the allantois is attached.

The inner surface of the amnion is covered by a number of minute white discs. These are epithelial thickenings on the inner layer of the amnion which serve for the storage of glycogen.

3516 A portion of the chorion and allantoic sac corresponding to one of the horns of the uterus of a Deer.

The specimen has been minutely injected by the hypogastric (allantoic) arteries and shows the high vascularity of the cotyledons. These are oblong and vary in size; and are scattered irregularly over all parts of the chorionic sac.

3517   A small portion of the chorion of, apparently, the same species of Deer, showing a cotyledon of oblong form and ordinary size, and a second of a sub-circular form and of much smaller dimensions.

3518   A section of the chorion and allantois of a Ruminant, exhibiting two foetal cotyledons minutely injected; they are of a circular form and are composed of very delicate elongated filamentary processes, less branched and sub-divided than those of the Cow or Deer.

3519   A section of the chorion of the same Ruminant, exhibiting a single foetal cotyledon, of which the arteries have been partially filled with red injection and the veins with injection of a blue colour.

3520   A portion of the foetal cotyledon of a large Ruminant, minutely injected, with the villi partially unravelled. By this means the elaborate branching of these absorbent processes is clearly demonstrated.

3521   The foetal cotyledon of a Ruminant with a small part of the chorion surrounding it.
        The allantoic and trophoblastic layers of which the chorion is composed have been separated from one another up to the circumference of the cotyledon, showing the blood vessels that ramify in the mesenchyme between them. The villi of the foetal cotyledon have not been completely drawn from the maternal crypts and are to a large extent surrounded and compacted together by the remains of the crypt walls.

3522   A portion of the pregnant uterus of a Ruminant, including one cotyledon, to which the corresponding foetal cotyledon with a portion of the surrounding chorion and epithelial wall of the allantois is attached. The uterine vessels have been filled with a red injection.
        The inner wall of the chorionic sac has been reflected from the chorion and foetal cotyledon and can be seen hanging from the lower parts of the specimen. This removal of the allantoic wall has exposed the soft mesenchymal tissue naturally interposed between it and the chorion; embedded within this tissue lie the allantoic vessels from which branches ramify over the surface of the cotyledon and break up to form capillaries in the foetal villi.
        The species from which this preparation has been taken was not given in the

Manuscript Catalogue, but the parts correspond in form and structure with those of a Cow.

3523   A uterine cotyledon, of the same Ruminant, in section, showing its pedunculate attachment to the uterine wall and the form and arrangement of the crypts from which the villi of the foetal cotyledon have been withdrawn.

The crypts are deep and narrow, with their walls continued into each other so as to give a reticulate character to the surface of the cotyledon. They radiate to the convex surface of the cotyledon from the connective tissue centre or base into which the pedicle is continued.

3524   A similar section of a cotyledon of the same Ruminant including both its uterine and foetal components.

The foetal portion has been minutely injected; its vascular branching villi are clearly contrasted by their colour against the uninjected walls of the crypts of the uterine portion and can be seen extending from the surface of the cotyledon to its pedunculate base.

At the periphery of the cotyledon some of the villi have been withdrawn from the crypts and show well their delicate, branching form.

The wall of the allantois has been removed to expose the network of coarse and fine allantoic vessels that cover the convex surface of the cotyledon.

3525   A portion of the uterus and chorion of a Ruminant including a placental cotyledon, in section. The uterine vessels have been injected.

In this specimen the mode of attachment of the uterine cotyledon to the wall of the uterus by a narrow peduncle carrying the maternal blood vessels is well shown, and at the upper margin of the cotyledon the distinction between the various membranes that form the chorion and foetal cotyledon is particularly clear.

The united chorion and allantoic wall, as they approach the margin of the cotyledon diverge from one another, the allantois passing smoothly from the convex surface of the cotyledon without taking part in its structure, the chorion passing towards its peduncle of attachment and being there reflected to form the main part of the foetal cotyledon.

Between the two lies a mass of soft fibrous mesenchyme.

3526   A similar section of the complete cotyledon of a Ruminant, with the maternal vessels injected.

In this preparation the various membranes—allantois, vascular mesenchyme and trophoblast—that take part in the formation of the foetal cotyledon can clearly be distinguished upon the section surface.

3527   A small portion of the uterus of a Ruminant, including a complete cotyledon, with the surrounding chorion and allantoic wall.

The uterine cotyledon resembles in its form and in the mode of its attachment that of the Ewe, but is somewhat larger. The maternal and foetal blood vessels have been injected and upon one side the wall of the uterine cotyledon has been partly cut away to expose the mass of placental tissue contained within its concavity.

A number of foetal villi situated along the margin of the cotyledon have been withdrawn from their crypts to show their delicate arborescent structure.

Opposite the cotyledon the mesenchyme layer that separates the allantoic wall from the trophoblast is inflated, so that the allantoic wall projects as a hemispherical sac into the cavity of the allantois, thus affording a clear demonstration of the independence of the trophoblastic and allantoic layers of the chorion.

3528   A portion of the chorion and allantois of a Ruminant, probably a Cow, including two cotyledons.

The foetal cotyledon, when removed from its uterine counterpart has the form of a hemispherical pouch of chorion, invaginated towards the allantoic cavity. The mouth of the invagination is comparatively narrow, corresponding no doubt with the narrow pedunculate attachment of the maternal cotyledon; its inner surface is beset with long branching villi which are shown in the upper cotyledon by the eversion of the chorionic pouch. The reverse of the specimen presents a smooth surface formed by the wall of the allantois.

Some of the following seventeen preparations, illustrating the generative processes in the Sow, are the subjects described by Hunter in the following notes (*Works*, vol. v, p. 196):

'*Experiments on Sows*

'December 24th, 1781.—In a sow which took the boar on Tuesday and was killed the Thursday sennight following, in the morning, which was about ten days after, the glands of the ovarium (ovisacs or Graafian vesicles) were swelled a little, and, when cut into, contained coagulated blood. Some of them contained pieces bigger than a cherry-stone, others were less. The horns of the uterus seemed preparing for the ova, being divided into partitions by a tightness or stricture, but of unequal lengths, some being as long again as others; and those divisions corresponded with the number of glands in one (the ovarium of that) side, being eleven in number; (those of) the other side could not be counted, owing to its being opened later, by which means the parts were not so distinct.

'A sow that had taken the boar, April the   , was killed April   , viz.   days after.

'(The dates are lost; however, it is not material; it shows the progress and difference in the same animal, some being further advanced than others.—J. H.).

'The following appearances were observed:—The ovarium of the right side was larger than that of the left. There appeared several ova (ovisacs) that were more vascular and larger than the others. These were eleven in number, each of which had a part projecting like a nipple, which was more evident in some than in others. The remaining number had this appearance beginning to take place; the other ova (ovisacs) were smaller, of a yellowish white, harder and firmer in consistence. When cut into, they appeared of the same colour (throughout) their whole substance.

'One of the eleven (ovisacs) appeared as if it had burst. When cut into, it had an irregular appearance of a cavity, in which there was extravasated coagulated blood. On cutting into the other ova (ovisacs) which seemed impregnated (viz. those which had the projecting appearance), they seemed to be taking on more the appearance of a cavity; which in some of them contained a yellowish serum, in others coagulated blood, but of irregular form, like extravasation into the substance. This was much more in some than in others.

'In the other (ovisacs) that had not the above projection, their cavities appeared more circumscribed and perfect; their inner surfaces were very vascular with partial exudations of coagulated blood, and they contained a serum. The left ovarium had seven of the ova (ovisacs) of a red colour, four of which had a projection. One of them seemed ready to burst; and in cutting into its substance, one cavity, whose surface was vascular, was covered with coagulated blood; and contained also serum. The other three were not so much advanced; but all contained coagulated blood, which might be separated from all sides of the cavity.

'In the uterus of a sow sixteen days gone, the foetus was formed, and its purse-shaped membrane (chorion and allantois) was above a foot long in some. This membrane, with the foetus nearly in the middle between each end, occupied nearly the whole length of the cavity of the uterus, like a tape-worm in the intestines. Through the whole course of the uterus was a white

C.H.M.—I

mucus almost like cream; and where the foetus lay, this was most in quantity. (See Nos. 3538-3541.)

'In two other sows that were only allowed to go ten days, I could not observe any change whatever, and there was none of the mucus to be found in either uterus.

'The connexion between the outer covering of a (foetal) pig and the uterus appears to be only one of contact; for they separate with as much ease as any two wet substances can do that have no connexion but that of having lain together. Upon close examination, there appears not to be the least violence committed upon separation. The inside of the uterus is thrown into circular rugae, and so is the external surface of the outer membrane of the foetus, which appears to confine the membranes in their situation.

'There are on the outer surface of the external membrane of the foetus a vast number of small circular spots, which are rather whiter or paler (from being thicker) than the parts of the same membrane, with a darker centre. These spots do not appear to be more vascular upon injecting, than any other part of the same membrane.

'In the year 1777 I spayed a young sow of one ovarium only. When she was of age, I gave her the boar, and she brought forth six pigs. The second time she had eight (I slit her ear to know her); the third litter was only six; the fourth litter of ten; the fifth litter, March 1782, she had ten; the sixth litter, September 1782, she had nine pigs. In this instance she had been served with the wild boar; five of the nine were like the father, three like the mother, and one like neither.

'The sister of the above sow, although not spayed, did not take the boar so early as the spayed one did. When she did so, I only allowed the boar to serve her once (as was also the case with her spayed sister). This was with a view to see if once was sufficient to impregnate several ova, and she brought forth nine pigs, being three more than her sister's first litter. The second time she had only six pigs, being two fewer than her spayed sister. The third time she had eight; the fourth litter, December 1781, was of thirteen pigs; the fifth litter, June 18th, 1782, was of ten pigs; the sixth litter, December 6th, 1782, was of sixteen pigs.'

In 1787, Hunter read a paper at a meeting of the Royal Society giving an account of 'An Experiment to determine the effect of extirpating one ovarium upon the number of young produced' (*Phil. Trans.*, **77**, p. 233) from which the following extract is taken:

'In all animals of distinct sex, the females, those of the Bird-kind excepted, have, I believe, two ovaria, and of course the oviducts are in pairs.

'By distinct sex I mean when the parts destined to the purposes of generation are of two kinds, each kind appropriated to an individual of each species, distinguished by the appellation of male and female, and equally necessary to the propagation of the animal. The testicles, with their appendages, constitute the male; the ovaria, and their appendages, the female sex.

'As the ovaria are the organs which, on the part of the female, furnish what is necessary towards the production of the third, or young animal, and as females appear to have a limited portion of the middle stage of life allotted for that purpose, it becomes a question, whether those organs are worn out by repeated acts of propagation, or whether there is not a natural and constitutional period to that power on their part, even if such power has never been exerted? If we consider this subject in every view, taking the human species as an example, we shall discover that circumstances, either local or constitutional, may be capable of extinguishing in the female the faculty of propagation. Thus we may observe when a woman begins to breed at an early period, as at fifteen, and has her children fast, that she seldom breeds longer than the age of thirty or thirty-five; therefore we may suppose, either that the parts are then worn out, or that the breeding constitution is over. If a woman begins later, as at twenty or twenty-five, she may continue to breed to the age of forty or more; and there are, now and then, instances of women, who, not having conceived before, have had children as late in life as fifty or upwards. After that period few women breed, even though they should not have bred before; therefore, there must be a natural period to the power of conception. A similar stop to propagation may likewise take place in other classes of animals, probably in the female of every class, the period varying according to circumstances; but still we are not enabled to determine how far it depends on any particular property of the constitution, or of the ovarium alone.

'As the female, in most classes of animals, has two ovaria, I imagined, that by removing one it might be possible to determine how far their actions were reciprocally influenced by each other, from the changes which by comparison might be observed to take place, either by the breeding period being shortened, or perhaps, in those animals whose nature it is to bring forth more than one at a time, by the number produced at each birth being diminished.

'There are two views in which this subject may be considered. The first, that the ovaria, when properly employed, may be bodies determined and unalterable respecting the number of young to be produced. In this case we can readily imagine, that, when one ovarium is removed, the other may be capable of producing its determined number in two different ways: one, when the remaining ovarium, not influenced by the loss of the other, will produce its allotted number, and in the same time; the other, when affected by the loss, yet the constitution demanding the same number of young each time of breeding, as if there were still two ovaria, it must furnish double the number it would have been required to supply, had both been allowed to remain, but must consequently cease from the performance of its function in half the time. The second view of the subject is by supposing, that there is not originally any fixed number which the ovarium must produce, but that the number is increased or diminished according to circumstances; that it is rather the constitution at large that determines the number; and that, if one ovarium is removed, the other will be called upon by the constitution to perform the operations of both, by which means the animal should produce, with one ovarium, the same number of young as would have been produced if both had remained.

'With an intention to ascertain those points, as far as I could, I was led to make the following experiment; and for that purpose gave pigs a preference to any other animal, as being easily managed, producing several at a litter, and breeding perfectly well under the confinement necessary for experiments. I selected two females of the same colour and size, and likewise a boar-pig, all of the same farrow; and having removed an ovarium from one of the females, I cut a slit in one ear, to distinguish it from the other; they were well fed and kept warm, that there might be no impediment to their breeding; and whenever they farrowed, their pigs were taken away exactly at the same age.

'About the beginning of the year 1779 they both took the boar; the one which had been spayed, earlier than the perfect female. The distance of time, however, was not great, and they continued breeding at nearly the same times. The spayed animal continued to breed till September 1783, when she was six years old, which was a space of more than four years. In that time she had eight farrows; but did not take the boar afterwards, and had in all seventy-six pigs. The perfect one continued breeding till December 1785, when she was about eight years old, a period of almost six years, in which time she had thirteen farrows, and had in all one hundred and sixty-two pigs; after this time she did not breed; I kept her till November 1786.—

'—The perfect animal bred till she was eight years of age; and if conception depended on the ovaria, we might have expected that she would bring forth double the number at each birth; or, if not, that she would continue breeding for double the time. We indeed find her producing ten more than double the number of the imperfect animal, although she had not double the number of farrows; but this may perhaps be explained by observing that the number of young increased as the female grew older, and the perfect sow continued to breed much longer than the other.

'From a circumstance mentioned in the course of this experiment it appears, that the desire for the male continues after the power of breeding is exhausted in the female; and therefore does not altogether depend on the powers of the ovaria to propagate, although it may probably be influenced by the existence of such parts.

'If these observations should be considered as depending on a single experiment, from which alone it is not justifiable to draw conclusions, I have only to add, that the difference in the number of pigs produced by each was greater than can be justly imputed to accident, and is a circumstance certainly in favour of the universality of the principle I wished to ascertain.*

'From this experiment it seems most probable, that the ovaria are from the beginning destined to produce a fixed number, beyond which they cannot go, although circumstances may tend to diminish that number; but that the constitution at large has no power of giving to one ovarium the power of propagating equal to both; for in the present experiment, the animal with one ovarium produced ten pigs less than half the number brought forth by the sow with both ovaria. But that the constitution has so far a power of influencing one ovarium as to make it produce its number in a less time than would probably have been the case if both ovaria had been preserved, is to be inferred from the above-recited experiment.'   *Works*, vol. iv, p. 50.

3529 The ovary and oviduct of a Sow (*Sus scrofa*) injected. The ovary is of large size and lobulated by the protrusion of a number of ripe Graafian follicles. A bristle has been inserted into the orifice of the Fallopian tube which is surrounded by a voluminous crenellated funnel.

3530 A segment of one of the uterine horns of a Sow, minutely injected, showing the vascularity of the lining membrane, ten days after impregnation.

This preparation may be from the first Sow mentioned in Hunter's manuscript note, which was killed ten days after having taken the Boar, and in which 'the horns of the uterus seemed preparing for the ova, being divided into compartments by a tightness or stricture'. In two other Sows killed also at ten days after coitus Hunter states that he could not observe in the uterus creamy white mucus such as he found in an individual killed 16 days after the coitus.

---

* 'It may be thought by some that I should have repeated this experiment; but an annual expense of twenty pounds for ten years, and the necessary attention to make the experiment complete, will be a sufficient reason for my not having done it.'

3531   A similar preparation of a portion of the uterus of a Sow, injected.

3532   The ovaria, oviducts, and commencement of the uterine horn of a Sow: the large
       and lobulated ovarium is attached by a small part of its circumference near the
       mouth of the purse-like duplicature of the peritoneum; the ovarium has been
       cut away from the opposite side and a bristle inserted into the fimbriated portion
       of the oviduct or Fallopian tube; morbid hydatid cysts are developed in some
       parts of the mesometry.

3533   The ovary, Fallopian tube, and adjoining portion of the uterine horn of a Sow
       killed sixteen days after the coitus, injected.
          The ovary is strongly lobulated and shows upon the surface of its prominences
       several shallow depressions due to the collapse of the thin outer walls of ripe
       ovisacs.   A section has been removed from one side of the ovary to show a
       corpus luteum with the remains of the vacated ovisac in its centre, communicat-
       ing by a narrow slit with the cicatrised orifice through which the ripe ovum
       escaped.
          The uterine horn has been laid open to show the vascularity of its transversely
       plicated lining membrane and a strand of white matter adherent to its mes-
       enterial surface.   This white strand was described by Owen in his Catalogue
       (Vol. v, p. 132) as 'an ovum' but in its present condition it is difficult to de-
       termine whether it is a partly disintegrated early blastocyst or a strand of
       coagulated secretion of the uterine glands.   By the fourteenth day of gestation
       the blastocysts of the Pig 'fill the whole length of the uterus'.
                     F. H. A. Marshall, *The Physiology of Reproduction*, 2nd ed., 1922, p. 427.

          In the Hunterian manuscript it is stated that in a 'sow sixteen days gone, the
       foetus was formed and its purse-like membrane was about a foot long in some.
       This membrane, with the foetus nearly in the middle, between each end, lay
       nearly the whole length in the cavity of the uterus, like a tape-worm in the
       intestines.   Through the whole course of the uterus was a white mucus almost
       like cream; and where the foetus lay this was most in quantity.'

3534   A segment of one of the horns of apparently the same uterus as that shown in the
       preceding preparation.
          It is laid open longitudinally and shows several strands of the same white
       material as that shown in the preceding specimen.

3535   A similar preparation of the uterine horn of a Sow.

The white membranous strands are more distinct and show more clearly than in the previous specimens indications of young embryos and of the membranous walls of the blastocyst.

3536 A similar specimen, showing an increased rugosity of the lining membrane of the uterus and thickening of the submucous connective tissues.

3537 A transverse section of the horn of the uterus of a Sow, injected, showing the cavity completely occupied by opposite folds of the lining membrane, and the great depth of the submucous connective tissue.

3538 A young foetus, about 15 lines (31·5 mm.) in length, with part of its membranes, of a Sow.

The foetus has been exposed by the reflexion from its dorsal aspect of the chorion (which here consists of trophoblast and mesenchyme) and the amnion.

Upon the opposite side of the specimen the chorion has been laid open longitudinally to expose the cavity of the allantois and the funnel-shaped allantoic canal or urachus (indicated by a bristle) by which the cloaca of the foetus communicates with this cavity.

A duplicature of the allantoic wall, carrying some of the allantoic vessels, extends from the neighbourhood of the mouth of the allantoic canal to the opposite wall of the chorion. The blood vessels of the chorion though uninjected, are very conspicuous by transmitted light.

3539 A foetal Hog, two inches, nine lines (69·9 mm.) in length, with a portion of its membranes.

A section is removed from the chorion and allantois; the amnion has been laid open laterally and a portion of it reflected downwards together with the part of the allantoic wall adherent to it.

The foetus is displaced from the amniotic cavity, by which is exposed the short and straight umbilical cord, and the orifice of the allantoic canal where it expands into the allantois.

The foetal vessels have been injected by the hypogastric arteries. The vascularity of the exterior surface of the chorion is thus displayed. Numerous small uninjected spots resembling shallow follicles are scattered irregularly over the whole surface of the chorion. These are depressed areas opposite which the glands of the uterus open.

3540 A foetal Hog, about five inches (127 mm.) in length, with its membranes partially injected.

The amnion is entire, but only so much of the chorion is preserved as immediately surrounds the embryo. Upon the surface of the chorion can be seen (most clearly just in front of the hind leg of the embryo) several of the circular depressions which lie opposite the openings of the uterine glands, and serve to receive their secretion.

3541   A small portion of the chorion and allantoic wall of a foetal Hog, injected, but not very minutely, from the hypogastric arteries.

The surface of the chorion is beset by innumerable and exceedingly minute folds, except upon a number of irregularly scattered small circular spots. The folds enter into close contact with corresponding irregularities in the uterine mucosa forming a simple type of placenta. The smooth spots overlie the openings of the uterine glands.

At the lower end of the specimen the delicate allantois has been separated from the chorion.

3542   A foetal Hog with the whole of its membranes, showing the great length of the cylindrical chorionic sac, with which the allantois is nearly co-extensive.

The membranes are much broken, thus parts of the cavity of the chorionic sac are exposed here and there and the wall of the allantois may be readily distinguished in contact with, but not firmly adherent to the trophoblastic chorion, being separated from it by loose mesenchymatous tissue.

The membranes have been injected by the hypogastric arteries, bringing into prominence the numerous small white spots scattered over the surface of the chorion which overlie the areas upon the wall of the uterus at which open the ducts of the uterine glands.

3543   A segment of the horn of the uterus which contained the foetus shown in the previous specimen, minutely injected by the uterine arteries and everted.

Numerous small spots mark the position of the openings of the ducts of the uterine glands. The secretion of the glands is a nutrient fluid; it collects at the spots between the uterus and chorion and is absorbed by the latter for the nourishment of the foetus.

The rest of the surface of the uterus is highly vascular and is corrugated by minute reticular folds which interdigitate with corresponding irregularities of the surface of the chorion; the close contact thus effected between the maternal and foetal blood vessels forms a simple type of placenta through which the respiratory and probably also the excretory processes of the foetus are maintained.

3544 A short section of the same uterus, slit open, showing the coarse transverse folding of the mucosa, the minute corrugation of its surface and the small circular un-injected spots where lie the openings of the uterine glands.

3545 The ovary, ovarian pouch, and Fallopian tube of a Sow, described in the manuscript catalogue as 'having done breeding'.

The surface of the ovary is here rather minutely lobulated and traces of small round cicatrices, from which ripe ova have previously escaped, are very numerous. A section has been removed from one of the prominent ovisacs and its contents taken away. The mouth of the ovarian pouch has been distended by a bristle to display the position of the ovary relative to the entry to the Fallopian tube.

This preparation may have been made from one of the Sows which were the subjects of Hunter's experiments 'to determine the effect of extirpating one ovarium upon the number of young produced' (see Hunter's notes, above, p. 114).

The object of Hunter's experiment was to ascertain whether each ovary produced a determinate number of young or whether the number of young and the time during which they could be produced was dependent on some property of the general constitution. In the first case he expected that a pig from which one ovary had been removed would produce half the number of young produced by the control. This, in the one experiment he carried out, seemed to be the case and he concluded (tentatively) that 'the ovaria are from the beginning destined to produce a fixed number, beyond which they cannot go . . . that the constitution at large has no power of giving to one ovarium the power of propagating equal to both . . . but that the constitution has so far the power of influencing one ovarium, as to make it produce its number in a less time than would probably have been the case if both ovaria had been preserved.'

3546 The ovaries, Fallopian tubes, and uterus of an Ass (*Equus asinus*) at, apparently, a brief period after impregnation, injected.

Both ovaries are bisected; in one of them a large cavity is exposed, the irregular internal surface of which is stained with particles of extravasated injection. This is the ovisac from which the last ovum ripe for impregnation has escaped; near it is a previously vacated ovisac replaced by a corpus luteum.

A bristle is inserted into the abdominal aperture of each Fallopian tube; the uterus is laid open to show the prominent angular folds of its vascular lining membrane.

3547   The Fallopian tube, with the corresponding ovarian sac, ovary, and part of the uterus of an Ass (*Equus asinus*) injected.

A bristle is inserted into the ostium of the Fallopian tube, which is in the centre of the radiating folds that line the Fallopian funnel. The ovary lies completely within the concavity of the ovarian sac.

3548   The right ovary and Fallopian tube of a Mare (*Equus caballus*).

The ovary is bisected, exposing the cavity of a large ovisac. A bristle is inserted into the mouth of the subspiral radiating folds that line the Fallopian funnel.

3549   The apex of the horn of the uterus of the same Mare, showing the minute aperture (marked by a bristle) through which the Fallopian tube is in communication with it.

The lining membrane of the uterus is minutely injected.

3550   The left ovary, Fallopian tube, and contiguous extremity of the uterine horn of the same Mare.

The ovary is bisected and shows on the section surfaces a recent and an ancient corpus luteum and likewise a large vacated ovisac.

The recent corpus luteum is highly vascular and is situated in that part of the ovary to which the Fallopian funnel is attached.

Bristles have been placed in the mouth of the Fallopian tube and into its orifices of communication with the uterus.

3551   An embryo Foal, with its membranes; it is described in the Hunterian manuscript catalogue as being a month old.

The embryo has been exposed from the dorsal aspect by opening the allanto-chorionic sac and the composite membrane formed by the union of the inner wall of the allantois with the amnion.

The cervical and cranial flexures are well pronounced; the eye is in the stage of an optic cup with the lens occupying the whole of its concavity; and the limbs are elongated buds without definite limitation of their several segments.

3552   A foetal foal about 8 inches (204 mm.) in length, with the vessels of the chorion injected.

The chorion has been opened and turned away from the allanto-amnion, so that it is inverted and shows for the most part its allantoic surface, though in places between its torn edges parts of the trophoblastic chorion with its villous absorptive surface come into view.

The chorion can be seen to be composed of two membranes, an outer (the trophoblast) bearing upon its external surface innumerable tufts of small absorbent villi, and an inner delicate and smooth membrane—the distal wall of the allantois. Between these two membranes and between the proximal wall of the allantois and the amnion lie the nutritive blood vessels of the foetus which towards the upper parts of the specimen can be seen uniting into larger and larger trunks as they make their way to the umbilical cord. In this region the allantoic membrane is loose and distinct and bounds a considerable cavity (part of the extra-embryonic body cavity) between the trophoblastic chorion and the amnion in which lie the main trunks of the foetal vessels, the dilated extremity of the yolk-sac, and the distal end of the allantoic stalk.

3553   A small portion of the chorion of an Ass (*Equus asinus*) with the allantoic arteries and veins injected respectively with red and white.

The chorion consists of an outer layer of trophoblast, and an inner layer formed by the smooth and delicate distal wall of the allantois. Between the two is a stratum of mesenchyme carrying the tortuous allantoic blood vessels.

The external surface of the trophoblast is covered by innumerable clusters of small arborescent vascular villi; these are somewhat irregularly disposed, but cover the whole surface of the chorion, giving it the appearance of plush.

'Experiment on an Ass

'On Friday, the 2nd of October, 1789, the ass took the male, and I killed her on the Tuesday following, about seven in the morning, making in all what is called four days, but only ninety-two hours. The uterus was immediately taken out, and it was observed that one ovarium was much larger than the other. It was injected in both sides, and by both veins and arteries. When injected, the increased ovarium was much redder than the other, as also was the horn of the uterus on that side. I cut through the small ovarium first, to see if it led to the better exposing of the other which was in a line.

'I then slowly divided the other, in which I cut across several small hydatids (ovisacs?), but I came to a glandular substance distinct from the surrounding parts in structure; and, dividing that, along with the other parts, I came to a kind of cavity in which there seemed to be a kind of fine and loose cellular membrane, in the centre of which was a small rounded body, which was a little bag; for in dividing this part, I had cut off a little of the side of the bag, into which hole a small globule of air had entered. Within this was an oblong body, which, when taken out, looked like a little coagulable lymph.

'The secondines of a mare and an ass are the same. The urachus in the foetus of a mare and in that of an ass is a small canal, which passes along the (umbilical) cord, and opens (into the allantois) between the amnios and chorion, which membranes do not adhere anywhere; so that the urine must lie between those two membranes.'   *Works*, vol. v, p. 199.

3554   A similar preparation of the chorion of an Ass (*Equus asinus*).

3555   A similar preparation of a part of the chorion of a Foal (*Equus caballus*) in which the placental villi are numerous and are set closer together than in the preceding specimens.

3556   A specimen described in Owen's *Catalogue* (Vol. 5, p. 139) as 'A section of the chorion and allantois of a foetal Foal, showing portions of the tortuous hypogastric vessels.'

3557   A specimen described by Owen as a 'preparation showing a part of the chorion where the villosities are not developed'.
       It seems probable that these two preparations are not of the chorion but of the proximal (inner) wall of the allantois where it spreads out from the umbilical cord over the amnion and that the two membranes between which the vessels lie are the allantois and the amnion.

3558   The proximal end of the umbilical cord of a Foal. The amnion that covers the cord is beset (as in the foetal Hippopotamus) by minute filiform processes.
       At the ends of the specimen can be seen the allantoic vessels and the patent stalk of the allantois or urachus cut across. A bristle has been passed along the urachus.

3559   A foetus of a Walrus (*Trichechus rosmarus*) measuring between two and three inches (67 mm.) in length.
       The limbs show the peculiarities of the adult in the webbing of the digits to their extremities and in the backward rotation of the hind limbs parallel to the body axis and their envelopment to beyond the knees in the common integument of the trunk.
       The abdomen is laid open showing the numerous convolutions of the intestine. The surface of the umbilical cord is smooth.

3560   The foetus of a Walrus measuring five inches (127·5 mm.) in length.

The eyes and the passage of entry to the auditory meatus are closed by epithelial fusion. The position of the auditory meatus is indicated by a small projection about half an inch (12·7mm.) behind the eye.

The nostrils, which are open, have the form of two linear crescentic fissures having their convexities turned towards each other and diverging dorsally.

Vibrissae are beginning to be developed upon the swollen upper lips; a little posterior to the umbilicus may be observed the orifice of the prepuce, which is flush with the general surface of the body. The nails upon the pectoral flippers project (as do those of the adult) from the extensor surface a short distance proximal to the finger tips and margin of the web.

The body has the general characters of that of the adult, but is in proportion stouter and shorter than in the earlier foetus shown in the previous specimen.

3561   The foetus of a Walrus seven inches (178·5 mm.) in length.

This foetus differs but little except in size from that shown in the previous specimen.

It is to be observed that in the formation of the pectoral flipper, the extension of surface has been effected, as in the Manatee, by the growth of an integumentary fold along the ulnar margin of the limb to the tip of the little finger.

3562   A segment of the impregnated horn of the uterus of a Cat (*Felis domestica*) including a placenta with a foetal kitten and its membranes.

The uterine wall and chorionic sac are divided longitudinally and spread apart to expose the foetus lying within the unruptured amnion.

The placenta consists of a thin, lobulated layer of vascular tissue which surrounds the middle part of the chorionic sac in the form of a broad circular band or hoop. It has been in part detached from the uterine wall, carrying with it, as shown by the injection of the uterine vessels, the superficial parts of the maternal submucosa with its capillaries.

Continuous with either margin of the placental zone is the thin membranous non-placental chorion, which forms a capacious sac enclosing the embryo and its amnion.

3563   A segment of the impregnated uterus and chorionic sac of a Cat cut open. The foetus with its amnion has been removed.

The allantois is seen expanding from the distal end of the umbilical cord to line the inner surface of the chorion and placenta; it forms here and there broad duplicatures, within the margins of which run the larger branches of the allantoic vessels.

The lobulated foetal surface of the placenta can be well seen through the thin transparent wall of the allantois.

3564   The greater part of the chorionic sac of a Cat with the foetus and its amnion removed.

The preparation includes one pole of the non-placental chorion, the placenta, and a small part of the other non-placental pole.

The maternal vessels have been injected red and an attempt has been made to inject the foetal vessels with yellow.

The external surface of the placental zone has a soft raw appearance due to the rupture of the maternal tissues that are incorporated with it. Its margins are sharply defined towards the non-placental simple chorion that constitutes either pole of the chorionic sac.

3565   A small segment of the wall of the uterus of a Cat, with a portion of the placenta attached to it.

The placenta has been partially detached from the outer layers of the uterine wall that take no direct part in its formation.

3566   A small piece of the placenta of a Cat, with a piece of the non-placental chorion continuous with its border.

3567   The ovary, Fallopian tube, and corresponding horn of the uterus of a Bitch (*Canis familiaris*).*

One half of the peritoneal sac which encloses the ovary and the fimbriated extremity of the Fallopian tube around the circumference of the sac is indicated by bristles; the parts have been injected and sections have been removed from the projecting lobes of the ovary; the uterine horn is laid open showing the longitudinal folds of its lining membrane.

3568   A section of the ovary and of the corresponding horn of the uterus of a Bitch, killed one month after having taken the Dog.

The uterus is laid open, showing the condition at this stage of the maternal portion of the placenta. The mucosa of the uterus is swollen and pitted by humerous crypts, the larger of which are scattered at intervals of from 1-3 mm.

The margin of the placenta is bordered by a simple fold of the mucous membrane.

The foetus is mounted below.

---

* The period of gestation in the Bitch is sixty-three days.

In the Dog the blastocyst lies free in the uterus for about 20 days, surrounded by a prochorion formed from the secretion of the uterine glands; after that period the chorion produces villi upon its surface, first over a discoid area. The villi invade the uterine mucosa (in some cases entering the crypts) and destroy its epithelium, replacing it by a trophoblastic syncytium.

F. H. A. Marshall, *The Physiology of Reproduction*, 2nd ed., 1922, p. 444.

3569   A small portion of the uterus of probably the same pregnant Bitch, showing the modification of the lining membrane to form the maternal part of the placenta.

The orifices of the larger crypts, mentioned in the description of the previous specimen measure about 3 mm. in diameter. The surface of the mucous membrane between the crypts is minutely reticulated.

The specimen has been injected.

3570   A similar specimen of the placental area of the wall of the uterus of probably the same Bitch.

3571   The ovary, Fallopian tube, and greater part of one of the horns of the uterus, injected, of a pregnant Bitch, including four placental zones, with (attached to the second from the distal extremity of the horn) a foetus five and a half inches (140 mm.) in length with its membranes and placenta.

The chorion, allantois, and amnion have been laid open and the greater part of the foetal placenta torn from its uterine attachment, showing on the raw surface an intermixture of non-injected foetal and injected maternal tissue.

The placenta, as in the Cat, presents the form of a thin annular band.

3572   The foetus of a Hyæna, eight inches (240 mm.) in length.

3573   The posterior half of a pregnant Mole (*Talpa europaea*)* with the uterus and three foetuses, each about half an inch (12·7 mm.) in length, exposed *in situ*.

The ovary is contained in a thin, transparent peritoneal capsule around which the Fallopian tube may be seen passing in the form of an opaque, white, narrow band.

Where each foetus is situated the uterine cavity is expanded opposite its mesometric border, forming a pouch-like sac to contain the foetus and its membranes. The dilatation next the left ovary has been cut open and the foetus exposed enveloped by its membranes; the other dilatations have been left entire.

---

* The period of gestation is at least two months; the young are usually born in April.

3574   The posterior extremity of a pregnant Mole, with the uterus and five foetuses displayed *in situ*. The uterine arteries are injected.

One of the dilated chambers of the left uterine horn is laid open and the foetus exposed lying within its membranes and suspended from the placenta.

The placenta is a dense vascular oval mass composed mainly of foetal tissue attached to the anti-mesometric wall of the uterus with its long axis parallel to that of the foetus.

Another of the uterine chambers is laid open in the right horn of the uterus and the contained foetus exposed by cutting through its chorionic sac and amnion. The foetus hangs from the placenta by the remains of the membranes.

This specimen is figured by G. E. Dobson in his *Monograph of the Insectivora*, 1882, Pl. 22, Fig. 16.

3575   The reproductive organs of a pregnant Mole with four foetuses, each one an inch and a quarter (32 mm.) in length.

One of these foetuses is exposed *in situ* in its uterine dilatation; two others hang from the placenta still surrounded by their membranes; the fourth is freed of its membranes and hangs from the placenta by its umbilical cord.

In the first foetus it is noticeable that the capacity of the chorion is very little larger than the foetus which it contains.

In one of the second pair the deciduous part of the placenta is partly separated from the uterine wall showing the interdigitation of the foetal villi with the mucosa of the uterus. The maternal blood vessels have been injected but no portion of the injection has passed into the foetal villi which are here exposed.

In the fourth foetus the short umbilical cord and the characteristic form of the body and particularly of the short fossorial fore-limbs may be discerned. The external apertures of the eyes and ears are completely closed.

3576   The reproductive organs of a pregnant Hedgehog (*Erinaceus europaeus*).*

Four foetuses have been developed in the left horn of the uterus and two in the right, and have attained the length of half an inch (12·7 mm.).

At this period of development the foetus lies within a deep concavity in a massive, cup-shaped placenta which is formed (as a decidua reflexa) by an outgrowth of the uterine mucosa, the epithelial portion of which is replaced by foetal trophoblast derived from the chorion. The left horn of the uterus has been cut open to show, in one of its foetigerous dilatations, the placenta attached by a small part of its convex surface to the wall of the uterus and containing the

---

* The period of gestation in the Hedgehog is supposed to be ten weeks; the young are usually born in June.

embryo within its concavity. In the next uterine compartment and in one of those in the right uterine horn the foetus and its placenta have been removed showing the slightly concave thickening of the uterine mucosa to which the placenta was attached.

3577 A foetal Hedgehog near the conclusion of gestation.

Its spines are just beginning to protrude through the dorsal integument. They are soft and flexible in the new-born animal, but become hard in the course of a day or two.

3578 The impregnated uterus of a large Fruit Bat (*Pteropus sp.*) with the foetus that it contained removed and tied to it.

The horn of the uterus that contained the foetus forms a large thin-walled sac continuous with the dilated corpus uteri. The non-impregnated horn projects from one side of the foetigerous sac. It is marked by a black bristle.

The foetus which is far advanced in development, is enveloped in a thin transparent chorionic sac. At a point opposite the ventral surface of the foetus the chorion is developed to form a subcircular disc-like placenta, which is slightly convex towards the uterus and presents upon this surface a soft villous appearance.

3579 An advanced foetus of apparently the same species of Bat with its membranes and placenta hanging from it by the straight and relatively short umbilical cord.

The tissues of the disc-like placenta, owing probably to maceration, have become dissociated and present a fluffy appearance as though composed of delicate branching villi. In the Bats the placenta is formed of a mass of foetal trophoblastic tissue permeated by lacunae in continuity with the uterine vessels, and infiltrated by the capillaries of the allantoic vessels.

The foetus is hairless, but has assumed the peculiar characters of the adult; the nostrils, eyes, and ears are closed.

3580 The impregnated uterus of a large Fruit Bat (*Pteropus sp.*) with the single foetus that it contained.

The uterus has been cut open and the foetus with its placenta and a small part of the surrounding chorion removed. The foetus is apparently ready to be born, being covered with hair and with the eyes open. The nostrils present the formation peculiar to the adult; the claws and wing membranes are fully developed.

The placenta shows the flattened disc-form noted in the preceding specimens.

C.H.M.–K

3581   A young foetus of a Fruit Bat, with the placenta and the wall of the uterus in connection with it.

The foetal surface of the placenta is flat and shows numerous large allantoic vessels radiating across it from the umbilical cord which is attached to its centre. The opposite (uterine) surface is strongly convex.

The foetus is considerably younger than those shown in the previous specimens, and shows a relatively undeveloped condition of the wings. The fingers though long, are short compared with those of the adult; a narrow web runs from the root of the thumb to the basal phalanx of the first finger and thence along the side of the second finger to its apex and to the tips of the succeeding digits and to the foot.

3582   The foetus of a Lemur at the conclusion of gestation.

The foetus is covered by a coating of fine hair which, though but slightly developed in comparison with the adult, is fairly strong upon the dorsal surfaces of the head and trunk and tail. The eyes, nostrils, and ears are open.

3583   Part of the chorionic sac and amnion, including the double disc placenta and umbilical cord of a Rhesus Monkey (*Macacus rhesus*); red injection had been thrown into the umbilical arteries of the cord.

Flaky portions of the decidua remain attached to the outer surface of the placenta and chorion.

A section has been removed from the smaller lobe of the placenta; the cut surface shows the floccular appearance presented by the placental tissues due to the intermixture of foetal capillaries and vacuolated trophoblast.

3584   The angular section of the placenta and chorio-amnion removed from the previous specimen.

A bristle is inserted into a fissure of the uterine surface of the placenta, below which is shown a uterine vein emerging from that surface. Below this vein and abutting on the cut edge of the section is another vein which has been laid open, leading into the substance of the placenta.

The decidua, which forms a denser membrane than in the human subject, is reflected from part of the uterine surface of the placenta and surrounding chorion.

The amnion has been separated from the chorion, exposing the delicate mesenchymal tissue by which the two membranes are united.

3585   The foetus which was attached to the placenta shown in Nos. 3583, 3584.

It is apparently ready to be born and differs in its external characters in no important respect from the adult.

Nos. 3583, 3584, and 3585 are the subjects of the following observations by Hunter:

'Monkeys always copulate backwards: this is performed sometimes when the female is standing on all fours, and at other times the male brings her between his thighs when he is sitting, holding her with his fore paws.

'The female has her regular periods for the male, but she has commonly too much complaisance ever to refuse him. They carry this still further, for they receive the male when with young, even when pretty far gone; at least this was the case with the one of which I am going to give an account.

'A female Monkey, belonging to Mr. Endersbay, in the summer 1782, had frequently taken the male. The keeper observed that after the 21st of June she became less lively than usual, although it was not suspected that she had conceived; but some time after appearing to be bigger in the belly, it created a suspicion of her being with young. Great attention was paid to her, and great care was taken of her. She went on gradually increasing in size; and at last something was observed to move in her belly at particular times, and the motion could even be felt through the abdominal muscles. She became indolent, and did not like to leap or perform her usual feats of activity. Towards the latter part of the time they perceived the breast and nipple to have become rather fuller, and that a kind of water could be squeezed out at the nipple. Some time before she brought forth she became red about the hips and posteriors, which redness extended to the inside of the thighs. It being now certain that she was with young, I desired that she might be particularly attended to when there were signs of approaching delivery, both on her own account and that of the young one, and requested that the after-birth might be carefully preserved, as that part would assist to ascertain the mode of uterine gestation. These directions were attentively followed; and when in labour it was observed that she had regular pains; that when the young one was partly come into the world she assisted herself with her fore paws, and that it came with the hind parts first. This happened on the 15th of December 1782, in all about six months after conception; and when she brought forth her young one it showed signs of life, but died immediately, owing probably to the unfavourable mode of its being brought into the world. When delivered she took the young one up, and although it was dead clasped it to her breast.

'The afterbirth was preserved entire, and was perfectly fit for examination. It consisted of placenta, with the membranes and navel-string, which all very much resembled the corresponding parts in the human subject, as will now be described.

'The placenta had the appearance of being divided into two oblong bodies, united by their edges, each terminating in an obtuse point at the other end, which were of course at some little distance from one another.

'It is probable that these two points were placed towards the openings of the Fallopian tubes, where the uterus assumes a form resembling two obtuse horns.

'The two lobes above mentioned were made up of smaller ones, united closely at their edges, which were more apparent and distinct at some parts than at others. Some of these lobes were divided by fissures which seem to be derived from one centre, while there were others near the edges passing in a different direction, in which fissures are placed veins or sinuses that receive the blood laterally from the lobes. The substance of the placenta seems to be cellular, as in the human subject; this structure allows a communication to be kept up between different parts of each lobe, and the sinuses allowing of a communication between the different lobes of which the placenta is composed, the blood passes into the fissures before it enters the veins; in which respect it differs from the human placenta.

'The arteries from the uterus, on the surface of the placenta, were visible, but too small to be injected: I cannot therefore say how they terminated in the placenta.

'The principal veins arose in general from the fissures beginning from the surface, as in the human placenta; but besides these, there were other small ones; all which, we may suppose, pass through the decidua and enter the substance of the uterus, most probably in the same way as in the human subject.

'The membranes are the amnios, the chorion, and the membrana decidua. These appear to be much the same as in the human, except that the decidua is considerably thicker, especially where it passes between the uterus and the placenta.

'The navel-string in the monkey is not proportionally so long as in the human, and is very much and very regularly twisted.

'There is no urachus, and of course no allantois; not even the small ligament that appears to be a drawing-in of the bladder at its attachment to the navel, the bladder here being rounded.'   *Works*, vol. iv, pp. 71-73.

3586 A human ovary, with the ovarian extremity of the Fallopian tube, showing the relative position of the fimbriated extremity of the Fallopian tube to the ovary and the aperture of the tube itself, in which a bristle is placed.

The ovary is bisected, showing its dense capsule enclosing the stroma in which the ovarian vesicles and ova are developed. Two ovisacs or Graafian follicles are laid open showing the condensation of the stroma that forms a tunic around them.

3587 A similar preparation of the ovary and Fallopian tube of a pregnant woman, showing the elongated form of the ovary and the shortening of the broad ligament owing to the encroachment of the expanding uterus between the layers of the peritoneum which compose that 'ligament'.

3588 A similar preparation of the ovary and Fallopian tube of a woman who had borne seven children.
     One-half of the ovary was removed and the blood vessels have been injected.

3589 The Fallopian tube of a pregnant woman, laid open to show the wavy longitudinal folds of the lining membrane.

3590 The left ovary, Fallopian tube and corresponding half of the uterus of a young woman, supposed to have been in the first month of her pregnancy, injected.
     A thin slice has been removed from the middle of the ovary and the remaining portions are divaricated, showing the two lateral parts of a large corpus luteum, which occupies nearly one third of the entire ovary; the cavity from which the ripe ovum escaped is completely occluded. The corpus luteum is adherent to the tunica of the Graafian follicle which it has replaced and is permeated by vessels introduced by ingrowths from this tunic.
     The tissue between it and the attachment of the ovary is highly vascular.
     Upon the cut surfaces of the ovary may be observed several large Graafian follicles in section.
     The Fallopian tube has been laid open and the cavity of the uterus exposed. The tissues next the cavity of the uterus are swollen but have received very little injection.

3591 The right ovary, Fallopian tube, and half of the uterus of the same young woman.
     The ovary is bisected showing Graafian follicles of various size scattered throughout its vascular stroma; the largest are near the periphery.
     In this half of the uterus the swollen mass of slightly vascular tissue lining its cavity projects further towards the cervix uteri and there terminates in a free jagged and irregular extremity. Some vessels can be seen passing from the

deeper and more vascular layers of the uterine wall into this relatively non-vascular tissue.

3592   A thin slice from the middle of the posterior wall of the same uterus, showing the relation of the swollen non-vascular lining with the general lining membrane of the cervix uteri and the entry into it of a few blood vessels.

The three preceding preparations formed the subject of Hunter's account of the case of a young woman who poisoned herself in the first month of her pregnancy:

'*The case of a young Woman who poisoned herself in the first month of her pregnancy*: by Thomas Ogle, Surgeon, Great Russell Street, Bloomsbury. '*To which is added, an Account of the Appearances after death, by the late John Hunter.**

'Mary Hunt, servant to a gentleman in Charlotte-Street, Bedford-Square, twenty-five years of age, had for some time shown a partiality for one of the footmen in the same family. She became all at once exceedingly dejected, which was supposed to proceed from his neglecting her; and on Thursday, the 19th of April, at twelve o'clock at night, took half an ounce of white arsenic, and immediately afterwards drank a quart of wine; about one o'clock she had so much pain in her stomach as to be obliged to call for assistance.

'The symptoms were excruciating pain in the stomach, sickness, vomiting, excessive thirst, and a small tremulous pulse; these were followed by pain in the bowels, and several purging stools.

'She drank brandy and water, wine and water, and several quarts of plain water, to relieve the thirst and ease the pain. Some hours after taking the arsenic she became easier, expressed a desire to be left alone, being inclined to sleep, and remained several hours in a dosing or comatose state, from which she did not recover, and died about one o'clock on Friday, thirteen hours after taking the arsenic.

'Upon inspecting the body after death there were found the following appearances.

'In the cavity of the abdomen there was an appearance of the effects of slight inflammation on the peritoneal coat of the small intestines.

'The stomach contained a greenish fluid, with a curdy substance in it, in all amounting to about twelve ounces.

'On the internal surface of the great curvature near the cardia a portion of the villous coat, about the size of a crown-piece, was partly destroyed, and of

---

* Originally published in the *Transactions of a Society for the Improvement of Medical and Chirurgical Knowledge*, vol. ii, p. 63. Communicated to the Society by Everard Home, and read on the 5th of August, 1794.

a dark red colour, with a regularly defined edge, and some of the arsenic adhering to different parts of its surface. The rest of the stomach was in a natural state. This appearance in the stomach was an effect produced by the arsenic.

'The uterus was a little enlarged, and had the vessels unusually loaded with red blood.

'There was an uncommon quantity of blood in the vessels of the ovaria and Fallopian tubes, but principally in those of the ovarium, and morsus diaboli of the left side.

'The organs of generation being carefully removed, and both ovaria being slit open, there was found in the left a corpus luteum.

'It was evident, from this circumstance, that conception had taken place; which led to an enquiry respecting the last appearance of her menses, which appeared by the evidence of the family to have been little more than a month before her death.

'With the dread upon her mind of being with child, the usual period of menstruation had hardly elapsed without its appearing, which confirmed her suspicions, before she, in a fit of despair, put an end to her life.

'From this evidence, the period of conception could not exceed a month, and probably was much within that time.

'As it was interesting to have the parts accurately examined, to see what information might be acquired respecting the foetus at so early a period, they were given to Mr. Hunter for that purpose, whose observations upon them are contained in the following account.

'The arteries of the uterus were injected, and the smaller vessels were filled to so great a degree of minuteness that the whole surface became extremely red.

'The cervix uteri and os tincae were of their natural size; but the body, or that portion of the uterus next the fundus, was a little enlarged, and more prominent externally in the middle. The spermatic vessels were also enlarged.

'On cutting into the substance of the uterus, it had more of a laminated structure than in the unimpregnated state: this appearance of lamellae appeared upon examination to be formed by veins somewhat enlarged, compressed and transversely divided. The uterus was unusually soft in texture, and terminated on the internal surface in a pulpy substance.

'The blood-vessels of the uterus passed into and ramified upon this pulpy substance, which was continued across at the cervix uteri, so as to make the cavity of the uterus a circumscribed bag; and at this part the pulpy substance was so thin as to resemble the retina.

'This cavity had a smooth but irregular internal surface, and the pulpy substance upon which it was formed was evidently blood coagulated and varied in its thickness in different parts. Upon a longitudinal section of the uterus, the posterior part of the coagulum, which was the thickest, was nearly half an inch; where it terminated towards the cervix it was pendulous and unattached. There were also several loose processes, all turned towards the cervix, one of them very thin, as broad as a silver penny, and only attached by one edge to the fundus near the opening of the right Fallopian tube.

'On slitting open the Fallopian tubes, the coagulum was found to pass some way into them, and to extend more than half an inch on the left side, which had the corpus luteum. The coagulum was thickest at the orifice of the tube, and there adhered to the inner surface for the eighth part of an inch; beyond which it became smaller and terminated in a point. In the left tube the coagulum was in two places coiled or folded upon itself, as if thrown back by the action of the tube. The portions of the coagulum at the orifices of the tubes were hollow.

'When the inner surface of the cavity of the uterus was examined with a magnifying glass it was found extremely vascular, and dotted with innumerable whitish spots too small to be seen by the naked eye.

'In the examination of this uterus and Fallopian tubes, as Mr. Hunter's chief object was the detection of the embryo, no precaution was omitted which could be devised to prevent it being overlooked or destroyed.

'The uterus was opened in a bason of clear water, the incision was conducted with great circumspection, and very slowly continued, till the whole of the cavity was exposed. Every part of the internal surface was minutely examined with magnifying glasses; but in no situation was there anything resembling an embryo to be found.

'The presence of a corpus luteum, the enlargement of the uterus, the newly-formed vascular membrane or decidua, lining the cavity, and the history of the case, sufficiently prove conception to have taken place; and the embryo being nowhere detected by an examination so accurate and conducted by an anatomist so skilful in minute investigation, would induce a belief that the foetus had not been sufficiently advanced to take on a regular form.

'The appearances in the uterus, here described, the late Dr. Hunter, in his lectures, mentioned to have seen at a very early period after impregnation: so far they are not entirely new. The accuracy of the examination renders this case valuable, as it seems to enable us to decide a point hitherto not at all understood—that certain changes in the uterus not only take place previous to the reception of the foetus, but that the foetus does not acquire a visible form for some time after these changes have been made.'   *Works*, vol. iv, pp. 55-57.

3593 The ovaries, Fallopian tubes, and uterus of a Woman, apparently a short time after impregnation.

The right ovary is in part bisected by two separate incisions, exposing a large corpus luteum half of which has been dissected out, displaying the smooth surface of the ovarian stroma which was in contact with its external surface.

A section has been removed from the left ovary. The uterus is slit open.

3594 A section of the gravid uterus and chorion at a more advanced stage of pregnancy, when the perionic* or true uterine cavity is obliterated by the confluence of the decidua reflexa with the decidua vera. It thus results that a single layer of loose decidual tissue separates the chorion from the muscular wall of the uterus. Whether this single decidual layer when fully formed is composed of both the decidua reflexa and the decidua vera or of decidua vera alone, the decidua reflexa having been absorbed, is uncertain.

3595 A section of the same uterus, on one side of which the chorion has been slightly separated from the inner surface of the uterus and the loose texture of the decidual tissue better displayed.

3596 A section of a gravid uterus at the same period of gestation, in which a portion of the chorion has been stripped from the underlying decidua and turned down.

3597 A portion of a gravid uterus, the arteries of which have been minutely injected.

A part of the chorion is reflected to show several minute arteries distributed to the decidual tissue upon its surface.

3598 A portion of the wall of a gravid uterus about the same period of gestation, minutely injected by the arteries and veins.

The amnion, chorion, and two superficial layers of the vascular decidua are successively reflected from the inner surface of the specimen.

3599 A small portion of the wall of a gravid uterus, with red wax injected into the arteries and yellow wax into the veins.

A portion of the chorion and amnion has been reflected from its inner surface, showing the loose reticulate texture of the decidua which is interposed between the muscular walls of the uterus and the chorion.

The large size of the uterine veins can be seen on the cut edges of the specimen.

* A term coined by Albert Breschet (1784-1845) (from the Greek, meaning 'around the egg').

3600   A similar preparation, but uninjected.

3601   Part of the wall of a gravid uterus showing (in section) the great thickness of its
        muscle coats.

3602   A similar preparation.

3603   A portion of the right wall of a gravid uterus, to which the broad and round
        ligaments and the ligament of the ovary are attached, showing the increase in
        the size and strength of the supporting ligaments of the uterus in an advanced
        stage of pregnancy.

3604   A gravid uterus at the sixth month of gestation with the placenta, chorion and
        amnion lining its interior and exposed to view by the removal of the greater
        part of its anterior (ventral) wall.
            The uterine veins have been filled with a white injection; their size is well
        seen as they leave the uterus between the folds of the broad ligament; within
        the walls of the uterus they are abundant, of large size and flattened between
        the muscle bundles owing to the pressure exerted by the growing foetus and its
        membranes, and thus giving to the uterine wall a characteristic laminated
        appearance.
            The uterus is lined completely by the placenta and foetal membranes. The
        limits of the placenta are clearly defined by the high vascularity and swollen
        appearance of its tissues. From its centre emerges the umbilical cord covered
        by a reflection of the amnion; within it can be seen one of the spirally coiled
        umbilical arteries, injected red. The umbilical vein has been filled with a blue
        injection, its factors may be seen on the surface of the placenta, deep to the
        corresponding arteries; converging towards the commencement of the umbilical
        cord.
            Upon the dorsal aspect of the specimen the os tincae and vagina have been
        laid open.
        See 'On the Structure of the Placenta', *Works*, vol. iv, pp. 60-73.

3605   A longitudinal section of a uterus at the seventh month of gestation, with a red
        injection thrown into the uterine arteries and a yellow injection into the uterine
        veins.
            Upon the cut edges of the specimen the large size and abundance of the veins
        are well displayed; they are specially developed in the area occupied by the
        placenta.

The foetal membranes and placenta are retained in place.

Parts of the amnion, chorion laeve, and decidua have been separated and reflected; a portion of the placenta has likewise been detached from the uterine wall so as to expose its outer surface with the ruptured ends of the uterine arteries and veins embedded in it. Parts of the placenta are coloured by the injection introduced into the uterine vessels; the foetal vessels are not injected.

3606 A longitudinal section of the cervix uteri and os tincae at the latter period of pregnancy, showing the tumescence of the mucous membrane of this passage and the oblique valvular folds projecting into its lumen.

3607 A similar section of the cervix uteri, with a small portion of the vagina, at a less advanced period. It shows the longitudinal raphe from which the oblique folds of the lining membrane emerge.

3608 A longitudinal section through the cervix uteri and os tincae and part of the vagina at the period of parturition.

The lining membrane of the cervix is not cast off during this process, as is the decidua that lines the uterus.

The lips of the os tincae are swollen and covered with vesicles and punctures which probably are due to the enlargement of the numerous glands.

3609 A smaller section of the os tincae at a similar period, showing more clearly the vacuolated and swollen condition of the lips.

3610 A portion of the wall of the uterus at the close of gestation to which the placenta was attached and from which it and the decidua basalis have been torn away.

The veins had been filled with a dark injection (most of which has fallen out) and the arteries with red.

Upon the surface and the cut edge of the specimen can be seen the large size, the abundance and the plexiform arrangement of the veins underlying the placenta. The ruptured extremities of the arteries on the raw inner surface of the preparation may be observed in general to form a short spiral coil, as described by Hunter in his account of the vascular communication between the uterus and placenta.   *Works*, vol. iv, p. 66.

3611 The anterior wall of the uterus and part of the vagina, with the urinary bladder, soon after parturition, injected to show the raw surface of the uterus from which the decidua has been cast off.

The cervix uteri has been flattened out with an almost entire obliteration of the os tincae.

3612   A longitudinal section of a uterus soon after parturition, showing the great increase in the thickness of its walls that results from its rapid and strong contraction.

The veins, which are filled with a pale injection, have reassumed a circular outline in cross-section.

The inner surface is ragged and covered with flakes of ruptured decidual tissue.

3613   A small section of the fundus of a uterus at the same period, showing the thickness of its walls, the circular form of the larger veins in cross-section and the compression and diminution in size of the veins near the surface from which the decidua has been detached.

3614   A small portion of the wall of a uterus soon after delivery.

The specimen shows in its centre a circular recess or orifice; fluid injected into this recess emerged freely at the cut surface of the ligament which is attached to the outer surface of the wall of the uterus; this circumstance suggests that the recess is the aperture by which the Fallopian tube communicates with the cavity of the uterus. In Owen's description of the specimen (*Physiology Catalogue*, vol. v, p. 161) this central recess is regarded as 'a preternatural condition' and the piece of uterine wall is said to include the 'part to which the centre of the placenta was attached'.

3615   A section of the wall of a uterus (including the body and cervix) a short (but unknown) time after parturition.

The inner surface of the corpus uteri is the area from which the placenta was detached; it is extremely irregular and rugose.

3616   A longitudinal section of the uterus and head of the vagina soon after parturition: the exact period is not recorded.

The walls of the uterus are thick and solid, and the inner surface soft and irregular. The os tincae is well marked and prominent.

3617   A sagittal section of the uterus, vagina, and urinary bladder at a later period after delivery, showing considerable diminution of the size of the uterus by contraction. Its walls are still thick and spongy, riddled with a plexus of large veins.

The ovary has been divided, showing the corpus luteum. This body is much diminished in size as compared with those shown in Nos. 3590, 3593, at the onset of pregnancy; a white line which runs along its centre and sends processes into its substance, indicates the situation of the obliterated cavity of the ovisac.

3618　The opposite section of the same uterus, vagina, and urinary bladder.

3619　A uterus at a later period after parturition, with the commencement of the vagina laid open.

The uterus has now more nearly reassumed its normal resting condition; its inner surface is smooth, as though now lined by a newly formed epithelium.

3620　The chorionic sac of a young embryo, slit open.

This specimen as described by Owen (*Catalogue of the Physiological Series*, vol. v, p. 162) included the embryo measuring four lines in length; the embryo has been lost.

The chorionic sac is lined by the amnion and is covered by a dense growth of branched villi by which a connection is formed with the surrounding decidua.

3621　A section of the amnion, chorion, and decidua reflexa of an embryo, at apparently about the same period of development as the preceding. Upon one margin of the specimen the decidua has been stripped off to expose the flocculent mass of chorionic villi. Upon the lower part of the chorion the villi are few and separately scattered.

3622　A portion of the amnion, chorion, and decidua reflexa of an embryo at about the same period of development.

3623　A portion of the chorionic sac and decidua reflexa of an embryo at apparently the same period of development as the preceding specimen.

A bunch of branching villi of the chorion is excellently shown.

3625　The chorionic sac, consisting of amnion and chorion, at a similar period of development, inverted, showing the smooth surface of the amnion that forms the lining of the sac, and the delicate branching chorionic villi that cover its outer surface.

3626　One-half of a similar chorionic sac, to the outer surface of which is attached a portion of the decidua reflexa.

3627   A Human embryo, bctween four and five lines in length (8·4-10·5 mm.) enclosed
        within its amniotic sac.   An embryo of this length would be from 4-5 weeks old.
        See C. M. Jackson: 'On the prenatal growth of the human body and the relative
        growth of the various organs and parts', *Am. J. Anat.*, 1909, p. 155.

        Most of the chorion has been dissected from the outer surface of the amnion
        but here and there fragments of it are left, showing its branched villous pro-
        cesses.

3628   The chorionic sac of an embryo which measured five lines (10·5 mm.) in length.
        The sac has been opened and from its outer surface parts of the chorion have
        been removed.

        In the description of this specimen in Owen's *Catalogue* (vol. v, p. 163) it is
        stated that the embryo is attached to the chorion by an abnormally short
        umbilical cord and that the yolk-sac can be seen attached to the outer surface
        of the amnion.   The yolk-sac is, however, not now visible and in a manuscript
        note by Sir William Flower it is recorded that the embryo was absent in 1872.

3629   The chorionic sac, with parts of the decidua reflexa adhering to it, of a young
        embryo.

        The sac has been opened showing within it the amnion loosened from the
        inner surface of the chorion.   In the lower left corner of the specimen may be
        seen a small vesicle (indicated by black paper) hanging by a thread-like pedicle
        between the amnion and chorion.   From its general form and position this must
        be the yolk-sac.

        The branching villi upon the outer surface of the chorion are admirably shown.

3631   An embryo, five lines (10·5 mm.) in length appended by a thick straight umbilical
        cord an inch (25·5 mm.) in length to the inner surface of the chorionic sac.

        The sac has been laid open to expose the embryo and to show the smooth
        surface of its amniotic lining.   Portions only of the villous chorion remain
        attached to the external surface of the amnion.

3632   An embryo six lines (12·6 mm.) in length, with its amnion, chorion and decidua
        reflexa, which is thickened and loaded with coagulated blood.   (An embryo of
        this length would be about 6 weeks old.)

        The embryo is suspended by a thick umbilical cord, about its own length.
        Part of the wall of the abdomen of the embryo has been removed to expose the
        liver and intestines.

3633   A Human embryo, ten lines (21 mm.) in length, at about the seventh week of
       gestation, with its chorionic sac and parts of the decidua vera and reflexa.

       The decidua vera which forms the inner lining of the original uterine cavity
       presents a reticulate appearance due to the distension of the uterine glands in
       its deeper ('spongy') layer.

       The chorionic sac has been laid open, exposing the embryo suspended by a
       short wide umbilical cord. Between the smooth and delicate amnion and the
       villous chorion can be seen a layer of soft gelatinous mesenchyme tissue.

3634   The chorionic sac of a Human embryo, with the decidua reflexa around it and
       parts of the decidua vera.

       The sac is laid open by a crucial incision, showing within it the remains of a
       damaged embryo and its umbilical cord. The cord is attached to the anterior
       pole of the sac and around this point the chorion is strongly villous (chorion
       frondosum); elsewhere, as shown where the decidua reflexa is turned back
       along the edges of the incision, villi seem to be practically absent (chorion
       laeve). The area of the chorion frondosum is involved in the formation of the
       placenta.

       The line of reflection from which the decidua vera bulges to form the decidua
       reflexa is clearly shown. The decidual membrane is here minutely reticulate;
       many orifices (possibly the openings of glands) may also be observed upon the
       portion of the decidua vera which has been turned upwards to expose the
       decidua reflexa.

3635   Twin embryos, each about 26 mm. in length, included within their amniotic sacs
       in a common chorion.

       This membrane is attached to the decidua reflexa, which is morbidly laden
       with coagulated blood.

       The embryos are exposed within their respective amniotic sacs, each suspended
       by a relatively slender umbilical cord some 13 mm. in length. Embryos sur-
       rounded by independent amnions, but a common chorion, are derived from a
       single ovum and are known as similar twins.

       The embryos are each at a similar stage of development, with the different
       segments of the limbs and the digits established, the eyelids commencing by a
       slight fold at the inner angle of the eye, the nostrils represented by two minute
       punctures and the tongue well formed and projecting from between the jaws,
       which are not yet bordered by separate lips.

       An embryo of this length would be about eight weeks old.

3636   The chorionic sac of an embryo fourteen lines (29·4 mm.) in length, with (mounted above it) the decidua reflexa.

The sac has been inverted; between the amnion and chorion at a distance of one inch (25 mm.) from the point of attachment of the umbilical cord, may be seen the yolk-sac in the form of a flattened, opaque, oval disc a line and a half (3 mm. in length).

The outer surface of the chorion is covered, especially towards the upper end of the specimen, by richly branching villi.

Originally (see Owen's *Catalogue*, vol. v, p. 166) this preparation included the embryo, but this has become detached from its long slender umbilical cord and lost.

3637   An embryo one inch and a quarter (31·9 mm.) in length, at between the eighth and ninth week of gestation, displaced from the amniotic sac, from which a section has been removed. The delicate mesenchymatous tissue that connects the amnion to the chorion is well displayed along the cut edge of the lower part of the sac.

Opposite the attachment of the umbilical cord to the chorion, the decidua is much thickened and, as may be seen along the section surface of this part, is deeply penetrated, or rather replaced, by abundant chorionic villi. Towards the lower part of the sac, villi are few and small.

The umbilical cord is long and narrow; within its foetal extremity may be seen a coil of intestine.

3638   An embryo at a corresponding period of development, with the amnion and chorion laid open by a crucial incision.

The amnion has been detached from the inner surface of the chorion and thus shows its delicate structure to advantage.

3639   A foetus between the fourth and fifth month of uterine gestation enclosed within its amnion and the non-placental part of the chorion (chorion laeve).

The specimen is suspended by the extremity of the umbilical cord where it leaves the amnion to join the placenta.

At some distance from this point is a narrow selvage indicating the line of union of the placental with the non-placental area of the chorion. Along this line the non-placental chorion laeve shows a few isolated branching villi, elsewhere it is perfectly smooth.

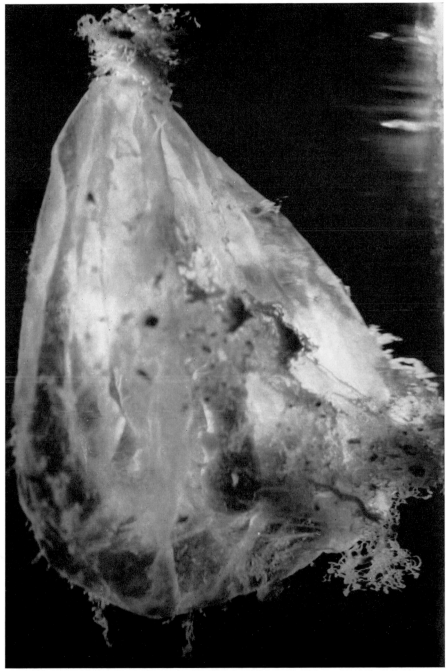

FIG. 9

A Human embryo between four and five weeks old, enclosed within its amniotic sac.
Specimen No. 3627, magnified approximately 7 times.

3640 A section of the uterus and placenta at about the sixth month of gestation, including the point of attachment of the umbilical cord.

Upon the section surface can be seen the mass of placental tissue clearly distinguished by its soft spongy texture from the muscular walls of the uterus that overlie it.

The inner surface of the placenta is covered loosely by the delicate amniotic membrane and at its edges it is continued without direct connection with the uterine wall as a relatively thin double membrane consisting of chorion and amnion and forming the chorion laeve of the chorionic sac.

The umbilical cord is long and slender and shows through its semi-transparent walls the spirally twisted blood vessels.

3641 A portion of the placenta showing the deep lobulation of its outer (uterine) surface.

Upon the cut edge of the specimen can be seen numbers of the larger foetal vessels ramifying over the foetal surface of the placenta, which unlike the outer surface is perfectly smooth.

3642 A longitudinal section of a gravid uterus of the seventh month, showing the relation of the placenta and foetal membranes to the uterine walls.

The cut surface of the placenta shows clearly the deep subdivision of its substance into lobules by the intrusion into it of laminar processes of the decidual membrane. The foetal surface, though convex and projecting considerably into the amniotic cavity, is not lobulated; its chorionic layer, which gives rise to the villi of the placenta, forms a narrow dense zone, just external to the amnion, occupied by the larger branches of the allantoic vessels; several of these can be seen radiating from the point of attachment of the umbilical cord.

The amnion has been in part separated from the chorion, showing that it is reflected from the placental end of the umbilical cord and forms a complete lining to the chorion. In the non-placental region the chorion has been separated from the decidua vera and the latter membrane isolated and split to show its laminated structure. This might be regarded as an indication that at this age the decidua vera represents a combination of decidua reflexa and decidua vera, but it is more likely that the decidua reflexa, after it has become pressed against the decidua vera by the growth of the chorionic sac, is absorbed.

The uterine arteries and veins have been filled respectively with red and yellow injection, showing their abundance and large size, particularly in the region of the placenta and their intrusion into the tissues of the placenta in the folds between its lobules.

C.H.M.–L

Hunter's description of the human placenta, which is illustrated by this and subsequent preparations, is as follows:

'The necessary connexion subsisting in all animals between the mother and foetus, for the nourishment of the latter, as far as I know, takes place in two ways. In some it is continued, and subsists through the whole term of gestation; in others the union is soon dissolved; but an apparatus is provided, which at once furnishes what is sufficient for the support of the animal till it comes forth.

'The first of these are the viviparous, the second the oviparous animals, both of which admit of great variety in the mode by which the same effect is produced.* In the first division is included the human species, which alone will engage our present attention. But before I describe this connexion, it may be necessary that the reader should understand my idea of generation: I shall therefore refer him to what I have said upon that subject in my account of the free-martin.†

'In the human species, the anatomical structure of the mother and embryo, relative to foetation, being well known, it will only be necessary fully to describe the nature of the connexion between them, which is formed by the intermediate substance called placenta. For this purpose we must first consider the placenta as a common part; next, the uterus as belonging to the mother, yet having an immediate connexion with the placenta, from which the nourishment of the foetus is to be derived, which will lead us lastly to a consideration of those peculiarities of structure by means of which the foetus is to receive its nourishment, and which likewise constitutes its immediate communication with the placenta. It is the structure of this intermediate substance, and its connexion with the child and the uterus of the mother, which have hitherto been so little understood, and without an accurate knowledge of which it was impossible any just idea could be formed of its functions.

'The placenta is a mass lying nearly in contact with the uterus; indeed it may in some degree be said to be in continuity with a part of its internal surface. On the side applied to the uterus the placenta is lobulated, having deep irregular fissures. It is probable, from this structure of the placenta, that the uterus has an intestine motion while in the time of uterine gestation,

---

* 'It may be remarked here, that the oviparous admit of being distinguished into two classes, one where the egg is hatched in the belly, as in the viper, which has been commonly called viviparous; the others, where the eggs have been first laid and then hatched, which is the class commonly called oviparous, such as all the bird tribe; and many others, as snakes, lizards, &c.'

† *Works*, vol. v, p. 34.

not an expulsive one; which those lobes of the placenta allow of; but all these lobes are united into one uniform surface on that surface next to the child, where its umbilical vessels ramify. When we cut into the placenta its whole substance appears to be little else than a network, or spongy mass, through which the blood-vessels of the foetus ramify, and indeed seems to be principally formed by the ramifications of those vessels; it exhibits hardly any appearance of connecting membrane; but we cannot readily suppose it to be without such a membrane, as there is so much regularity in its texture. The cells, or interstices of each lobe, communicate with one another, even much more freely than those of the cellular membrane in any other part of the body; so that whatever fluid will pass in at one part, readily diffuses itself through the whole mass of lobe; and all the cells of each lobe have a communication at the common base.

'This structure of the placenta, and its reciprocal communication with the two bodies with which it is immediately connected, form the union between the mother and foetus for the support of the latter. Prior to the time I have mentioned above,* anatomists seem to have been wholly unacquainted with the true structure of the placenta. By notes taken from Dr. Hunter's lectures, in the winter 1755-6, it appears that he expressed himself in the following manner.† "The substance of the placenta is a fleshy mass, which seems to be formed entirely of the vessels of the umbilical rope." In another part, mentioning the appearances when injected, he says: "and upon a slight putrefaction coming on, you will find the whole appearing like a mass of vessels"; then says, "there is always a white uninjected substance between the vessels; but whether lymphatics or what I cannot tell." This uninjected substance, mentioned by Dr. Hunter, is what forms the cellular structure.

'The placenta seems to be principally composed of the ramifications of the vessels of the embryo, and may have been originally formed in consequence of those next to the uterus laying hold by a species of animal attraction of the coagulable lymph which lines the uterus. It might take place in a manner resembling what happens when the root of a plant spreads on the surface of moist bodies, with this difference, that in the present instance the vessels form the substance through which they ramify, as in the case of granulations.

'At the time, or perhaps before, the female seed enters the uterus, coagulable lymph, from the blood of the mother, is thrown out everywhere on its inner surface, either from the stimulus of impregnation taking place in the

---

* 1754 (p. 60).

† 'These quotations were taken from Mr. Galhie's MS. of Dr. Hunter's lectures, who is one of the gentlemen that favoured Dr. Hunter, upon a former occasion, with the use of his notes. See Dr. Hunter's Commentaries.'

ovarium, or in consequence of the seed being expelled from it.   But I think the first the most probable supposition; for we find in extra-uterine cases that the decidua is formed in the uterus, although the ovum never enters it, which is a proof that it is produced by the stimulus of impregnation in the ovarium, and that it is prior to the entrance of the ovum into the uterus.   When it has entered the uterus it attaches itself to that coagulable lymph, by which, being covered and immediately surrounded,* there is formed a soft pulpy membrane, the decidua, which I believe is peculiar to the human species and to monkeys, I never having found it in any other animal.   That part which covers the seed or foetus, where it is not immediately attached to the uterus, and likewise forms a membrane, was discovered by Dr. Hunter, and is by him called decidua reflexa.†   The whole of this coagulable lymph continues to be a living part for the time; the vessels of the uterus ramify upon it; and where the vessels of the foetus form the placenta there the vessels of the uterus, after passing through the decidua, open into the cellular substance of the placenta, as before described.   As this membrane lines the uterus and covers the seed, it is stretched out, and becomes thinner and thinner, as the uterus is distended by the foetus growing larger, especially that part of it, called decidua reflexa, which covers the foetus; as there it cannot possibly acquire any new matter, except we could suppose that the foetus assisted in the formation of it.   This membrane is most distinct where it covers the chorion; for where it covers the placenta it is blended with coagula in the great veins that pass obliquely through it, more especially all round the edge, where innumerable large veins come out; but the chorion and decidua can be easily distinguished from one another, the decidua being less elastic.

'From the description now given, I think we are justified in supposing the placenta to be formed entirely by the foetus, which is further confirmed by extra-uterine cases, and by the formation of the membrane in the egg, there being no living organic part to furnish them; and the decidua we must suppose to be a production of the mother: of both which the circumstance of the decidua passing between the placenta and uterus may be considered as an additional proof.   For if the vessels of the foetus branched into a part of the decidua, we might conceive the whole placenta to be formed from that

---

* 'This is somewhat similar to another operation in the animal oeconomy.   If an extraneous living part is introduced into any cavity it will be immediately inclosed with coagulable lymph.   Thus we find worms inclosed, and hydatids, that have been detached, afterwards inclosed; but in those cases this is a consequence of the pressure of the extraneous body, whereas in the uterus it is preparatory.'

† 'The placenta is certainly a foetal part, and is formed on the inside of the spongy chorion, or decidua.   How far the decidua reflexa is a uterine part I do not yet know; if it is, then the ovum must be placed in a doubling of the coagulum, which forms the decidua; but if the ovum is attached to the inside of the decidua, then the decidua reflexa is belonging to the foetus.'

exudation; the portion of it, where the vessels had ramified like the roots of a plant, becoming thicker than the rest, and forming the placenta. If that were the case, this membrana decidua, when traced from the parts distinct, and at a distance from the placenta, should be plainly seen passing into its substance all round at the edges, as a continuation of it. But the fact is quite otherwise; for the decidua can be distinctly traced between the placenta and uterus, hardly ever passing between the lobuli, the vessels of the foetus never entering into it, and of course none of them ever coming in absolute contact with the uterus. But what may be considered as still a stronger proof that the decidua is furnished by the uterus is, that in cases of extra-uterine conception, where the foetus is wholly in the ovarium or Fallopian tube, we find the uterus lined with the decidua, having taken on the uterine action; but no placenta, that being formed by the foetus, and therefore in the part which contained it.

'The vessels of the foetus adhering, by the intervention of the decidua, to a certain portion of the uterus when both are yet small, as the uterus increases in every part of its surface during the time of uterine gestation, we must suppose that this surface of adhesion increases also; and that by the elongation of those vessels of the foetus in every direction this substance should likewise be increased in every direction. This is in some degree the case, yet the placenta does not occupy so much of the enlarged surface of the uterus as one at first would expect.

'The vessels of the uterus in the time of the gestation are increased in size nearly in a proportion equal to the increased circumference of the uterus, and consequently in a proportion much greater than the real increase of its substance. But when we reflect that the uterus ought not to be considered as hollow, but as a body nearly solid, on account of its contents, which derive support from this source, and that a much greater quanitity of blood must necessarily pass than what is required for the support of the viscus itself, we cannot be at a loss to account for the greatly increased size of its vessels.

'The arteries which are not immediately employed in conveying nourishment to the uterus go on towards the placenta, and, proceeding obliquely between it and the uterus, pass through the decidua without ramifying; just before they enter the placenta, after making two or three close spiral turns upon themselves, they open at once into its spongy substance without any diminution of size, and without passing beyond the surface, as above described. The intention of these spiral turns would appear to be that of diminishing the force of the circulation in the vessels as they approach the spongy substance of the placenta, and is a mechanism calculated to lessen the quick motion of the blood in a part where a quick motion was not required. These curling arteries at this termination are in general about half the size of a crow's quill, and sometimes larger.

'The veins of the uterus appropriated to bring back the blood from the placenta commence from this spongy substance by such wide beginnings as are more than equal to the size of the veins themselves. These veins pass obliquely through the decidua to the uterus, enter its substance obliquely, and immediately communicate with the proper veins of the uterus. The area of these veins bears no proportion to their circumference, the veins being very much flattened.

'This structure of parts points out at once the nature of the blood's motion in the placenta; but as this is a fact but lately ascertained, a just idea may perhaps be conveyed by saying that it is similar, as far as we yet know, to the blood's motion through the cavernous substance of the penis.

'The blood, detached from the common circulation of the mother, moves through the placenta of the foetus; and is then returned back into the course of the circulation of the mother, to pass on to the heart.

'This structure of the placenta, and its communication with the uterus, leads us a step further in our knowledge of the connexion between the mother and foetus. The blood of the mother must pass freely into the substance of the placenta, and the placenta most probably will be constantly filled; the turgidity of which will assist to squeeze the blood into the mouths of the veins of the uterus, that it may again pass into the common circulation of the mother; and as the interstices of the placenta are of much greater extent than the arteries which convey the blood, the motion of the blood in that part must be so much diminished as almost to approach to stagnation. So far and no further does the mother appear to be concerned in this connexion.

'The foetus has a communication with the placenta of another kind. The arteries from the foetus pass out to a considerable length, under the name of the umbilical arteries, and when they arrive at the placenta ramify upon its surface, sending into its substance branches which pass through it, and divide into smaller and smaller, till at last they terminate in veins; these, uniting, become larger and larger, and end in one, which at last communicates with the proper circulation of the foetus.

'This course of vessels, and the blood's motion in them, is similar to the course of the vessels and the motion of the blood in other parts of the body.'

Works, vol. iv, pp. 62-67.

3643   The ovaries, Fallopian tubes, and gravid uterus with its contents, at the seventh month of gestation; the uterine vessels have been minutely injected.

The right ovary is bisected through the corpus luteum which is near its margin and undergoing reduction.

The anterior walls have been removed, exposing the thin decidua vera, a large portion of which has been dissected off to lay bare the underlying chorion laeve. Near the cervix uteri the chorion has been reflected to show the amnion.

On the opposite side of the specimen a part of the uterine wall has been turned up to show the chorion laeve and the lower half of the placenta. The large orifices of numerous veins may be seen on the deep surface of this reflected portion of the uterine wall and on the corresponding surface of the placenta the same veins are apparent leaving the decidua; some of these are indicated by bristles inserted into them.

At the border of the placenta several large uterine veins have been laid open and upon its exposed surface may be seen a few minute tortuous branches of the uterine arteries.

Near the cervix uteri the decidua has been removed from the underlying chorion and the chorion reflected to expose the amnion.

3644 The ovaries, Fallopian tubes, and gravid uterus with its contents, at the eighth month of gestation.

The left ovary is bisected and a section has been removed from the right ovary in which the corpus luteum is situated. The place of exit of the ripe ovum is indicated by a vascular spot or cicatrix.

The posterior walls of the uterus have been removed, together with the corresponding part of the decidua and foetal membranes to show the foetus in its natural position; it occupies practically the whole of the uterine cavity with its body and limbs strongly flexed. The back of the foetus is directed towards the left and the head towards the cervix uteri.

The uterine arteries have been injected whereby the vascularity of the decidua is demonstrated in the parts of this membrane that project beyond the cut edges of the uterus.

3645 A section of the deeper layers of the walls of the uterus at the ninth month of gestation, with a portion of the placenta connected with it.

The uterine wall is honey-combed by a meshwork of large veins separated from one another by thin layers of muscle and intercommunicating at acute angles. These veins have been filled with a dark injection which has passed from them onto the blood spaces of the placenta within which the foetal chorionic villi lie. The intermingling of white non-injected branching foetal villi and black injection-filled spaces is very clearly shown on the section surfaces, and it is possible also to see here and there the orifices through which the blood spaces are continuous with the veins.

This is the first of the series of important specimens by which Hunter proved that the fluid contained in the intervillous spaces of the placenta is maternal blood.

3646   A smaller portion of the same injected uterus and placenta.

The reticulate arrangement and their connection with the intervillous blood spaces of the placenta are shown upon the section surfaces.

3647   A section of a placenta in which the intervillous blood spaces have been filled with a black injection, the allantoic arteries with red and the allantoic vein with white.

The black injection is visible here and there in the intervillous spaces through which the maternal blood of the placenta circulates.   A few of the chorionic villi which lie in these spaces show signs of the red injection and a few on the edge of the section are filled by the white injection.

At the upper margin of the specimen is displayed a bunch of isolated arborescent chorionic villi.

3648   A section of a placenta in which the uterine arteries have been filled with a red injection and the corresponding veins (less successfully) with black.

The intervillous spaces of the placenta are filled almost entirely by the red injection, and upon the uterine surface may be seen a few small, contorted terminal arterioles.

One of the interlobular fissures has been widened to show a uterine vein passing through it from the substance of the placenta.

3649   A section of a twin placenta.   A deep cleft indistinctly divides the placental tissue into two parts, one belonging to each foetus.   Opposite this cleft lies the boundary line between the two independent amnions.   The chorion is apparently single, indicating that the twins developed from one ovum.

3650   A large segment of a placenta, including a portion of its border from which extends a section of the chorion laeve dissected to show its chorionic and amniotic layers.

The amnion has been removed from the foetal surface of the placenta to show the larger branches of the allantoic vessels ramifying over it.

The arteries have been filled with red injection and the veins with white.

3651 A section of a placenta including the point of attachment of the umbilical cord.

A yellow substance has been injected into the allantoic arteries and a red injection into the corresponding veins.

Over a large area of the section-surface, the venous injection may be seen occupying the chorionic villi. The larger branches of the allantoic vessels are exposed upon the foetal surface of the placenta by the removal (from the upper half of the specimen) of the amnion; and are also shown in cross-section at the extremity of the cord distal to the line at which the amnion is reflected from its surface.

In their passage across the placenta the arteries lie superficial to the veins.

From the lower margin of the specimen hangs a small portion of the chorion laeve.

3652 An adjoining section of the same placenta.

3653 Another section of the same placenta.

3654 A section of the same placenta including a considerable extent of its circumference, from which is continued the decidua vera and chorion laeve.

The amnion has been removed.

3655 A small portion of a placenta, including part of its margin, injected by the allantoic vessels.

The amnion has been raised from the surface of the placenta and at its margin is separated from the chorion laeve which in turn is detached from the overlying decidua vera.

3656 A similar section of a placenta showing the amnion, chorion, and decidua continued from its margin.

3657 A large portion of a placenta, injected by the allantoic vessels and subsequently macerated to show the complex, bushy, villous processes of the chorion that in nature lie in the intervillous spaces through which the maternal blood circulates.

3658 An entire placenta of large size, showing by maceration the form and abundance of the branching chorionic villi.

THE HUMAN EMBRYO

In estimating the approximate age of the following Human embryos and foetuses, the relation between the length from vertex to breech and the probable age given by C. M. Jackson ('On the prenatal growth of the Human Body', *Am. J. Anat.*, Vol. 9, 1909, p. 155) has been adopted. References are also given in many cases to figures of embryos and foetuses at similar stages of development published by Wilhelm His (*Anatomie menschlicher Embryonen*, 1880, *Atlas*), Franz Keibel (*Normentafel zur Entwicklungsgeschichte des Menschen*, 1908) and Gustav Retzius ('Zur Kenntnis der Entwicklung der Körperformen des Menschen', *Biol. Untersuch.*, N.F. XI, 1904, p. 33).

A tabular statement of the chief structural features of the embryos to 26 mm. vertex-breech length is given by Keibel (l.c. pp. 90-151).

3661   A female foetus, which corresponds very nearly with the foetus of 54 mm. vertex to breech length figured by Retzius in Pl. 15, Fig. 4, and is, according to Jackson's estimate, probably about nine weeks old.

3662   A male foetus, a little further advanced; some coils of intestine protrude through the umbilical aperture of the abdomen.

3664   A female foetus, at about the end of the third month of development.
      It corresponds with the foetus of 68 mm. vertex to breech length figured by Retzius in Pl. 15, Fig. 6, and on Jackson's estimate should be 82 days old.

3665   A female foetus at about the beginning of the fourth month of gestation.
      It corresponds very nearly with the foetus of 94 mm. vertex-breech length figured by Retzius in Pl. 15, Figs. 7-8, which, according to Jackson's estimate should be 97 days old.

3666   A female foetus at about the beginning of the fifth month of development.
      It exactly resembles the foetus of 117 mm. vertex-breech length figured by Retzius in Pl. 15, Fig. 9, and on Jackson's estimate should be 115 days old.

3667   A male foetus at approximately the same stage of development as the previous specimen.

3668   A male Negro foetus at about the fourth month of gestation.
      The dark pigment and the characters of the expanded alae of the nose and the thickened lips already begin to be manifest.

3669   A male foetus at a similar stage of development as the two previous specimens.

3670   A male foetus at a slightly more advanced stage of development about the middle of the fifth month.
        It corresponds with the foetus of 131 mm. vertex-breech length figured by Retzius in Pl. 18, Fig. 10, and by Jackson's estimate should be 130 days old.

3671   A female foetus probably at the end of the fifth month, or the beginning of the sixth month, of development.
        It corresponds with the foetus of 151 mm. vertex-breech figured by Retzius in Pl. 21, Fig. 1, which by Jackson's estimate should be 140 days old.

3672   A male foetus of about the same age as the previous specimen.

3673   A female foetus in the sixth month of gestation.
        It corresponds nearly with the foetus of 161 mm. vertex-breech length figured by Retzius on Pl. 21, Fig. 12, and by Jackson's estimate should be 155 days old.

3674   A male Chinese foetus, between the fifth and sixth months of development.
        Note the comparatively large size of the hands.

3675   A female foetus at about the end of the sixth month of development.
        It corresponds with the foetus of 175 mm. vertex-breech length figured by Retzius on Pl. 22, Figs. 1-2. According to Jackson's estimate a foetus this length should be 160 days old.

3676   A male foetus at about the same stage of development as the previous specimen.

3677   A female foetus early in the eighth month of development. It corresponds with the foetus of 206 mm. vertex-breech length figured by Retzius on Pl. 22, Figs. 3 and 4. Jackson estimates that a length of 200 mm. should indicate an age of 185 days.

3678   A female foetus at about the eighth month of development.

3679   A female foetus, between the eighth and ninth months of gestation.

3680   A female foetus at the termination of gestation.

3681   Five female foetuses, the produce of the same gestation, and successively brought
       forth at the same period of parturition; three were still-born; two of these may
       be distinguished by their shrivelled and distorted aspect; two were born alive,
       but survived their birth but a short time.

       The size of each foetus and the condition of the eyelids, ears, and external
organs of generation correspond with the state of development usually exhibited
at about the fifth month of uterine gestation.

       A record of this case of multiple gestation is published by Dr. Garthshore in
the *Philosophical Transactions*, Vol. 77, 1787, p. 344, together with a summary of
recorded cases of multiple births. In this account it is stated that the mother
of the above children, who was 21 years of age, and had previously borne a
single child, conceived again in December 1785, and on April 24th, 1786 brought
forth these five foetuses, the time of delivery occupying 50 minutes. Each foetus
was enclosed in its own amnion, and was attached by a separate umbilical cord
to a common undivided placenta.

       This specimen was sent to Canada soon after the birth of the Dionne quin-
tuplets, was kept there during the period of World War II, and returned to the
College in 1947.

Corpora lutea

When at certain periods of the year, corresponding in Lower Mammals with the
sexual season and in Man with (or near) the menstrual periods, the Graafian follicles
burst and the ripe ova are shed into the body cavity, certain changes take place in the
evacuated Graafian follicles.

The cells of the epithelium that line the follicle increase enormously in size and the
resulting masses of cells become permeated by a rich network of capillaries derived from
the connective tissue capsule of the follicle. The body thus formed is known as the corpus
luteum, and is probably a gland of internal secretion. It reaches its full development
early in pregnancy about the time that the blastocyst becomes attached to the uterine
wall and persists throughout pregnancy. At or shortly after parturition, degenerative
changes take place and the body is gradually absorbed.

In a general way (though not apparently without exception) during the time the
corpus luteum is present in the ovary, no growth or maturation of the ova takes place.
It has therefore been assumed that one function of the corpus luteum is to fix the time of
ovulation. It has also been observed that in the absence of the corpora lutea the mammary glands do not undergo their proper increase in size during pregnancy, from which
it has been concluded that the corpora lutea exert some influence on the production of
milk. Further it has been shown by experiment and clinical observation that the corpora

lutea are in some way intimately associated with the changes in the uterus incident to pregnancy and the fixation of the embryo, and from the fact that the period during which the corpora lutea are present in the ovary coincides in many cases with the duration of pregnancy, it has also been suggested that these structures may in some way determine the time of parturition.

Excellent reviews of the work that has hitherto been done on the structure and functions of the corpora lutea are given by Charles H. O'Donoghue in *Science Progress*, Vol. 8, 1913, p. 721; and by F. H. A. Marshall in *The Physiology of Reproduction*, 2nd ed., 1922, pp. 137 and 365, and *Q. Jl. Micr. Sci.*, Vol. 49, 1905, p. 189.

3682   The right ovary, oviduct, and corresponding extremity of the uterus of a Ewe (*Ovis aries*) which had been killed probably less than three days after the coitus.

Two vacated ovisacs are shown; the orifice in each, from which the ovum has escaped, is still patent and is surrounded by a circular lip, formed by the tumid and everted theca, with probably parts of the epithelial lining of the follicle.

A section has been made of each ovisac, exposing its cavity, into which a portion of a small quill is introduced; the parts have been minutely injected and the vascularity, thickness, and the corrugation of the fibrous and epithelial walls of the sac are well demonstrated.

A bristle is inserted into the abdominal aperture of the oviduct.

3683   One of the ovaries and oviducts of a Ewe, at a later period after impregnation, minutely injected.

The point whence the impregnated ovum escaped is indicated by a vascular mammilloid prominence on the surface of the ovary; but no trace is left of the orifice which is now healed over.

Two parallel sections have been made through the ovary, one through the centre, the other by the side of the mammilloid prominence; both of them show the large size and spherical form of the epithelial and fibrous mass which forms the corpus luteum.

A thin layer of loose fibrous tissue intervenes between the surface of the corpus luteum and the general stroma of the ovary.

The remains of the original cavity of the follicle, very much reduced, may be seen in the central section a little below the centre of the corpus luteum; it is occupied by a reticulum of fibrous tissue derived from the theca interna.

The substance of the ovary, beneath the corpus luteum, consists chiefly of a plexus of large vessels.

3684   The two ovaries of a Ewe, minutely injected and bisected.

In one of these—the lower specimen—there is a corpus luteum, in an advanced condition. It consists of the greatly hypertrophied cells of the membrana granulosa of the Graafian follicles permeated by vascular off-shoots of the fibrous theca interna.

3685   The ovary and oviduct of a Ewe at apparently eight weeks after impregnation.

Two impregnated ova have escaped from this ovary and their vacated follicles have subsequently been transformed into corpora lutea. These are shown, by a section through the ovary, to consist of lobulated masses of epithelium separated by strands of connective tissue, which converge towards the centre, where they form a fibrous plug filling the remains of the original cavity of the follicles.

3686   A similar preparation in a less perfect condition.

3687   The ovary, oviduct, and corresponding extremity of the uterine horn of a Cow (*Bos taurus*).

The ovary is bisected, showing some of the ovisacs, enlarged and in the natural state before the discharge of the ovum. Towards the outer extremity is a vacated ovisac, showing the thickening of the walls by a great development of the cells of the membrana granulosa, though at this stage the cavity of the sac is still patent.

A black bristle is inserted into the abdominal aperture of the Fallopian tube.

3688   The ovary of a Cow, killed during the period of uterine gestation; it is described in the *Manuscript Catalogue* as having had a slink-calf *in utero*, but the size of the embryo is not stated. From the appearance of the ovary it may be concluded that not many weeks had elapsed since impregnation took place.

The ovary is bisected; nearly the whole of its substance is occupied by a corpus luteum. The place whence the ovum escaped is indicated by a mammilloid prominence. The corpus luteum is divided through the middle of its mammilloid eminence, the original cavity of the follicle is filled by a plug of connective tissue derived from the theca interna, and presenting the appearance of a linear white trace leading from the middle of the cut surface of the mammilloid eminence to the centre of the corpus luteum, slightly expanding as it proceeds.

From this trace, white lines diverge towards the surrounding capsule and indicate the path of intrusion of outgrowths of vascular tissue from the theca interna among the enlarged cells of the membrana granulosa, that form the mass of the corpus luteum.

3689 The two ovaries of a Cow killed apparently at an early period after gestation. The lower ovary in the bottle is that from which the impregnated ovum has escaped; a longitudinal section has been removed from it. In its size, in the form and condition of the mammilloid eminence and in the fibrous trace of the original follicle, this corpus luteum resembles the preceding one. Adjoining it is an ovisac of large size from which the ovum and the epithelial tunics of the follicle have been removed.

The thin, fibrous tunic here shown takes part in the formation of the corpus luteum after the escape of the impregnated ovum, by providing a vascular network among the enlarged cells of the membrana granulosa which constitute the main mass of the body.

The ovary mounted above shows the ordinary appearance of that organ.

3690 The ovary of a Cow, bisected through the middle of the mammilloid eminence and showing a corpus luteum similar in all respects to the two preceding specimens.

3691 The ovary of a Cow, showing a similar corpus luteum. It is stated in the *Manuscript Catalogue* to be from a Cow in which impregnation had taken place and the calf was a little advanced.

3692 The ovary of a Sow (*Sus scrofa*), removed ten days after coitus; the ovisacs from which the ripe ova have escaped have been laid open.

The aperture through which each ovum passed is still patent and leads into a small cavity surrounded by a thick compact layer formed by the hypertrophy of the membrana granulosa. Within the cavity is a flocculent-looking material, which is probably the remains of the liquor folliculi, with possibly some admixture of blood.

3693 Two sections of the ovary of a Sow, at a later period after impregnation of the ovum, showing in each a few small ovisacs and one corpus luteum. In the latter the original cavity of the follicle is still a considerable size, though the altered cells of the membrana granulosa that constitute the bulk of the luteal tissue are much more developed than in the preceding specimen.

3694 The ovary of a Sow, removed apparently a short time after impregnation and minutely injected.

The ova have escaped from some of the ovisacs, the point of exit being marked by a nipple-like prominence, formed mainly of the everted vascular and tumid internal theca of the follicle. In one instance the summit of the prominence is occupied by a white non-vascular substance, which is apparently a plug formed by the coagulation of extruded liquor folliculi of the epithelial lining of the follicle. In another instance (seen on the right) the passage through which the ovum escaped seems to have closed, but the cavity of the follicle still persists.

3695 The other ovary of (apparently) the same Sow, in which the corpora lutea present similar conditions.

In one of the corpora lutea (on the left) which has been vertically bisected, the cavity of the ovisac is nearly obliterated by the growth of the luteal tissue which, advancing centripetally from each side and below, has reduced the vertical section to a linear triradiate figure. In other ovisacs from which sections have been removed, the remains of the follicular cavity present the same size as in the corpora lutea of the preceding specimen.

3696 A portion of the ovary of a Sow, sixteen days after coitus, injected.

Five of the corpora lutea are shown in section; the section passes through the cicatrix that marks the exit of the ovum and through the remains of the follicular cavity. This cavity is reduced to a linear fissure by the ingrowth of the modified cells of the membrana granulosa and the vascular fibrous tissue of the theca interna. The deeper parts of the original cavity are occupied by a plug of connective tissue derived from the theca interna; the more distal, open, part contains a certain amount of extravasated injected mass.

A transverse section has been removed from the corpus luteum below the one just described; here the remains of the original follicular cavity are filled by what appears to be a plug of connective tissue. The radiate arrangement of the vascular strands of connective tissue intruding from the theca interna towards the remains of the follicular cavity is well shown. It gives the substance of the corpus luteum the appearance of division into lobes (the acini of Haller).

3697 A longitudinal section of the ovary, with the corresponding Fallopian tube, of a Sow.

The section exposes four corpora lutea in which the cavity of the ovisac is completely obliterated.

The specimen has been minutely injected, showing the great vascularity of the corpora lutea.

3698 A section of the ovary of a Sow, at apparently a later period after coitus.

Five corpora lutea are shown in section. The original cavity of the ovisac has in each case been completely obliterated by the centripetal growth of the vascular and epithelial tissues of the follicular walls. The specimen has been injected to show the great vascularity of the corpora lutea and the sharp differentiation of their tissue from the surrounding general stroma of the ovary.

3699 The ovary and adjoining parts of a Mare (*Equus caballus*). A longitudinal section has been removed from the ovary and a thin slice reflected from the cut surface; this exposes the cavities of a few ovisacs from which the ovum and its surrounding fluid have been removed; it likewise shows three corpora lutea, in each of which the original cavity of the ovisac has been completely obliterated by the growth of the luteal tissue. Its position is occupied (in the corpus luteum on the left) by an irregular branching mass of vascular connective tissue. The small corpus luteum in the centre of the specimen shows the vascularity of the connective tissue that permeates and supports the luteal cells.

3700 The ovary and ovisac of a Mare, four weeks after impregnation. The ovary is laid open by an incision through the vacated ovisac, a small part of the cavity of which still remains unobliterated by the surrounding luteal tissue. The cavity is occupied by a loose reticulum, probably consisting of the coagulated remains of the liquor folliculi.

The cerebriform plication of the corpus luteum due to the meshwork of connective tissue that supports the luteal cells is well displayed in this preparation.

3701 The ovary, Fallopian tube, and contiguous portion of the uterine horn of an Ass (*Equus asinus*).

A section of the ovary has been made through the corpus luteum, showing that the original cavity of the ovisac has been obliterated by the ingrowth of the hypertrophied cells of the membrana granulosa of the follicle, except a small vestige occupied by a delicate reticulum.

The appearance of the corpus luteum presented in this preparation corresponds with that described by Hunter in the following note:

'On Friday the 2nd of October, 1789, my she-Ass took the male, and on the Tuesday following I killed her about seven in the morning, making in all what is called four days, but only ninety-two hours. The uterus was immediately taken out, and it was observed that one ovarium was much larger than the other. It was injected on both sides, and in both veins and arteries. When injected, the increased ovarium was much redder than the other, as

C.H.M.—M

also was the horn of the uterus on that side. I cut through the small ovarium
first, to see if it led to the better exposing of the other.

'I then slowly divided the other, in which I cut across several small hydatids
(ovisacs), but I came to a glandular substance distinct from the surrounding
parts in structure; and dividing that, along with the other parts, I came to a
kind of cavity in which there seemed to be a kind of fine and loose cellular
membrane, in the centre of which was a small rounded body, which was a
little bag; for in dividing this part I had cut off a little of the side of the bag,
into which hole a small globule of air had entered. Within this was an oblong
body, which, when taken out, looked like a little coagulable lymph.'

Works, vol. v, p. 199.

3702   The ovary of a Quadruped of unknown species. It had recently been impregnated
and a great portion of the ovary is occupied by a single corpus luteum.

The parenchymoid capsule of the ovisac appears unusually dense. The small
remains of the primitive cavity of the ovisac, having a smooth surface, may be
seen on one side of the section.

3703   Two ovaries with their oviducts and the corresponding extremities of the horns of
the uterus of an unnamed quadruped, but which from the form and structure
of the ovarian capsules and ovaries, and their relative positions to each other,
must have been a species of *Canis*, most probably the domestic Dog.

The animal had recently been impregnated; one ovary presents the still
patent orifices of five vacated ovisacs; four of these (lower specimen) are left
entire; their margins though raised and slightly thickened, are less tumid and
everted than in the Sheep (3682); a small portion of coagulum protrudes from
each. In the fifth ovisac, which has been vertically bisected, the original cavity
of the ovisac can be traced as a narrow chink from the external aperture to the
middle of the mass of luteal tissue.

In the other ovary a section has been removed from each of the vacated
ovisacs, showing a similar condition of the corpus luteum.

In each specimen a bristle has been passed through the restricted orifice of
the ovarian capsule.

3704   The ovary, oviduct, and corresponding portion of the horn of the uterus of a
species of *Canis*,* most probably a pregnant Bitch.

Half of the ovarian capsule has been cut away to expose the contained ovary
and Fallopian funnel.

---

* Called in Home's Catalogue 'ovarium and horn of the Sow'.

In this case gestation has further advanced than in the preceding. The orifices of the vacated ovisacs have cicatriced. Two of the corpora lutea are in section to show the complete obliteration of the original cavity of the ovisac by the hypertrophy of the luteal cells derived from the membrana granulosa of the follicles.

3705 A section of the ovary of a young Woman, in the fourth week of pregnancy; it includes a slice of the middle of the corpus luteum. This body occupies more than one third of the entire ovary; immediately above it, in the preparation, are the evident remains of a previous corpus luteum with its centre occupied by a plug of whitish connective tissue and the whole surrounded by a vascular layer of ovarian stroma.

Several undischarged ovisacs are likewise laid open; in three of these the ovarian vesicle is preserved; in the fourth it has been removed, showing the lining of the follicle from which after impregnation the corpus luteum is produced.

3706 A section of a Human ovary at the ninth month of pregnancy; it has been minutely injected and shows in close juxtaposition an empty ovisac which has contained an ovum ripe for impregnation and a corpus luteum. The walls of the unimpregnated ovisac are comparatively thin and unvascular, its cavity on the contrary, is considerable. The periphery of the corpus luteum is occupied by a dense, highly vascular tissue in which the blood vessels are radially disposed.

In the centre is a mass of whitish unvascular tissue.

3707 A Human ovary bisected to show a large corpus luteum.

The trace of the original cavity of the ovisac presents the form of a small, white, opaque, irregular streak of condensed fibrous tissue from which lines radiate into the epithelial mass of the corpus luteum.

3708 A human ovary, bisected to show a large corpus luteum, at a similar stage of development to the preceding specimen.

3709 A human ovary and oviduct with the ovary bisected to show a corpus luteum similar to those seen in the two preceding preparations.

One half of the corpus luteum has been turned out of its cavity in the ovarian stroma, showing the condensed layer of the connective tissue of the ovary by which the corpus luteum is surrounded.

3710   A human ovary and oviduct with the ovary divided through a corpus luteum
similar to those previously shown.

   The central mass of connective tissue still bears trace in its centre of the
original cavity of the ovisac.

3711   A human ovary and oviduct finely injected.

   The bisected ovary shows well the vascularity of the tissue of the corpus
luteum and the radial disposition of the connective tissue framework that
supports the luteal cells.   In the centre is a conspicuous cavity—the remains
of the original cavity of the ovisac.   The lacerated orifice by which the ovum
escaped is not cicatriced.

3712   The ovary and oviduct of a Woman at an advanced stage of pregnancy, or
immediately subsequent to parturition.

   The parts have been injected and the ovary bisected to show the corpus
luteum.   In the centre of the corpus luteum is a small remnant of the original
cavity of the ovisac immediately surrounded by a layer of white unvascular
connective tissue, which sends radiating processes outwards into the substance
of the luteal tissue.

3713   The ovary and oviduct of a Woman, apparently removed at an advanced stage
of gestation, or soon after parturition.   A corpus luteum has been mesially
divided, showing in its centre an extensive cavity three lines in diameter, which
is lined by a delicate membrane and surrounded by a dense layer of non-vascular
tissue.

   Around this lies a vascular zone of luteal cells, in which the blood vessels are
radially disposed.

3714   The ovary, oviduct, and a section of the uterus of a Woman at the close of
gestation.

   The ovary has been bisected and a corpus luteum divided nearly through its
centre; it exhibits a cavity similar to that of the preceding preparation but
larger and with its lining membrane more immediately coherent with the white
non-vascular layer that lies within the covering zone of luteal tissue.

Foetal Peculiarities

3715   A foetal Dog (*Canis familiaris*) with the abdominal wall removed from the left side
to show the vitelline blood vessels passing from the umbilicus to the mesentery

of the small intestine. In the original description (Owen's *Catalogue of the Physiological Series*, Vol. V, p. 195) one of these vessels is identified with the vitelline duct but a close examination shows that this cannot be correct, as both pass on to the mesentery and neither forms a direct attachment to the gut.

In the pelvic region may be seen the fusiform urinary bladder extending between the two large allantoic arteries to the umbilicus; and from the umbilicus the voluminous allantoic vein (marked by a black bristle) may be traced passing towards the posterior surface of the liver.

3716 A foetal Dog with the abdominal walls and small intestine removed, showing the elongated form of the urinary bladder and its continuation by the urachus into the umbilical cord.

The position of the ovaries attached to the lower end of the kidneys may be observed; they are not yet enclosed in peritoneal capsules as they are in the adult.

The horns of the uterus are filamentary. On the left side a bristle has been passed behind the round ligament.

3717 The heart of a young Porpoise (*Phocaena communis*), soon after birth.

Parts of the walls of the auricles and ventricles, and of the aorta and pulmonary artery have been removed, showing the foramen ovale or open passage in the upper part of the inter-auricular septum, through which the two auricles are in communication in the foetus.

The foramen is a large oval window partly screened from below by a delicate lip of membrane, so set that its free edge projects as a valve into the left auricle.

The ductus arteriosus, or open passage between the pulmonary artery and aorta, which in the foetus carries the blood from the right ventricle into the systemic circulation, is in progress of obliteration, though still patent.

3718 A portion of the ventricles of the heart of a foetal Calf (*Bos taurus*) including the origins of the aorta and pulmonary artery.

The walls of these two vessels are of great thickness and at this period show no marked disparity in this respect.

In later life the pulmonary artery is thin in comparison with the aorta.

3719 The heart of a Human foetus, from which the apex has been removed to show the nearly equal thickness of the walls of the ventricles at this period, though those of the left ventricle are denser and less reticulate than those of the right.

From the great size and capacity of the ductus arteriosus the descending aorta appears rather as a continuation of the pulmonary artery than of the aortic arch.

3719A The heart of a Human foetus, injected, dried and preserved in turpentine.

The auricles have been opened to show the foramen ovale of which the lower two thirds are closed by membrane and the upper third is patent.

The ductus arteriosus is large.

This specimen probably belonged to Hunter's Kew Collection. (See above, p. 27).

3720 A foetal Nine-banded Armadillo (*Tatusia novemcincta*) with the ventral walls of the abdomen and the small intestine removed, principally to show the abdominal position of the testes, which they retain throughout life in this species.

3721 The lower half of the body of a foetal Calf (*Bos taurus*) with the ventral walls of the abdomen and all the viscera removed excepting the testes and urinary bladder, the kidneys, adrenal bodies, and rectum.

The preparation is made to show the abdominal position of the testes, which are suspended by a fold of peritoneum analogous to the broad ligament of the female. Posterior to the testes the fold bifurcates; within the outer division lies the gubernaculum, a fibrous strand comparable to the round ligament of the female; the inner division contains the vas deferens and is continued towards the mesial line behind the neck of the bladder.

3722 A foetal female Lamb (*Ovis aries*) similarly dissected to show the ovaria lying within the abdomen in a position comparable to that occupied by the testes at their first appearance. In most Mammals the testes later leave the abdomen, whereas the ovaries remain there permanently.

The peritoneal fold by which the ovaries and oviducts are suspended shows a bifurcation posteriorly, the outer subdivision of which contains the round ligament, and the inner the oviducts, thus presenting a condition similar to that shown in the male in the preceding specimen.

3723 The testis of a Foal (*Equus caballus*) before it has passed into the scrotum, with the abdominal ring and the pouch of peritoneum (processus vaginalis) projected through the ring towards the scrotum by the growth of the gubernaculum.

The gubernaculum may be seen descending from the posterior pole of the testis, bound up with the epididymis and continuing, from the point of reflexion of the vas, into the vaginal peritoneal pouch to its extremity.

The genital arteries have been injected.

3724 The opposite abdominal testis of the same Foal, with the vaginal peritoneal pouch inverted, to show the smooth continuity of its lining with the peritoneum that lines the wall of the abdomen and covers the gubernaculum and the suspensory ligament of the testis.

3725   The right testicle of a Ram (*Ovis aries*) which never passed into the scrotum.
        This testicle is figured *in situ* in *Animal Oeconomy*, 2nd ed., Pl. LV where the parts are thus described by Hunter (p. 29):

> 'A side view of the pelvis of a young Ram, to show the right testicle remaining in the cavity of the abdomen, after the left had come down, but which is removed with that half of the pelvis. The testicle which lies in the loins is flatter than common, and is only attached by one edge, which is principally by the epididymis; there is also a ligament passing from the upper part of the common attachment which binds the testicle to the posterior part of the abdominal muscles; this is analogous to the ligament that attaches the ovarium to the same part in the female quadruped. The epididymis passes along the outer or posterior edge, and at the lower part becomes larger and pendulous, making a little twist upon itself where it becomes vas deferens. The vas deferens is a little contorted, and passes down obliquely over the psoas muscle to the bladder. From the lower end of the testicle there is a ridge continued along the psoas muscle through the abdominal ring, going on to the scrotum which is most probably the gubernaculum; but it was so much covered by a hard suety fat, that I could not exactly ascertain its structure: at the lower part of this ridge, about an inch and a half from the ring, I found the termination of the cremaster, which was a tolerably large muscle; part of its fibres seemed to arise in common with the internal oblique, while the rest appeared to come from the psoas and iliacus internus behind it; the outer portion passed inwards and downwards, and spread upon the fore-part of the ridge, or gubernaculum, where the greatest part of its fibres were lost, and the rest of them were continued into the back part of it. The posterior portion got upon the inside of the ridge, and was lost in the same manner as the former.'

3726   The lower part of the trunk of a Human foetus, at the eighth month of gestation, with the ventral walls of the abdomen and most of the abdominal viscera removed.
        The walls of the left side of the scrotum have also been dissected away to show the left testis descended into that cavity; a bristle is passed through the peritoneal or abdominal canal along which it has passed, which still remains unobliterated.

The right testis may be seen within the abdomen resting upon the internal abdominal ring through which the gubernaculum is continued (it may have been artificially retracted within the abdomen).

3727   The ovary, Fallopian tubes, and uterus of an Infant, showing the narrow elongated angular form of the ovaries and their smooth external surface at this period of life.

3728   A foetal Dolphin (*Delphinus delphis*) about 200 mm. long, partially dissected.

The tip of the lower jaw and tongue has been cut off, exposing the roof of the mouth marked longitudinally close to either edge by the alveolar groove within which the teeth are developed.

In the cross section of the lower jaw may be seen, in a similar position, the intrusion of the soft tooth-forming gum into the dental groove of the mandible.

The ventral walls of the chest and abdomen have been removed, exposing the heart, with the large solid thymus body covering the roots of the large vessels, and on either side the lungs, from one of which a section has been removed to show its solid structure before use in respiration.

The left end of the thymus body is lifted by means of a bristle; and the ventral wall of the pericardium has been removed to show the acutely pointed single apex of the ventricles, a form retained in the heart of the adult.

Beneath the diaphragm may be seen the simple, non-lobulated liver with the umbilical vein (indicated by a black bristle) entering the notch between its two halves; another bristle is placed behind the elongated urachus. Between this and the liver lie the large and minutely lobulated kidney and the complex coils of the small intestine. The clitoris is more prominent than in the adult; a short distance behind it is the minute anal opening. The exposed surface of the umbilical cord is covered by small thorn-like processes.

3729   The foetus of a Walrus (*Odobaenus rosmarus*), about 160 mm. in length, with the ventral body walls and the greater part of the alimentary canal removed.

In the chest may be seen the hinder margin of the thymus body, covering the origin of the large vessels and the greater part of the auricles.

The ventricles are wide and flat with their apices far separated and clearly distinguishable superficially.

The liver is deeply lobulated; in the cleft between its two halves may be seen the umbilical vein cut across and supported by the falciform ligament.

The urachus and allantoic arteries have been cut across. On the left side of the abdominal cavity may be observed the minutely lobulated kidney with the smooth gonad lying along its postero-lateral margin.

Bristles are inserted into the cut ends of a loop of the small intestine. Externally the foetus shows closure of the eyelids and auditory orifices; the nostrils are open and soft bristles are present on the broad truncated muzzle.

Membrana Pupillaris

During the development of the eye a capsule of vascular mesenchyme is formed round the lens for its nourishment.

The anterior portion of this capsule extends between the lens and the iris, forming a vascular membrane (membrana pupillaris) spread across the pupil. In the human foetus it is most highly developed during the seventh month. Later it degenerates and at birth is completely lost.

The pupillary membrane and the rest of the vascular capsule of the lens is vascularised by the hyaloid artery of the vitreous, which radiates over its surface, being most richly arborescent at the equator of the lens.

3731   The anterior half of the coats of the eye of a Human foetus of the seventh month, injected.

Although in the original description this specimen is said to show the pupillary membrane and its vascularisation, no signs of the membrane can now be seen.

3733   The anterior parts of the sclerotic and choroid membranes of the eye of a foetus at full term, minutely injected.

In the original description of this specimen shreds of the membrana pupillaris were said to be attached to the free margin of the iris. These cannot now be seen.

3734   The tunica of the eye of a Human infant with the cornea removed; no trace of the membrana pupillaris remains.

3735   The iris, ciliary process and part of the choroid of an adult, minutely injected to show the complete absence of the membrana pupillaris.

Mammary Organs and Parts having an Analogous Office

'The nourishment of animals admits, perhaps, of as much variety in the mode by which it is to be performed as any circumstance connected with their oeconomy, whether we consider their numerous tribes, the different stages through which every animal passes, or the food adapted to the support of each in their distinct conditions and situations. We are likewise to include in this view that endless variety in the means by which this food is procured, according to the class of the animal and the particular stage of its existence. If the food was the same through every period of the life of an animal; if every individual of a tribe lived on the same kind, and procured it by the same mode, our speculations would then admit of a regular arrangement. But when we see that the food adapted to one stage of an animal's life is rejected at another, and that animals of one class in some respects resemble those of another, by hardly having any food peculiar to themselves, the subject becomes so complicated that it is not surprising if we are at a loss to arrange the various modes by which animals are nourished.

'Animal life may not improperly be divided into three states or stages. The first comprehends the production of the animal and its growth in the foetal state; the second commences when it emerges from that state by what is called the birth, yet for a certain time must, either mediately or immediately, depend on the parent for support; the third may be said to take place when the animal is fit and at liberty to act for itself. The first and third stages are perhaps common to all animals; but there are some classes, as fishes, spiders, &c., which seem to have no second stage, but pass directly from the first to what is the third in other animals. Of those requiring a second stage, the polypus and the viviparous animals continue to derive their nourishment immediately from the parent; while the oviparous are for some time supported by a substance originally formed with them, and reserved for that purpose.

'There is infinite variety in the means by which Nature provides for the support of the young in the second stage of animal life. In many insects it is effected by the female instinctively depositing the egg, or whatever contains the rudiments of the animal, in such a situation that, when hatched, it may be within reach of proper food; others, as the humble-bee and black-beetle, collect a quantity of peculiar substance, which both serves as a nidus for the egg, and nourishment for the maggot, when the embryo arrives at that state. Most birds, and many of the bee-tribe, collect food for their young; when at a more advanced period the task of feeding them is performed by both male and female, with an exception in the common bee, the young ones of which are not fed by either parent, but by the working-bees, which act the part of the nurse. There is likewise a number of animals capable of supplying immediately from their own bodies the nourishment proper for their offspring during this second stage, a mode of nourishment which has hitherto been supposed to be peculiar to that class of animals which Linnaeus calls Mammalia; nor has it, I imagine, been ever suspected to belong to any other.

'I have, however, in my inquiries concerning the various modes in which young animals are nourished, discovered that all of the dove kind are endowed with a similar power. The young pigeon, like the young quadruped, till it is capable of digesting the common food of its kind, is fed with a substance secreted for that purpose by the parent animal; not, as in the Mammalia, by the female alone, but also by the male, which, perhaps, furnishes this nutriment in a degree still more abundant. It is a common property of birds, that both male and female are equally employed in hatching, and in feeding their young in the second stage; but this particular mode of nourishment, by means of a substance secreted in their own bodies, is peculiar to certain kinds, and is carried on in the crop.

'Besides the dove kind, I have some reason to suppose parrots to be endowed with the same faculty, as they have the power of throwing up the contents of the crop, and feeding one another. I have seen the cock parroquet regularly feed the hen, by first filling his own crop, and then supplying her from his beak. Parrots, maccaws, cockatoos, &c., when they are very fond of the person who feeds them, may likewise be observed to have the action of throwing up the food, and often do it. The cock pigeon, when he caresses the hen, performs the same kind of action as when he feeds his young; but I do not know if at this time he throws up anything from the crop.

'During incubation the coats of the crop in the pigeon are gradually enlarged and thickened, like what happens to the udder of females of the class Mammalia in the term of uterine gestation. On comparing the state of the crop when the bird is not sitting, with its appearance during incubation, the difference is very remarkable. In the first case it is thin and membranous; but by the time the young are about to be hatched, the whole, except what lies on the trachea, becomes thicker, and takes on a glandular appearance, having its internal surface very irregular. It is likewise evidently more vascular than in its former state, that it may convey a quantity of blood sufficient for the secretion of the substance which is to nourish the young brood for some days after they are hatched.

'Whatever may be the consistence of this substance when just secreted, it most probably very soon coagulates into a granulated white curd, for in such form I have always found it in the crop; and if an old pigeon is killed just a the young ones are hatching, the crop will be found as above described, and in its cavity pieces of white curd, mixed with some of the common food of the pigeon, such as barley, beans, &c. If we allow either of the parents to feed the brood, the crop of the young pigeons when examined will be discovered to contain the same kind of curdled substance as that of the old ones, which passes from thence into the stomach, where it is to be digested.

'The young pigeon is fed for a little time with this substance only, as about the third day some of the common food is found mingled with it: as the pigeon grows older the proportion of common food is increased; so that by the time it is seven, eight, or nine days old, the secretion of the curd ceases in the old ones, and of course no more will be found in the crop of the young. It is a curious fact that the parent pigeon has at first a power to throw up this curd without any mixture of common food, although afterwards both are thrown up according to the proportion required for the young ones.

'I have called this substance curd, not as being literally so, but as resembling that more than anything I know; it may, however, have a greater resemblance to curd than we are perhaps aware of, for neither this secretion, nor curd from which the whey has been pressed, seems to contain any sugar, and do not run into the acetous fermentation. The property of coagulating is confined to the substance itself, as it produces no such effect when mixed with milk.

'This secretion in the pigeon, like all other animal substances, becomes putrid by standing, though not so readily as either blood or meat, it resisting putrefaction for a considerable time; neither will curd much pressed become putrid so soon as either blood or meat.'   *Works*, vol. iv, pp. 122-125.

The four following preparations illustrate the alteration that takes place in the structure of the crop of Pigeons of both sexes during the breeding season, for the purpose of secreting a food material, analogous to milk, for the nourishment of the nestlings:

3737   The anterior half of a Pigeon (*Columba aenas*) with the bilobed crop exposed and
          opened to show that at the non-breeding season its walls are thin and their
          surface smooth and even.

3738   A similar preparation of a Pigeon at the breeding season.
          At this season the lining membrane of the two lateral diverticula of the crop
          is increased in thickness, plication and glandular structure.

3739   The lower portion of the oesophagus of a Pigeon, including the crop with its two
          lateral diverticula and part of the proventricular chamber of the stomach,
          everted.

The walls of the crop are thin and smooth, in the condition usual at the non-breeding season.

This specimen is figured by Hunter (*Animal Oeconomy*, 2nd ed., Pl. XV).

3740   The corresponding parts of the male of the same species of Pigeon, similarly prepared to show the condition of the crop peculiar to the breeding season.

The walls of the two lateral diverticula are swollen and deeply corrugated by a complex network of folds.

Both parents contribute a nutritious secretion from the crop for the sustenance of the callow young.

This specimen is figured by Hunter (*Animal Oeconomy*, 2nd ed., Pl. XVI).

3741   A portion of the white curdy secretion of the thickened glandular membrane lining of the crop of the parent Pigeon, together with some grains which have been swallowed.

3742   One of the mammary glands and the integument supporting it, with the milk reservoir and nipple, of a large species of Dolphin (*Delphinus tursio*).

The gland is an elongated, sub-cylindrical, flattened mass of lobulated tissue extending forward deep to the blubber and the panniculus muscles from a point some few inches in front of the small slit in the integument, within which is lodged the nipple.

Between the gland and the nipple is a milk reservoir formed by a dilatation of the common duct into which open the collecting ducts of the gland. This reservoir has been slit open and marked by a large rod placed within it. A smaller rod has been passed from the reservoir through the small conical nipple by which the milk reaches the exterior.

The nipple, which may be seen on the reverse of the specimen, is bluntly conical and perforated by a single large channel. It projects from between the lips of a small longitudinal depression of the integument into which it can be withdrawn when not in use.

Hunter's description of the mammary apparatus of the Cetacea was based upon dissections of this species of Whale and in all probability upon this particular specimen, which was made from an animal caught near Berkeley with its young one. Dr. Edward Jenner dissected the animal.

The original Hunterian description of the Cetacean mammary apparatus runs as follows:

'The glands for the secretion of milk are two, one on each side of the middle line of the belly at its lower part. The posterior ends, from which go out the nipples, are on each side of the opening of the vagina, in small sulci. They are flat bodies lying between the external layer of fat and abdominal muscles and are of considerable length, but only one-fourth of that in breadth. They are thin, that they may not vary the external shape of the animal, and have a principal duct, running in the middle through the whole length of the gland, and collecting the smaller lateral ducts, which are made up of those still smaller. Some of these lateral branches enter the common trunk in the direction of the milk's passage, others in the contrary direction, especially those nearest to the termination of the trunk in the nipple. The trunk is large, and appears to serve as a reservoir for the milk, and terminates externally in a projection, which is the nipple. The lateral portions of the sulcus which incloses the nipple are composed of parts looser in texture than the common adipose membrane, which is probably to admit of the elongation or projection of the nipple. On the outside of this there is another small fissure, which, I imagine, is likewise intended to give greater facility to the movements of all these parts.

'The milk is probably very rich; for in that caught near Berkeley with its young one, the milk, which was tasted by Mr. Jenner and Mr. Ludlow, surgeon, at Sodbury, was rich, like cow's milk to which cream had been added.

'The mode in which these animals must suck would appear to be very inconvenient for respiration, as either the mother or young one will be prevented from breathing at the time, their nostrils being in opposite directions; therefore the nose of one must be under water, and the time of sucking can only be between each respiration. The act of sucking must likewise be different from that of land animals; as in them it is performed by the lungs drawing the air from the mouth backwards into themselves, which the fluid follows, by being forced into the mouth from the pressure of the external air on its surface; but in this tribe, the lungs having no connection with the mouth, sucking must be performed by some action of the mouth itself, and by its having the power of expansion.'   *Works*, vol. iv, p. 392.

3743 The mammary recess, with the small conical nipple lying within it, and a section of the milk reservoir of a young Piked Whale (*Balaena boops*).

The reservoir is covered externally by a thin layer of gland tissue, into which numerous large and small channels extend from its main cavity. Some of these channels open into the reservoir (as remarked by Hunter) in the direction of the flow of the milk, but the majority in the opposite direction.

In some of these channels rods have been inserted. Between the blubber and the gland and its reservoir is a layer of muscle, which thickens as it approaches the outlet of the reservoir. It is apparently part of the panniculus and (to judge by the condition in the Porpoise) forms a relatively narrow band of transversely set muscle bundles extending on either side of the mid-line for a certain distance towards the anterior end of the mammary gland. Its purpose would seem to be the expulsion of the milk.

3744 The mammary recess, nipple and part of the milk reservoir from the opposite side of the same Whale.

3745 The long conical nipple of some Quadruped.
The blunt extremity is perforated by several lactiferous ducts, into three of which bristles have been inserted.

3746 A section of the abdominal integument with two of the nipples of a Quadruped, probably a Sow, at the period of lactation; bristles are passed through the two large lactiferous ducts which traverse and open upon each nipple.

3747 One of the nipples of a Sow (*Sus scrofa*) at the period of lactation, from one side of which a section has been removed.
The nipple, which is covered by delicate wrinkled skin, is flaccid and sub-globular in shape. Upon its apex may be seen the independent openings of a number of lactiferous ducts.

3748 The extremity of the nipple of a Quadruped. The surface of the nipple is covered with deeply wrinkled papillate integument. Upon the apex are two circular areas punctured by lactiferous ducts, the punctures in each being arranged in a circle surrounding a central one.
On the section surface numerous bristles have been inserted into the lactiferous ducts.

3749 This preparation is described by Owen (*Catalogue of the Physiological Series*, 1840, Vol. 5, p. 207) as 'a portion of the integument including the base of the "preputium clitoridis", and the two nipples situated one on each side of that part of the Mare'.
It is difficult to associate the sleeve-like protrusion of skin lying between the nipples as any part of the female external genitalia. It might, however, well be the basal parts of the scrotum; in which case the nipples are those of the rudimentary mammae of the Horse.

3750   A portion of skin, with two small conical nipples and the corresponding mammary
       glands, said to be of the Horse.
           Bristles are inserted into the two lactiferous ducts which open at the end of
       each nipple.

3751   A section of part of the mammary gland and one of the teats of a Cow (*Bos taurus*).
           The teat is occupied by a large cylindrical receptacular cavity, constricted at
       its opening to the exterior and communicating at the base by large orifices with
       the collecting ducts of the gland.

3752   A Bandicoot Rat (*Mus giganteus*) showing the number and position of the nipples,
       which are six on each side, extending from the pectoral to the inguinal region.

3753   A Mouse (*Mus musculus*) showing the number and situation of its nipples; three on
       each side of the pectoral and three on each side of the inguinal regions.

3754   A large species of Fruit Bat (*Pteropus sp.*) with the hair and cuticle removed showing
       its two large nipples situated one beneath each axillary region.
           The nipples have the characteristic flattened sub-pedunculate form shown in
       the other specimens of Fruit Bats.

3755   A section of the integument from the pectoral and axillary region of a Fruit Bat
       (*Pteropus sp.*) showing the large and compressed sub-pedunculate nipple.

3756   A section of the integument of the breast of a young woman, including the blunt
       conical nipple.
           It shows the orifices of the lactiferous ducts upon the obtuse apex of the cone,
       the wrinkled integument forming the sides of the cone and the circle of large
       sebaceous glands surrounding its base.

3757   The extremity of the breast of a Woman at the period of lactation.
           The nipple and areola have much increased in size in comparison with the
       resting condition.   (See No. 1429, *Catalogue of the Physiological Series*, Vol. I, 1970,
       p. 187).
           The orifices of the milk tubes upon the convex apex of the nipple are very
       conspicuous.

       Marsupial Pouch, Mammae and Mammary Foetus in the Mammalia

3758   The posterior half of a Tapoa Tafa (*Phascogale penicillata*) with the abdominal fold of integument forming the marsupial pouch artificially dilated and everted to show the nipples.

These are eight in number, arranged in a circle; they are elongated, sub-compressed with an obtusely rounded apex and appear to have been in use when the animal was caught.

A footnote in Owen's *Catalogue* (p. 209) states that 'the specimen which Hunter has sacrificed for this preparation, is the individual from which were taken the description and figure of the species, under the name of Tapao Tafa, given in the Zoological Appendix to "White's Journal of a Voyage to New South Wales", 4to, 1790' (p. 281).*

---

* '*The Tapoa Tafa, or Tapha*
'This animal is the size of a rat, and, has very much the appearance of the martin cat, but hardly so long in the body in proportion to size.
'The head is flat forwards, and broad from side to side, especially between the eyes and ears; the nose is peaked, and projecting beyond the teeth, which makes the upper jaw appear to be considerably longer than the lower; the eyes are pretty large; the ears broad, especially at their base, not becoming regularly narrower to a point, nor with a very smooth edge, and having a small process on the concave, or inner surface, near to the base. It has long whiskers from the sides of the cheeks, which begin forwards, near the nose, by small and short hairs, and become longer and stronger as they approach the eyes. It has very much the hair of a rat, to which it is similar in colour; but near to the setting on of the tail, it is of a lighter brown, forming a broad ring round it. The fore feet are shorter than the hind, but much in the same proportion as those of the rat; the hind feet are more flexible. There are five toes on the fore feet, the middle the largest, falling off on each side nearly equally; but the fore, or inner toe, is rather shortest; they are thin from side to side, the nails are pretty broad, laterally, and thin at their base; not very long but sharp; the animal walks on its whole palm, on which there is no hair. The hind feet are pretty long, and have five toes; that which answers to our great toe is very short, and has no nail; the next is the longest in the whole, falling gradually off to the outer toe; the shape of the hind toes is the same as in the fore feet, as are likewise the nails; it walks nearly on the whole foot. The tail is long and covered with long hair, but not all of the same colour.
'The teeth of this creature are different from any other animal yet known. The mouth is full of teeth. The lower jaw narrow in comparison to the upper, more especially backwards, which allows of much broader grinders in this jaw than in the lower, and which occasions the grinders in the upper jaw to project considerably over those in the lower. In the middle the cuspidati oppose one another, the upper piercers, or holders, go behind those of the lower; the second class of incisors in the lower jaw overtop those of the upper while the two first in the lower go within, or behind those of the upper. In the upper jaw, before the holders, there are four teeth on each side, three of which are pointed, the point standing on the inner surface; and the two in front are longer, stand more obliquely forwards, and appear to be appropriated for a particular use. The holders are a little way behind the last fore teeth, to allow those of the lower jaw to come between. They are pretty long, the cuspidati on each side become longer and larger towards the grinders; they are points or cones placed on a broad base.
'There are four grinders on each side, the middle two the largest, the last the least; their base is a triangle of the scalenus kind, or having one angle obtuse and two acute. Their base is composed of two surfaces, an inner and an outer, divided by processes or points: it is the inner that the grinders of the lower jaw oppose, when the mouth is regularly shut. The lower jaw has three fore teeth, or incisors, on each side; the first considerably the largest, projecting obliquely forwards; the other two of the same kind, but smaller, the last the smallest.
'The holder in this jaw is not so large as in the upper jaw and close to the incisors. There are three cuspidati, the middle one the largest, the last the least; these are cones standing on their base, but not on the middle, rather on the anterior side. There are four grinders, the two middle the largest, and rather quadrangular, each of which has a high point or cone on the outer edge, with a smaller, and three more diminutive on the inner edge. It is impossible to say critically, what the various forms of these teeth are adapted for from the general principles of teeth. In the front we have what may divide and tear off; behind those, there are holders or destroyers; behind the latter, such as will assist in mashing, as the grinders of the lion, and other carniverous animals; and last of all, grinders, to divide parts into smaller portions, as in the graminiverous tribe: the articulation of the jaw in some degree admits of all those motions.'
John White, *Journal of a Voyage to New South Wales*, 1790, p. 281.

C.H.M.—N

3759 An Opossum (*Didelphys opossum*) showing the two opposite lateral semilunar folds of integument that form the marsupial pouch, with the nipples, of which five were in use when the animal was killed. A young Opossum far advanced in growth, covered with hair, and with its eyes open, adheres to one of the nipples.

3760 A portion of the ventral walls of the abdomen and the pelvis of a Virginian Opossum (*Didelphys virginiana*), showing the large oval entry to the marsupial pouch, and at some little distance behind it the opening of the cloaca.

3761 The pouch young of an Opossum, showing its immature condition; naked and with the eyelids and ears closed. The mouth is reduced by concrescence of the lips to a small round orifice adapted to adhere closely to the teat.

The marsupial pouch is but slightly indicated by a low crescentic fold of the integument leaving exposed the mammary area with six teats.

3762 A large female mammary foetus of a Pigmy Flying Opossum (*Petaurus pigmaeus*) or Petaurist showing the entry to the marsupial pouch directed forwards in the mid-line of the abdomen.

3763 A young male Petaurist. The mouth has assumed the form natural to the adult; the eyelids are open; the fold of skin between the fore and hind-leg on each side, which constitutes the parachute characteristic of this genus, is displayed; the testes have descended into the pedunculate scrotum, which occupies the position characteristic of marsupials anterior to the penis.

The cuticle and hair have been removed from the specimen.

3764 The mammary foetus of a Vulpine Phalanger (*Trichosurus vulpecula*) apparently at a period shortly after birth.

The foetus is little more than an inch in length. The situation of the eyes is scarcely discernable; the ears are indicated by small projections; a fine white line, like a cicatrix, indicates the fused lateral ends of the oral slit, the central part of which only is open; the end of the tongue, which is bent with its concavity towards the roof of the mouth for the firm embrace of the nipple, may be seen close to the subcircular, terminal oval aperture.

The walls of the abdomen have been reflected downwards.

3765 A young female Phalanger (*Phalangista gliriformis*) at the stage when the eyes and ears are still closed, showing the position of the two lateral folds of skin that bound the immature marsupial pouch.

The mammary area of the skin lying between the marsupial folds includes the umbilicus.

3766   A portion of the dorsal wall of the marsupial pouch of a Kangaroo (*Macropus major*) with the mammary glands and teats.

   The lower nipple on the left side has been in use at the time when the animal was killed and, from its great length and size, the mammary foetus must have been far advanced; the other nipples are not larger than those shown in previous specimens and are all of about equal size.

   The mammary glands have been dissected to show their lobulated structure.

3767   The upper and lower nipples from one side of the marsupial pouch of a Kangaroo (*Macropus sp.*) which was suckling a mammary foetus with the lower nipple.

   Upon the reverse of the specimen a dissection has been made of the lower nipple, exposing the lactiferous ducts running within it, parallel to one another, to their openings upon its apex.

3768   A male mammary foetus of a Kangaroo (*Macropus sp.*), showing its general form and the position in front of the penis of the pedunculate scrotum, at about the spot occupied by the marsupial pouch in the female.

   The right side of the mouth has been removed to show the extent to which the nipple is received into the buccal cavity and how firmly it is grasped between the tongue and palate.

3769   A female mammary foetus of a Kangaroo (*Macropus sp.*), with the right half of the head removed to show the concavity in the dorsum of the tongue for the reception of the nipple and great development and pyramidal form of the epiglottis and its permanent protrusion into the naso-pharynx through the small circular aperture of the posterior nares. This fixation of the epiglottis within the nasal passage removes all risk of the trachea being invaded by milk which may be injected down the fauces of the foetus by the mammary compressor muscle of the parent.

3770   A section of the lower jaw and tongue, with the soft palate and larynx of a mammary foetus of a Kangaroo (*Macropus sp.*).

   The parts are attached to the extremity of the teat of the parent, showing the mode in which the nipple is grasped by the tongue and the position of the larynx relative to the soft palate.

The basal parts of the teat have been dissected to show the lactiferous ducts passing to their openings upon the apex of the nipple.

3771   A mammary foetus of a Kangaroo (*Macropus sp.*), from which the right half of the head and the abdominal walls have been removed.

The large urinary bladder has been reflected forwards to show its smooth, rounded fundus.

A bristle has been passed through the nasal meatus and comes out by the side of the larynx, which is in its natural position within the posterior nares grasped by the muscles of the soft palate. The nipple of the parent is left in the mouth of the foetus lodged in the groove on the dorsum of the tongue.

3772   A male mammary foetus of a Kangaroo (*Macropus sp.*), at a fairly advanced stage of development.

The peculiarities of the adult and in particular the disproportionate size of the hind legs have been acquired, though as yet they are not so pronounced as they will finally become.

The fusion of the lateral parts of the lips is breaking down, but the eyelids and ears are still closed.

3773   A female mammary foetus of a Kangaroo (*Macropus sp.*), at a slightly more advanced stage of development.

In the centre of the abdomen is the mouth of the marsupial pouch.

The lateral fusion of the lips is still maintained although it is in process of breaking down.

3774   A male mammary foetus of a Kangaroo (*Macropus sp.*), at about the same stage of development.

3775   A female mammary foetus of a Kangaroo (*Macropus sp.*), considerably further advanced in development.

The hind legs have nearly acquired their normal proportions.

The lateral fusion of the lips has disappeared, but the eyelids are still closed.

3776   A male mammary foetus of a Kangaroo (*Macropus sp.*), of still greater size, measuring twelve inches (306 mm.) from the snout to the tip of the tail.

The lips are free from end to end and the eyelids are now open, but there is as yet no trace of hair upon any part of the integument.

3777   A female Opossum (*Didelphys dorsigera*), with two of her young, showing the mode

FIG. 10

A Toad (*Bufo dorsigera*) carrying one of its young.   Specimen No. 3778.

by which they are transported from place to place by the mother, adhering to the fur of her back by means of their claws, and entwining their tails around hers.

In this as in many other of the small species of Opossum, the marsupial folds of the abdominal integument are so shallow as not to conceal the nipples nor to afford the parent the means of transporting her young in the mode which is peculiar to the rest of the order; it may be observed, however, that the marsupial bones are relatively as well developed as in those which possess a deep marsupial pouch.

Nidamental Structures

(Natural or artificial cavities for the incubation or protection of the young)

3778 A Toad (*Bufo dorsiger*) with one of its young, which are transported by the parent, clinging to her back, like the young of the dorsigerous Opossum.

The three following preparations illustrate the adaptation of the skin of the back of the female Surinam Toad for the protection of the developing young from the time that the egg is laid till they are of a size to fend for themselves.

The structure of the modified skin has been fully described by A. V. Klinckowström (*Zool. Jb.*, Bd. 7 (Anat.) 1894, p. 620); and the process of egg-laying by A. D. Bartlett (*Proc. Zool. Soc.*, 1896, p. 595).

In the act of coition, the male toad grasps the female in front of the hind legs, as do other Anura, but fertilisation probably takes place before the actual laying of the eggs. When these are about to be laid, the female everts her cloaca for an extent of one inch or more and, pushing it under the male, spreads the eggs as they are laid over the surface of her back, where they firmly adhere. In this process the male appears to assist by squeezing the everted cloaca from side to side. After egg laying, the male leaves the female and her cloaca is slowly withdrawn.

The skin of the back of the female over an area extending from a few cm. behind the snout to within two or three cm. of the anus becomes swollen after the deposition of the eggs till it attains 15-17 mm. in depth; beneath it lies one of the great subcutaneous lymph sinuses. Under each egg is formed a pit or cell, some 10-15 mm. in depth, which is lined by an epithelium continuous with that covering the general surface of the body, except for the absence of the spinelets characteristic of the ordinary integument.

The mouth of each cell is slightly narrower than the general cavity and is closed by a lid which differs in structure from the lining membrane of the cell and apparently is a secretion-product of the egg membranes.

The walls of each cell are highly vascular, with capillaries invading even the lining epithelium. Enclosed within these cells the eggs develop into tail-less tadpoles and young toads and eventually leave the cells to carry on their independent life.

3779   A female Surinam Toad (*Pipa monstrosa*) showing the tegumentary cells on the back in which the young are protected and transported by the parent during the whole period of their development.

3780   A similar specimen, exhibiting the incubating cells at their period of functional activity; many of the young are here seen in the act of extricating themselves from the cells, their metamorphosis having been completed.   The cells which still retain the larvae have their mouths covered over with a thin lid of some homogeneous material, whose origin is doubtful, but it is most probably the egg.

3781   The right half of a vertically bisected Surinam Toad with some of her young brood in the dorsal cells.

   The modified skin is separated from the muscles of the back by a wide lymph reservoir, similar to that found in ordinary Toads and Frogs.

3782   A female Cray-fish (*Astacus fluviatilis*) showing the broadening of the abdomen which is associated with the habit of carrying the impregnated eggs for their protection under cover of this segment of the body, attached by threads of hardened secretion to the abdominal appendages or pleopods.

3783   A female Cray-fish with numerous vacated egg-shells and newly hatched young attached to the pleopods or abdominal appendages.

   In the Cray-fish the eggs, as they are laid, are enveloped in a sticky secretion which adheres to the hairs of the pleopods and is drawn out to form a thread by which the egg is firmly anchored.   After hatching the ruptured egg-shells remain glued to the pleopods to which the young also become attached by grasping them with their chelae.   Here the young remain fixed till the first moult (ten days); after that, till twenty-eight days old, they leave the mother at will, returning to her for protection in case of alarm.

   By their attachment to the pleopods the eggs and young are not only afforded protection but by sharing in the movements of these appendages are duly aerated and cleansed.   T. H. Huxley, *The Crayfish*, 1880, p. 40.

3785   A male Pipe Fish (*Syngnathus typhle*) with the abdomen opened and the fold of the integument that covers the left half of the subcaudal brood pouch cut away.

   The brood pouch consists of a depression upon the under surface of the tail; arched over by two integumentary folds that spring from its latero-ventral margins.

   The removal of one of these folds has exposed the impregnated ova within the pouch massed together upon the ventral surface of the tail and partly embedded in delicate honeycombed tissue produced from the integument.

In this position, the ova and embryos are not only protected from harm but receive nourishment secreted by the tissues in which they are embedded.

Within the body cavity may be seen the testes much diminished in size after the completion of their function.

Rud. Kolster, 'Die Embryotrophe bei den Lophobranchiern', *Anat. Hefte*, Bd. 34, 1907, p. 401.

3786 A male Pipe Fish of the same species, with the folds of skin that enclose the sub-caudal brood pouch reflected to either side.

The brood pouch is empty except for a few ova at its anterior end.

3788 A Wag-tail (*Motacilla lugubris*) with her nest and callow brood.

3789 A Nightingale (*Luscinia philomela*) with her nest and young.

3790 The nest and models of the young of a Field-mouse (*Arvicola arvensis*).

II

Undissected Invertebrates

The specimens to which this part of the General Catalogue relates consist for the most part of entire or undissected animals, and constitute one of the three great divisions of preparations in spirit under the heading of Natural History.

This division originated in the preservation of natural objects sent to Hunter for the purposes of dissection; which, accumulating as his reputation increased and as the leisure for their examination became abridged, enabled him to exhibit in a series the most remarkable differences in the outward forms of the animal kingdom.

It does not appear, however, that they were at any time instrumental in illustrating his opinions of the natural disposition and relations of the several classes of animals; no other conclusion, indeed, could be drawn from their original position, than that they were intended to have been displayed in the ascending order.

In all the cases where a record has been preserved of the habitat of the specimen, this has been included in the description; but where that part of the history of the specimen is not available, the habitat is given on the authority of authors who have described that particular species.

There were originally 600 specimens in this series. As only 61 of these have survived, they have been renumbered with the identifying letter 'X'. The numbers given at the end of each description are from Owen's catalogue of 'The Preparations of Natural History in Spirit', 1830.

COELENTERATA

Hydrozoa

The Hydrozoa are Coelenterates lacking stomodaeum and mesenteries. The sexual cells are discharged directly to the exterior.

X1 A specimen of *Antennularia ramosa*, the 'Lobster's Horn Coralline'. The example grows from a common base and has more than a dozen branches. The species inhabits European seas.

(23)

Ellis's Corallines, pl. 9, fig. 14, from a dried specimen.

Anthozoa

The Anthozoa possess a stomodaeum and mesenteries and the sexual cells are discharged into the coelenteric cavity.

X2   A specimen of *Gorgonia pennata*, suspended with the attached base uppermost. The numerous branches remain separate and do not anastomose. 'Many of the small Polypes with their ciliated tentacula may be seen extending from the lateral pores.' Inhabits the warm parts of the Atlantic Ocean.   (36)

Ellis's Zoophytes, pl. 14, fig. 3.

X3   Three specimens of *Renilla americana*, the 'Sea Pansy'. The specific name should probably be *reniformis*. The zooids are confined to the surface that is uppermost in the living animal, i.e. to the surface opposite that to which the peduncle is attached. Inhabits shallow waters of both Pacific and Atlantic coasts of North America. These three specimens were originally mounted separately.

(59, 60, 61)

X4   Two clusters identified by Owen as *Zoanthus ellisii* (should probably be *Z. sociatus*). The upper specimen, which embraces a colony of some twenty individuals adhering to a mussel shell, is Owen's 75. The lower, embracing a much larger number of individuals clustered on all sides of a calcareous base, is his 74.

The habitat of these specimens is the West Indies.   (74, 75)

X5   Three specimens of a Sea Anemone, diagnosed by Owen as *Actinia crassicornis*. The lower specimen is fully expanded (Owen's 79). The middle one is completely retracted into its conical form (Owen's 80); and the upper one is partly expanded (Owen's 81).

This is one of the common Sea Anemones of European seas.

(79, 80, and 81)

ECHINODERMATA

This phylum includes the Star-fish, Sea-urchins, Brittle-stars and Feather Stars.

X6   A large Brittle-star of the genus *Ophiura*. It is described by Owen as 'a large and beautiful species' with 'the disc flat, subpentagonal, its diameter one inch two-thirds; the five inter-radial divisions terminating towards the mouth, each in a small round scale. The rays are five in number, cylindrical, gradually attenuated to their extremities, with transverse rows of small spines laterally, as if the squamae were ciliated.   The diameter, taken from the extremities of the extended rays, is sixteen inches.'

The specific diagnosis is doubtfully made by Owen as *Ophiura lacertosa*.   (89)

X7   A large and perfect specimen of a Sea Urchin, labelled *Acrocladia*.   This name appears to be obsolete.   This specimen is apparently not included in Owen's Catalogue.

Holothuroidea

Sea Cucumbers, Sea Slugs or Beche-de-Mer.

X8   Specimen of a Holothurian diagnosed by Owen as ?*Fistularia maxima*.

The specimen is now completely bleached.   A bristle is passed into the mouth.   The specimen is some ten inches in length and three in breadth and is somewhat flattened.   (112)

Coelomata

Polychaeta

A group of marine worms 'that either lead a free life, swimming in the open sea, or crawling along the bottom; or they pass their life in burrows or definite tubes of various kinds.'

X9   A specimen of *Polynoë squamata* (although formerly labelled *Hermione*).   Originally there were two specimens mounted in the same jar.   The remaining specimen is some two and a quarter inches in length.   There are twelve pairs of semi-transparent elytra.   The chaetae scarcely project beyond the elytra.   This is an Atlantic species.   (256)

X10   Two specimens of *Aphrodite aculeata*.   In Owen's Catalogue one specimen is included and is named *Halithaea aculeata*.   These are specimens of the 'Sea-mouse' in which the notopodial chaetae are brilliantly irridescent.   It inhabits the Atlantic and Mediterranean Oceans.   (255)

X11   A specimen of the Lug-worm (*Arenicola marina*), commonly used as bait by fishermen.   The specimen measures some eight inches in length and is dark in colour. By Owen it is designated as *Arenicola piscatorum* or *Lumbricus marinus*, of Linnaeus. The hinder end of the body, devoid of chaetae and known as the 'tail', is in this specimen divided into three well-marked lobes. It is a sand burrower found on the shores in European seas. (246)

MOLLUSCA

X12 The specimen is unnamed and not identifiable in Owen's Catalogue. Two specimens are included in the jar: (1) the suspended soft parts (above), and (2) the shell with one lateral half removed to show the contained animal. The species is a brown-banded, flattened, mollusc with a chitinous operculum, but the diagnosis appears uncertain.

X13 Two specimens of *Patella vulgata*, the Common Limpet. The upper specimen, Owen's 147, consists of the soft parts removed from the shell, and the lower one in which the soft parts are displayed within the shell is possibly Owen's 146, although it does not exactly accord with his descriptive notes. (146 and 147)

X14 Specimens of the 'Mutton Fish', *Haliotis*. These consist of: (1) an empty shell; (2) the soft parts probably removed from it; and (3) a smaller shell with the soft parts *in situ*. These are all mounted in one jar.

The only *Haliotis* listed in Owen's Catalogue is No. 149 and it appears to have been a single specimen of *H. tuberculata*, catalogued without comment. The specimens, as mounted, are intended to show the gross relations of the mollusc to its shell. (149)

X15 Two specimens mounted in the same jar. The upper one is the soft parts removed from the shell. The operculum, typical of a *Trochus*, is attached. This is evidently Owen's 156, diagnosed as *Trochus niloticus*. The lower specimen fits Owen's description of 157—'The shell is laid open to show the soft parts; the mouth is closed by the operculum'. Owen describes this as *Turbo pica*: but it is evidently a *Trochus* and probably the same species as the upper specimen. On the jar (105) both specimens are rightly named *Trochus*. (156 and 157)

Nudibranchiata

Molluscs that in their adult stage lack a shell.

X16 A specimen of a *Tritonia*, diagnosed by Owen as *Tritonia coronata*. The specimen shows well the double rows of arborescent cerata on the dorsal surface. The individual is about one inch long.

Inhabits Northern seas. (159)

CRUSTACEA

Cirripedia

Order including the Barnacles and 'Acorn Shells'.

X17   The specimen consists of two species of Cirripeds. A large *Coronula diadema* is fixed to a base of Whale's skin and on it is a colony of another species of barnacle in various stages of growth. These are diagnosed by Owen as *Otion cuvieri*. They have been preserved in various stages of expansion.   (282)

X18   A portion of Whale's skin to which is attached a colony of eighteen *Coronula diadema*. The barnacles are all contracted. The specimen shows well the way in which the barnacle becomes embedded in the Whale's skin.   (280)

Copepoda

Small Crustacea, mostly of parasitic habit.

X19   Three specimens of *Dichelestium sturionis*. These are parasitic on the gills of the Sturgeon. Their blood is red in colour but is said not to contain haemoglobin.   (285)

X20   Six specimens of a *Caligus*, possibly *C. nanus*, diagnosed by Owen as *Lernaea pectoralis*. The specimens are said to come from the pectoral fins of the Haddock.   (284)

Isopoda

X21   Two specimens, the upper one about one and a half inches and the lower about half an inch in length. They appear to be Bopyrids. Not identified in Owen's Catalogue.

Decapoda

X22   Specimen unnamed and unnumbered. This is a Loricata and although it corresponds with Owen's description of 310, it is smaller than the specimen so numbered. It is identified by Owen as *Scyllarus latus*.   (? 310)

ARACHNIDA

This phylum contains the Spiders, Scorpions, and Mites.

Typical Scorpions and Whips

X23   A large Scorpion 'in a pregnant state', diagnosed by Owen as *Scorpio afer*.   (342)

X24   A Scorpion labelled on the jar *Isometrus maculatus*. It appears to be Owen's *Scorpio gracilis*, habitat America.   (347)

X25   Somewhat damaged specimen of *Thelyphonus caudatus*. The first pair of legs are modified into tactile organs and are not ambulatory, a condition typical of the Pedipalpi. Habitat: Tropical America.   (348)

Araneae

Typical Spiders

X26   Two specimens rightly named on the jar as *Heteropoda venatoria*. In Owen's Catalogue there is some confusion concerning the nomenclature and it is difficult to determine if he uses the name *Mygale nidulans* as a synonym for *Aranea venatoria*.   (Probably Owen's 355 and 356, mounted together)

X27   A typical member of the Mygalidae, the large hairy Spiders often known as Tarantulas. By Owen it is named *Mygale avicularia*, or *Aranea avicularia* and is a tropical American form.   (350)

Acarina

Mites, Ticks, and Harvest Bugs

X28   Two ticks attached to the skin of a Pangolin (*Manis*). The species was not definitely identified by Owen.   (372)

MYRIAPODA

Millipedes and Centipedes

X29 A typical large Millipede nearly six inches long, diagnosed by Owen as *Julus crassus*. It has between fifty and sixty segments. The minute puncta are pores or outlets for the emission of a slimy secretion. Habitat: Asia.   (333)

X30 Two specimens of the Luminous Centipede, *Geophilus electricus*. The smaller specimen (about two inches long) is Owen's No. 338 'from Sumatra'; the longer one (about three and a quarter inches) is his No. 339 and has no locality assigned to it.   (338 and 339)

INSECTA

Orthoptera

This Order includes earwigs, cockroaches, mantises, stick and leaf insects, grass-hoppers, and crickets.

X31 An Australian cockroach which Owen, unable to identify, named *Blatta dilatata*. The outstanding features of the species are the narrow white margin to the burnished dorsal surface. This specimen was said by Owen to be a female. It is a wingless form. Habitat: New Holland.   (447)

X32 A large Phasma, over six inches in length. Diagnosed by Owen as ? *Phasma angulatum* or *Phasma gigas*. The wings are in a rudimentary state—so-called pupa state; and the left fore-wing has been removed to show the rudimentary hind wing.   (454)

X33 A specimen of *Schizodactylus monstrosus* (in Owen's Catalogue designated *Gryllus monstrosus*). The insect is an Indian species and is remarkable for the curled-up ends of its long elytra.   (469)

X34 A specimen of *Anostoma australasiae*. The insect is remarkable for its large head and powerful jaws. It is wingless and has a completely naked and unprotected body. This specimen is not identifiable in Owen's Catalogue.

X35 Two specimens of *Gryllotalpa*, the Mole Cricket. The modification of the front pair of limbs for the purpose of tunnelling in the earth have remarkable superficial parallels to the adaptations of the fore limb of the Mammalian Mole (*Talpa*). Owen states that No. 465 is an impregnated female. The ova are deposited in June and July in round cavities, six or seven inches below the surface of the ground.   (464 and 465)

Neuroptera

This Order includes the winged White Ants, or Termites, Stone flies, Dragon flies, May flies, Caddis flies, and Ant-lions, as well as the wingless biting lice or bird lice.

Mallophaga

Wingless 'biting-lice'

X36   The specimen consists of a piece of skin of a Turkey with a dozen biting lice attached to the feathers. The species is *Nirmus meleagridis*.   (378)

Termitidae

White Ants

X37   A specimen about two and a half inches in length, with a hugely distended body and a hard chitinous head armed with strong jaws. It was labelled on the bottle *Rhynchophorus*; but this appears to be an incorrect diagnosis. Possibly it is Owen's 508 or 509, a female of *Termes fatale* 'impregnated'.   (? 508 or 509)

Hymenoptera

This Order includes ants, bees, wasps, saw-flies, and Ichneumon flies.

X38   A specimen of *Xylocopa latipes*, the Broad-legged Carpenter Bee. The specimen comes from Sumatra.   (528)

X39   Seven specimens of the Humble bee *Bombus terrestris*. These were mounted separately in the old series. The specimens demonstrate the two sexes of the adult, as well as the larval and pupal states.   (534-540)

X40   Two wasps of which the lower specimen is imperfect. The individuals are difficult to assign to any definite number in Owen's series of *Vespa*.

(One of the series 521-527)

X41 A single specimen labelled on the jar as Sphex.   (517)

Coleoptera

Beetles

X42 Three specimens mounted in one jar. The upper one is a Stag Beetle (*Lucanus cervis*), which is Owen's No. 416. The lower left hand specimen of a larva, with the skin dissected from one side is Owen's No. 414 and the other larva his No. 415, which is a larva killed in the act of casting its skin. Habitat: Europe; in decayed wood.   (414, 415, and 416)

X43 Two specimens—the larva and imago—of a *Dynastes* beetle. The imago is Owen's No. 396, diagnosed as *Dynastes hercules*. The larva is of the same species, from the Heaviside Museum, and is Owen's No. 396A.   (396 and 396A)

X44 An imago and a larva of the Water Beetle (*Dytiscus marginalis*). The larva is Owen's No. 384: but in his catalogue there is no mention of an imago of this species. The specimen is a male. Habitat: Europe, in fresh waters.   (384)

X45 A specimen of a Buprestid Beetle mounted with the elytra raised and the membranous wings exposed. This would appear to be the specimen rather doubtfully diagnosed by Owen as *Buprestis chrysis*.   (Probably 389)

Lepidoptera

Butterflies and Moths

X46 A lepidopterous larva 'two inches, two-thirds long; on each segment (except the last, which has four, and the first, which has none) there are six short spines. Species not determined.   (586)

X47 Larva of a large American Moth (*Bombyx regalis*), known as the Hickory Horned Devil. Three long spines are developed on the dorsal aspect of the second and third segments. They are barbed in their distal portion and are recurved. The spines on the succeeding segments are smaller and erect.   (589)

X48 Two larvae of *Deilephila euphorbiae* (so diagnosed by Owen), the Spurge Hawk Moth. Originally mounted separately.   (555 and 556)

FIG. 11

A tropical American Spider.   Specimen No. X 27.

FIG. 12

Boltenia reniformis, collected by Sir Joseph Banks during his voyage round the world with Captain James Cook.   Specimen No. X 57.

X49   A larva of a Moth allied to the Lappet-Moth (*Gastropacha quercifolia*). The specimen is about five and a half inches long.   (593)

X50   An unidentified exotic lepidopterous larva. The specimen is three inches long, 'of a dun colour, and remarkable for short white bristles, which project in a radiated manner from a central stem; each segment bearing a transverse row of these fasciculi.'   (583)

X51   An unidentified lepidopterous larva, remarkable for its long silky hairs. The specimen is a broad-bodied larva, three inches in length.   (594)

X52   An unidentified lepidopterous larva remarkable for the numerous small, pearly, iridescent spots with which it is ornamented.   (551)

X53   An unidentified lepidopterous larva in its cocoon. The specimen is one of those presented by Sir Joseph Banks.   (599)

Homoptera

Cicadas, Lantern Flies, etc.

X54   A large Cicada, mounted with the wings slightly spread. This is probably the *Cicada septendecim* of Owen's Catalogue.   (probably 497)

X55   A smaller Cicada too disintegrated to identify or to locate in Owen's Catalogue.

X56   A large 'Lantern Fly', diagnosed by Owen as *Fulgora lanternaria*. Mounted with the wings spread. Given to Hunter by Sir Joseph Banks. Habitat: China.   (501A)

TUNICATA

This phylum contains the Sea Squirts and their allies, which as adults are degenerate forms produced from larvae that have many features suggesting kinship with the Vertebrates.

X57   A specimen of *Boltenia reniformis*, one of the solitary, fixed Ascidians. The stalk and the supporting mass to which it was fixed are present. The specimen was collected by Sir Joseph Banks during Cook's voyage round the world and presented by Banks to Hunter.   Habitat: probably the north-west coast of America.   (119)

X59   A specimen named on the jar *Perophora*, consisting of a ramifying stolon from which a number of small individuals arise.   (Not identified)

X62   Four specimens of Salpidae mounted in the same jar.   They differ in length from some three inches to less than an inch.   (120-123, mounted together)

X63   A specimen diagnosed as *Salpa maxima*, measuring nearly eight inches in length.
                                                                (Probably 125 or 126)

X64   A specimen of *Salpa maxima* opened up to show its internal structure.   (128)

X65   A specimen, labelled on the bottle *Ascidia conglomerata*.   A colony consisting of eight individuals.   Mounted above on a sheet of mica are seven tadpole larvae.
                                                                       (Not identified)

The following three specimens, although probably not of Hunterian origin, are included here to complete the series:

X58   A specimen of a *Polyclinum*, diagnosed by Owen as *P. constellatum*.   This is an example of a compound Ascidian in which the colony takes the form of a hollow sphere.   A hole has been cut in one side of the sphere in order to show the structure of the individuals in the section.   This specimen from St. Lucia appears to be post-Hunterian.

X60   Two fine specimens of *Pyrosoma atlanticum*, a free-swimming pelagic Ascidian which is noted for its brilliant phosphorescence.   Blue glass rods are passed into the cavity.   In Owen only one specimen is included, of which no provenance is given.

X61   A fine specimen of a *Salpa*.   It is a representative of the free-swimming 'Chain Ascidians', according with the description in Owen's Catalogue of a specimen presented by John Howship.

III

General Osteology of Man

The first printed list of Osteological specimens contained in the Museum was published in 1831 and was possibly the work of William Home Clift.

As the collection was increased by numerous additions new catalogues were prepared from time to time and the various Orders were catalogued in separate volumes. The numbering used in the present catalogue is taken from the one prepared by Sir William Henry Flower, Conservator of the Museum from 1861 to 1884, the first edition of which was published in 1870. The second edition, prepared by Professor Charles Stewart, Conservator from 1884 to 1907, was completed in 1907.

3   A foetal skeleton of two and a half inches (70 mm.) in height. The neurapophyses of the dorsal and lumbar vertebrae have begun to be ossified, and the middle phalanges of the fingers of the hand (three months).

11   A foetal skeleton seven inches (178 mm.) in height (five months).

19   The skeleton of a foetus ten and a half inches (267 mm.) in height (six months).

22   The skeleton of a foetus eleven inches in height (279 mm.) between the sixth and seventh months.

33   A skeleton eighteen inches (456 mm.) in height, being that of a foetus of nine months or a child at birth. The skull is missing.

36   The cranium of a child at or before birth.

61   The skull of a young European. The basilar suture is not closed. The second molars are fully developed, but the posterior molars are not yet in place. It shows a rather sloping forehead and slightly prominent upper jaw.

67   The articulated skeleton of a male European five feet, seven and a half inches in height.

68   The articulated skeleton of a male European, just over five feet, eight inches in height.

80   The skull of a European, male.

81   The skull of a European, male.

83   The cranium of a male European advanced in years.   The coronal, sagittal, and lamboidal sutures are partly obliterated.

84   The cranium of a European, female.

85   The cranium of a Chinese, male.

86   The cranium of a native of New Holland, male.

89   The cranium of a European, male.   Flower notes that the 'occipital region appears to have been artificially flattened in infancy, perhaps unintentionally'.

91   The skull of a very aged female, in which the alveolar processes are absorbed in consequence of the total loss of teeth in both jaws.   Though perfectly edentulous, none of the cranial sutures are obliterated.   This was probably the specimen used by Hunter in his work 'On the Natural History of the Human Teeth' to illustrate the effects of the loss of teeth in both jaws (Plate VII).

92   The cranium of an aged edentulous male.   The cranial sutures are very simple and partially consolidated.

94   The skull of an aged female.

107   A calvaria with numerous Wormian ossicles in the lamboidal and through the whole length of the sagittal and in the left coronal sutures.

110   The cranium of an Englishwoman, with a central and a pair of lateral large distinct ossifications in the supraoccipital.

113   A cranium with two large Wormian bones in the anterior end of the sagittal suture, besides three very symmetrically disposed in the upper part of the lamboidal suture.

115   The skull of a male African negro from which part of the basis cranii and the right
      zygoma have been broken away.   There are well-marked independent ossicles
      in the pterion on both sides.

116   An elongated and remarkably low and narrow skull, with an epipteric bone on the
      right side.

118   A male European cranium showing metopism (persistence of the frontal suture),
      with a somewhat projecting supraoccipital region.
         In Clift's Catalogue (Part III, *The Human and Comparative Osteology*, 1831, p. 7)
      is the following statement:
            'It was a curious remark made by Dr. Leach, and others who have examined
         that immense collection of crania and other bones in the catacombs at Paris,
         that the number of adult skulls in which the frontal suture remained un-
         obliterated was so considerable that, from a calculation made on the spot, he
         estimated the proportion to be at least one in eleven.'

124   The upper part of a calvaria, showing persistence of the frontal and obliteration of
      the left half of the coronal suture, with corresponding shortening of the left side
      of the cranium.   The sagittal suture is nearly obliterated; and ossification has
      advanced farther on the right side of the lamboidal than on the left.

135   A cranium affected with parietal synostosis, occipital protuberance, and great and
      unsymmetrical elevation of the frontal region.

137   A small skull of a female European, compressed and vertically elevated.   It exhibits
      synostosis of the coronal and posterior half of the sagittal suture.   The lamboidal
      suture is perfectly open and contains several Wormian bones.

143   The cranium of a native of Madagascar, but with all the characteristics of the
      European skull.   As an individual peculiarity it exhibits an almost symmetrical
      pair of tubercles on the inferior surface of the basioccipital.

175   A vertical transverse section of the human cranium.   It includes the coronal suture,
      with the contiguous parts of the frontal and parietals.   The minutely cellular
      structure included between the outer and inner compact layers of bone is
      termed the 'diploë': it is most abundant in the basioccipital and at the bases of
      the alisphenoids and is traceable throughout the frontals and parietals, but is
      absent in the greater part of the squamosal.

195   The upper portion of a bisected scapula, in which the texture of the coracoid and acromion is exposed in longitudinal section.

196   The upper portion of a similarly bisected scapula of a child. The coracoid element has not coalesced with the proper scapular one, and is wanting.

197   The upper portion of a similarly bisected scapula of an infant. By comparing this with the two preceding specimens it will be seen that the proportion of the cancellous texture near the glenoid cavity does not increase in the same ratio as the compact lamellar part of the bone but forms a larger proportion of the scapula in the infant.

198   The posterior half of a longitudinally bisected humerus. It shows the accumulation of the minute cancellous structure at the extremities, and the progressive thickening of the outer compact bone as it passes to the shaft, where it forms exclusively the walls of the medullary cavity. At the proximal end may be discerned the linear trace of the primary separation of the epiphysis formed by the great tuberosity; that of the epiphysis formed by the articular head is less conspicuous. At the distal end may likewise be discerned the linear trace of the confluence of the epiphysis with that plate of compact substance which separated the olecranal from the coronoid fossae.

203   The right os innominatum, with the ilium longitudinally bisected. The compact walls are thickest above the great ischiatic notch.

204   The right ilium of a child longitudinally bisected. It shows a larger proportion of the cancellous structure than in the adult.

205   The left os innominatum, longitudinally bisected through the acetabulum. A thick stratum of diploë or cancellous texture is included between the compact inner and outer plates of the ilium, of which the outer is the thickest: they recede from each other towards the acetabulum, where the cancellous structure is more abundant, except at its lower half, where it is almost absent. The compact wall of the pubis is very thin, and includes a light and delicate cancellous texture.

206   The left os innominatum, transversely bisected through the acetabulum. The compact wall of the cavity is thickest at the rim.

207   The hinder half of a longitudinally bisected right femur. The columnar cancelli

are arranged in decussating curves, like the arches in Gothic architecture, where they transfer the weight sustained by the head and neck of the bone upon the strong and compact shaft. Here the dense tissue is disposed as a hollow column and forms the walls of a medullary cavity. This is gradually obliterated by fine cancellous structure towards the distal end, where the compact wall progressively diminishes in thickness. Scarcely any trace of the confluence of the epiphysis can be discerned at the extremity of the bone.

208 The left femur longitudinally bisected.

209 The proximal part of a left femur, longitudinally bisected. A tract of cancellous structure, more compact than the rest, extends from the middle of the head to the under part of the neck.

215 The posterior half of a longitudinally bisected left tibia. The line of confluence of the proximal epiphysis may be readily traced and divides the finer cancellous texture of the articular expansion from the coarser texture of the shaft below. The inner compact wall of the medullary cavity is thicker than the outer one. The epiphyseal line is traceable across the distal cancellous structure.

223 The articulated skeleton of Charles Byrne, the Irish Giant (1761-1783).

Charles Byrne, afterwards called O'Brien, the famous Irish giant, was born about 1761 in Ireland, of which country his father was a native, but his mother was a Scotswoman. He visited various towns in England and Scotland for the purpose of exhibiting his huge person and when in Edinburgh he is said to have had great difficulty in getting up and down the narrow stairs of the Old Town, being obliged to crawl on all-fours. It is also related of him that he 'dreadfully alarmed the watchmen on the North Bridge, early one winter's morning, by lighting his pipe at one of the lamps; which he did with the greatest ease, without standing even on tiptoe'. Newspaper accounts advertising his appearances give his height variously as 8ft., 8ft. 2in., and 8ft. 4in., but these were manifestly exaggerations, as the actual height of the skeleton, in which due allowance has been given for the intervertebral substances, is only 7ft. 7in. Neither his father, mother, brother nor any other person of his family was of an extraordinary size.

He first came to London on April 11th, 1782, and the following advertisement appeared in a newspaper on the 24th of that month:

'Irish Giant. To be seen this, and every day this week, in his large elegant room, at the cane shop, next door to late Cox's Museum, Spring Gardens,

Mr. Byrne, the surprising Irish Giant, who is allowed to be the tallest man in the world; his height is eight feet two inches, and in full proportion accordingly; only 21 years of age. His stay will not be long in London, as he proposes shortly to visit the Continent. The nobility and gentry are requested to take notice, there was a man shewed himself for some time past at the top of the Haymarket and Piccadilly, who advertised, and endeavoured to impose himself on the public for the Irish Giant; Mr. Byrne begs leave to assure them, it was an imposition, as he is the only Irish Giant, and never was in this metropolis before Thursday, the 11th inst. Hours of admittance every day, Sundays excepted, from 11 till 3, and from 5 till 8, at half-a-crown each person'.

He attracted considerable interest, as the following extract from a newspaper dated May 6th, 1782, gives evidence:

'However striking a curiosity may be, there is generally some difficulty in engaging the attention of the public; but even this was not the case with the modern living Colossus, or wonderful Irish Giant; for no sooner was he arrived at an elegant apartment at the cane-shop, in Spring Garden-gate, next door to Cox's Museum, than the curious of all degrees resorted to see him, being sensible that a prodigy like this never made its appearance among us before; and the most penetrating have frankly declared, that neither the tongue of the most florid orator, or pen of the most ingenious writer, can sufficiently describe the elegance, symmetry, and proportion of this wonderful phaenomenon in nature, and that all description must fall infinitely short of giving that satisfaction which may be obtained on a judicious inspection.'

In the same year, the summer pantomime at the Haymarket Theatre was entitled 'Harlequin Teague, or the Giant's Causeway', with reference to Byrne.

Another advertisement appeared in a newspaper dated August 12th, 1782, and gives further details of the attention that his appearance had aroused:

'Just arrived in London, and to be seen in an elegant apartment, at the cane-shop, in Spring Garden-gate, next door to the house late Cox's Museum, the Living Colossus, or wonderful Irish Giant, only 21 years of age, measures eight feet two inches high. This extraordinary young man has been seen by abundance of the nobility and gentry, likewise of the faculty, Royal Society and other admirers of natural curiosities, who allow him to surpass anything of the same kind ever offered to the public. His address is singular and pleasing, his person truly shaped and proportioned to his height, and affords an agreeable surprise; he excels the famous Maximilian Miller, born in 1674,

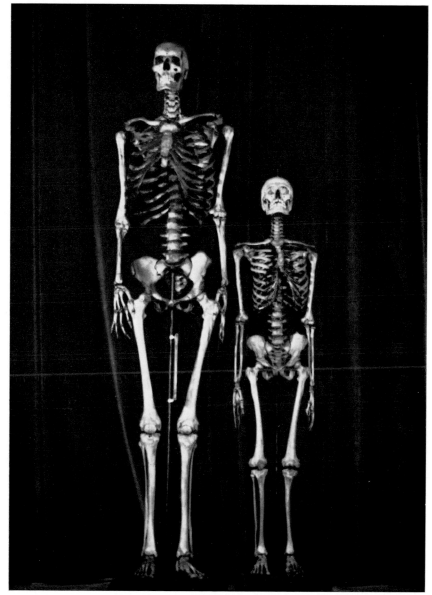

FIG. 13

The skeleton of Charles Byrne, the ' Irish Giant ', shown with one of average height. *General Osteology*. Specimen No. 223.

FIG. 14

An etching by John Kay of Charles Byrne with 'two other giants, also Irishmen'. The spectators are:
Lord Monboddo, whose head appears in the background; William Richardson, solicitor-at-law, on the left
behind; Mr Bell, engraver in front; and on the right, Bailie Kyd, a lady and a dwarf.

shown in London in 1733, and the late Swedish giant will scarce admit of comparison. To enumerate every particular would be too tedious, let it suffice to say, that he is beyond what is set forth in ancient or modern history. The ingenious and judicious, who have honoured him with their company, have bestowed the greatest encomiums on him, and on their departure have expressed their approbation and satisfaction. In short, the sight of him is more than the mind can conceive, the tongue express, or pencil delineate, and stands without a parallel in this or any other country. "Take him for all in all, we shall scarce look on his like again"—Shakespear. Ladies and gentlemen are respectfully informed that the hours of admittance are from eleven in the morning till four in the afternoon and from six to seven in the evening every day, Sundays excepted. Admittance 2s. 6d.'

A few months later he removed from Charing Cross to Piccadilly, as is apparent from the following newspaper notice dated November 29th, 1782:

'Irish Giant. The Irish Giant embraces, in the most respectful manner, the earliest opportunity of acquainting the nobility, gentry, &c., that he has removed from Mr. Mittenius's, Charing Cross, to the sign of the Hampshire Hog, No. 1 Picadilly, where he continues to be seen this and every day (Sundays excepted). This modern Colossus is but 22 years of age, measures upwards of eight feet two inches high, is well proportioned to his height, and is allowed by all who have seen him, to be the greatest natural curiosity ever seen in this or any other kingdom. Hours of admittance from eleven in the morning till four in the afternoon, and from six till seven at night. Admittance to ladies and gentlemen, 2s. 6d.; children and servants in livery, 1s.
N.B. To prevent any misunderstanding, no person will be admitted for one shilling, except children and servants in livery.'

It will be seen that most of our information about Byrne comes from newspaper notices and the following extract which appeared in 1783, gives a further change of address:

'Irish Giant. The Irish Giant respectfully informs the nobility, gentry and public in general, that he has removed to an elegant apartment at Mr. Hayne's, No. 12 Cockspur Street, where he is seen from 11 to 4 and 6 to 7, each day, Sunday excepted. This truly amazing phenomenon is indisputably the most extraordinary production of the human species ever beheld since the days of Goliath, as has been sufficiently demonstrated from the repeated approbation of numbers of the first characters in Great Britain and Ireland, as well as foreigners of the first distinction, from several of whom he has had the most pressing invitations to visit the continent. This astonishing Colossus is but 22 years of age, and measures upwards of eight feet two inches in height; nor does that size, however amazing, afford less satisfaction to the spectator, than his exact proportion in every respect. Admittance 1s.'

It is interesting to speculate why the charge for admission had been reduced from 2/6 to 1/- at this period. Perhaps after exhibiting for eight or nine months in London— for we have no evidence that he visited other places after he first appeared in London in April, 1782—he had satisfied the curiosity of those who were willing to pay 2/6 to view the phenomenon. Or was it that his custom was suffering from rival shows? A newspaper dated June 20th, 1782, and a handbill of the same period advertise the appearance 'at the late bird-shop, the corner of the Haymarket and Piccadilly, the astonishing Irish giant, whose height surpasses the Patagonian; with admirable symmetry of body, and esteemed to be the most proportioned ever seen' . . . 'who has had the honour of being shown to their majesties at Kew'. The advertisement goes on to describe a female dwarf, twenty-two years old, and thirty inches high, who was exhibited at the same place.

It may be that the giant mentioned in this last account was Patrick Cotter. The task of disentangling the life histories of Byrne and Cotter is made the more difficult since they both, for show purposes, called themselves O'Brien and each was referred to as 'The Irish Giant'. From 1785 until the end of the century, Cotter exhibited himself at various places in London and in other towns. At the same time, the 'Gigantic Twin Brothers', named Knipe, were on show in London.

Charles Byrne died on June 1st, 1783, in Cockspur Street, at the age of twenty-two years, and his death was said to have been hastened by excessive drinking, to which he was always addicted, but more particularly after the loss of almost all his property which he had invested in two bank notes, one being for £700 and the other for £70. An account of the theft is contained in a newspaper dated April 23rd, 1783, and is as follows:

> 'The Irish Giant, a few evenings since, taking a lunar ramble, was tempted to visit the Black Horse, a little public-house facing the King's mews; and before he returned to his own apartments, found himself a less man than he had been the beginning of the evening, by the loss of upwards of 700£ in bank notes, which had been taken out of his pocket.'

An extract from the *Gentleman's Magazine* for 1784, gives the information that on July 10th of that year 'a remarkable cause which was to have been tried at Guildhall was made up by compromise. It appeared that the late Mr. Byrne, the Irish Giant, had been robbed of two bank-notes; one of 700£, the other of 70£. That of 700£ was traced to Mr. Atkinson, who insisted that he had given value for it, viz. 400£ in cash, and 300£ in goods; but the executor to Byrne proving that notice had been given of the theft previous to his exchanging the notes, a compromise of 500£ was proposed and accepted, and each party paid their own costs.' This settlement shows the incorrectness of a story which relates that Byrne, apprehensive of being robbed, concealed his bank-note for 700£ in his fireplace before going to bed at night; and that a servant lighting a fire there in the morning, consumed the valuable document accidentally.

Shortly before his death Byrne requested that his remains should be thrown into the sea, in order that his bones might not be obtained by the surgeons, for it had come to his knowledge that several members of the medical profession were anxious to obtain his body. A newspaper dated June 5th, 1783, gives evidence of this in the following paragraph:

> 'The whole tribe of surgeons put in a claim for the poor departed Irish Giant, and surrounded his house just as Greenland harpooners would an enormous whale. One of them has gone so far as to have a niche made for himself in the giant's coffin, in order to his being ready at hand, on the "witching time of night, when church-yards yawn".'

Another newspaper, of June 13th, says:

> 'Since the death of the Irish Giant, there have been more physical consultations held, than ever were convened to keep Harry the Eighth in existence. The object of these Aesculapian deliberations is to get the poor departed giant into their possession; for which purpose they wander after his remains from place to place, and mutter more fee, faw, fums than ever were breathed by the whole gigantic race, when they attempted to scale heaven and dethrone Jupiter.'

Yet another journalist wrote on the same theme on June 16th:

> 'So anxious are the surgeons to have possession of the Irish Giant, that they have offered a ransom of 800 guineas to the undertakers. This sum if being rejected they are determined to approach the churchyard by regular works, and terrier-like, unearth him.'

On June 18th appeared the following account:

> 'Byrne's body was shipped on board a vessel in the river last night in order to be conveyed to the Downs, where it is to be sunk in twenty fathom water: the body hunters, however, are determined to pursue their valuable prey even in the profoundest depth of the aquatic regions; and have therefore provided a pair of diving bells, with which they flatter themselves they shall be able to weigh hulk gigantic from its watery grave.'

The Annual Register for 1783, after giving the information that the body had been conveyed to the Downs, goes on to say: 'We have reason, however, to believe that this report is merely a *tub* thrown out to the *whale*.'

A similar account of Byrne's death appears in *The Scots Magazine* for that year.

It has also been stated that Byrne was buried in St. Martin's churchyard and that his coffin was eight feet three inches long, two feet eight inches over the shoulders and twenty-one inches deep inside. Another version of the story, and one which seems better to agree with the known facts, is that John Hunter succeeded in bribing the undertakers with the sum of £500 (one account gives £800) when they were already part way on their journey to dispose of the body at sea, and that he brought back the giant to his own house and had the skeleton prepared for his Museum.

The following is a description of the skeleton as it appeared in the early catalogues:

The posterior molars are in place; and the epiphyses of the long bones are united, though the crests of the ilia and posterior borders of the scapulae are still free. The corresponding limb-bones of the opposite sides present great differences in dimensions. The bones of the cranium are thick and massive. The glabella, supraorbital ridges, mastoid processes, all the muscular ridges and the bones of the face, and especially the lower jaw, are greatly developed; but the alveolar arches and teeth are scarcely larger than those of a man of ordinary stature. The squamosal joins the frontal for more than half an inch on the left side, but does not quite reach it on the right. The frontal region is low and retreating, and the cranial cavity small for the external size of the skull.

Height:	2310—7 feet 7 inches
Clavicle:	r. 228, l. 220
Humerus:	r. 450, l. 430
Radius	r. 334, l. 325
Hand:	r. 255, l. 256
Femur:	r. 625, l. 642
Tibia:	r. 541, l. 537
Foot:	r. 325, l. 318
Cranium:	C. 593. L. 214. B. 148.
	Bi. 692. H. 147. Hi. 687.
	Ca. 1520.

A contemporary caricature sketch of Charles Byrne by Rowlandson can be seen in the Hunterian Museum and a boot, a slipper, and a glove belonging to him are also preserved there.

In 1783, Byrne's portrait by the engraver, John Kay, was published in Edinburgh; two other portraits by John Kay appear in *A series of original portraits and caricature etchings by John Kay*, published in 1837, and the description of Figure 14 is as follows:

'Three Giants, with a Group of Spectators

'This Print exhibits Charles Byrne, the Irish Giant, and two other giants, also Irishmen, who, although not in Edinburgh at the same time, have been placed by the artist in one group.

'The spectators are: Lord Monboddo, whose head appears in the background; William Richardson, solicitor-at-law, on the left behind; and Mr. Bell, engraver, in front; on the right, Bailie Kyd, a lady, and a dwarf.

'Byrne, the central of the three principal figures, was eight feet two inches in height, and proportionately thick. . . . In his last moments, he requested that his ponderous remains might be thrown into the sea, in order that his bones might be placed far out of the reach of the chirurgical fraternity; and it was reported that his body was shipped on board a vessel, to be conveyed to the Downs to be sunk in twenty fathoms of water.   In the *Edinburgh Evening Courant*, June 9 and 10, 1783, the following notices relative to the disposal of his body, arc to be found:

> ' "The coffin of Mr. Charles Byrne, the Irish giant, aged twenty-three years, measures eight feet five inches within side, and the outside case nine feet four inches, and the circumference of his shoulders measures three feet four inches".
>
> ' "Yesterday morning, June 6, the body of Byrne, the famous Irish giant, (who died a few days ago), was carried to Margate, in order to be thrown into the sea, agreeable to his own request, he having been apprehensive that the surgeons would anatomise him".'

. . . 'The two Irish giants, who are placed on each side of Byrne, visited Edinburgh in July 1784.   Their presence in the northern capital was announced by various advertisements, . . . These "interesting youths' left Edinburgh for Aberdeen in the month of August following, proposing "to stop in a few towns on their way", to astonish the natives.'

It is assumed that these 'interesting youths' are the Knipe brothers, who also exhibited themselves in London.

The other etching shows Byrne as the central figure, with Mr. Watson, Mr. M'Gowan, Mr. Fairholme, and Geordie Cranstoun as his companions.

A reference to the Irish Giant may be found in the *Diary and Letters of Madame d'Arblay (Frances Burney, 1778-1840)*.   This is to be found in the letter from Miss Burney to Mr. Crisp, dated October 15th, 1782, where she is referring to a conversation with Pasquale Paoli: 'Afterwards speaking of the Irish giant who is now shown in town, he said: "He is so large, I am as a baby!   I look at him—Oh!   I find myself so little as a child!

Indeed, my indignation it rises when I see him hold up his hand so high.   I am as nothing, and I find myself in the power of a man who fetches from me half-a-crown".'

REFERENCES

Catalogue of Human and Comparative Osteology (1831), No. 1.
Osteological Catalogue, Vol. II (1853), No. 5995.
Osteological Catalogue, Part I (1879), No. 223.
Giants and Dwarfs, Edward J. Wood (1868), p. 157.
Gentleman's Magazine.
Annual Register (1783).
The Scots Magazine (1783).
A series of original portraits and caricature etchings, John Kay (1837), Vol. I, Pt. I, Pt. II.

689   The cranium of a male Chinese.   It presents the moderate or medium proportion of length, height, and breadth.   The sagittal region is not unusually elevated. The chin is well marked, and the paraoccipital tubercles are well marked.   The chief distinction which this skull presents from the average form of those of European races is in the size and prominence of the malar bones.   The upper part of the supraoccipital is divided into three symmetrically arranged ossicles; and there are Wormian bones in both sides of the coronal suture.

690   The cranium of a male Chinese.

691   The cranium of a male Chinese.

772   The mutilated skull of a male Maori.

773   The much mutilated skull of a male Maori.   In this specimen a dislocation of the lower jaw has taken place, on the left side, by which the condyloid process has been dislodged from the glenoid cavity and, slipping forwards, has formed a new joint on the eminentia articularis.   That this displacement has been permanent seems apparent from the adaptation of the bony surfaces to each other and from the undue wearing of the teeth on that side of the jaw.

774   The skull of a female Maori, with the basis cranii mutilated.   It differs from those of the males in the smaller cranium and more protuberant super-occipital, in the less prominent supraorbital ridges and malars, which latter bones are smoothly rounded.   Traces of the maxillo-premaxillary sutures remain on the palate.

879   The skull of a male Carib from one of the Caribbean Islands.   It has a remarkably flat and receding forehead, probably from the effects of compression in infancy.

The nasals are large and prominent; the lower jaw is large, with a prominent chin.

880   The cranium of a Carib, said to be female, from one of the Caribbean Islands.   It shows the same low and receding forehead, but with a broader and more generally depressed cranium.

1221   The skull of a male African negro.   The left median incisor has been removed and its socket obliterated.   The first true molar on each side of the lower jaw has been similarly lost during life.   The two extremities of the coronal suture are obliterated.   The Eustachian process is well developed.   The cranium is narrow and the jaws prominent.   The molars are large.

COMPARATIVE OSTEOLOGY

This section has been numbered according to Flower's *Catalogue of the Osteology of Mammals* of 1884, and R. Bowdler Sharpe's *Catalogue of the Osteology of Birds* of 1901. These numbers have been used rather than the ones in the catalogue prepared by William Home Clift in 1831, as many of the specimens are impossible to identify from these early descriptions.   In later catalogues these specimens were sub-divided into 'current osteology' and 'fossils'.

1121   The cranium and horns of the Long-horned variety of the Common Ox (*Bos taurus*).   The nasal bones are missing.

1122   A similar specimen.

1144   The horns of a Transylvanian Ox (*Bos taurus*).

1184   The frontlet and horns of the Cape Buffalo (*Bubalus caffer*).

1214   The skull and horns of a male Musk Ox (*Ovibos moschatus*).

1215   A similar specimen.

1272   The skull and horns of the North American Argali or Rocky Mountain Sheep (*Ovis montana*).

1337   The cranium and horns of the Kudu or Striped Antelope (*Strepsiceros kudu*) from South Africa.

1339   Portion of the cranium and horns of the Kudu.

1341   The horns of the Kudu.

1343   A similar specimen.

1347   The skeleton of a Nilgai (*Boselaphus tragocamelus*). In the Museum before 1861 and probably Hunterian.

1411   The skull and horns of a Gnu (*Connochaetes gnu*).

1438   The long bones of a Giraffe (*Giraffa camelopardalis*). These bones, together with the skull and the skin, were brought to England by Lieutenant William Paterson, who had been sent by Lady Strathmore on a botanical expedition to Caffraria and other unexplored parts of Africa. The skin was stuffed and transferred to the British Museum.

  See William Paterson, *Narrative of Four Journeys into the Country of the Hottentots in 1777, 1778, 1779*, p. 126.

1498   The frontlet and antlers of a Red Deer (*Cervus elaphus*).

1528   The skull and antlers of a male Fallow-deer (*Cervus dama*).

1594   Limb bones of the Megaceros or Irish Elk (*Cervus hibernicus*) which inhabited Western Europe in the Pleistocene period.

1609   An antler of an old male Reindeer (*Cervus tarandus*) from Siberia.

1615   The left antler of a female Reindeer, with the brow-branch well developed.

1618   The calvarium and antlers of a female Reindeer from Greenland. The left brow-snag is longer and larger than the right. The beam is less curved than usual in both.

1686   The skull of a male Camel (*Camelus bactrianus*) vertically and longitudinally bisected. The cranium exhibits an instance of symmetrical morbid action, the

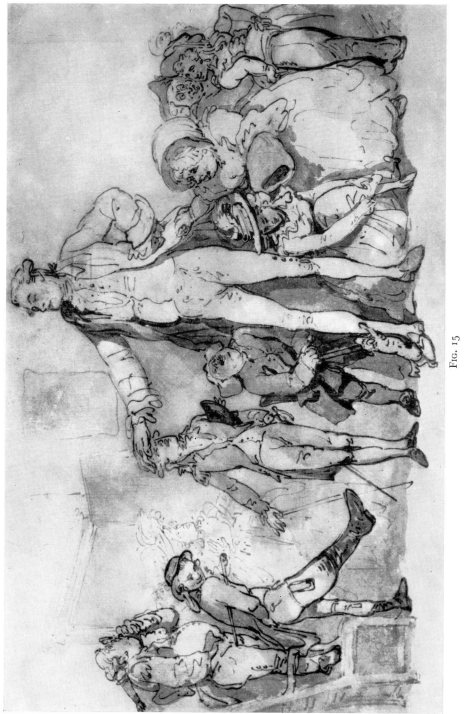

Fig. 15

Drawing by Thomas Rowlandson, acquired by John Hunter probably in 1783, now in the possession of the Royal College of Surgeons. See: *Catalogue of the Portraits* by William LeFanu. 1960, No. 296, p. 95.

Yr ... Camelopardalis in an upright position

FIG. 16

From a water-colour painting of John Hunter's Giraffe (Hunterian Drawing Book II, p. 171).
Artist unknown.

socket of the first true molar being more or less absorbed on each side. The socket of the first true molar on the right side of the lower jaw has begun to be affected by the ulcerative absorption.

1687   The skull (left ramus of lower jaw missing) and the incomplete skeleton of a Camel (*Camelus bactrianus*).

1688   The skull of a Camel (*Camelus bactrianus*).

1820   The skull of a Babirussa (*Babirussa alfurus*).

1862   The skull of a male Hippopotamus (*Hippopotamus amphibius*).

1867   The skull of a Hippopotamus.

1871   The cranium of a young Hippopotamus.

2018   The almost complete skeleton of a Horse (*Equus caballus*).

2133   The skull of a young Rhinoceros (*Rhinoceros sondaicus*). The premaxillae and most of the teeth are missing. The permanent premolars are still in their formative sockets.

2242   An imperfect skeleton, without the skull, of a nearly full-grown Elephant (*Elephas indicus*).

2248   The skull of an Elephant (*Elephas indicus*) (damaged).

2249   The skull of an Elephant (*Elephas indicus*).

2252 and 2253 are similar specimens.

2254   The skull of a young male Elephant (*Elephas indicus*). The molar teeth present a remarkable abnormality in both upper and lower jaws. The tooth in use, the antepenultimate, is joined to the one behind it by a thick mass of cement, the division between the two being only indicated by a slight constriction on each side.

2362   An ultimate upper molar of the right side (*Elephas indicus*). Said to be from the British Pleistocene beds.

C.H.M.—P

2377 Portion of a Mammoth's tusk (*Elephas primigenius*). From the Pleistocene beds of Flintshire.

2484 The proximal half of the right tibia of *Elephas antiquus*. The bone seems to have been imbedded in a reddish calcareous matrix, some of which still adheres to its posterior surface.

2498 The mandible of a female Elephant (*Elephas africanus*). The penultimate molars are in place; all their plates except the last two have been in use.

2503 A tusk of a young Elephant (*Elephas africanus*), considerably curved and with a slight tendency to a spiral direction.

2514 The left upper ultimate molar of an Elephant (*Elephas africanus*). It possesses nine plates, but is imperfect behind. The six anterior plates have been in use.

2574 A portion of the right ramus of a mandible of a Mastodon (*Mastodon americanus*) with the last molar much worn. From the Ohio.

2576 Part of the maxilla and palate of a Mastodon (*Mastodon americanus*) with the left ante-penultimate and penultimate molars *in situ*.

2926 A vertically bisected anterior caudal vertebra, probably of *Hyperoodon*.

2930 Caudal vertebra of a Cetacean. Locality unknown.

2939 The nearly complete skeleton of a Narwhal (*Monodon monoceros*).

Birds

1605 The skeleton of a Great Auk (*Alca impennis*).

1978 The skull of a Polish Fowl, showing the inflation and rarification of the bones of the cranial roof associated with the peculiar form of the brain and with the crest of feathers characteristic of the breed.

2375 The skeleton of a Pondicherry or Royal Vulture (*Haliaetus*); habitat Bengal, Java and Sumatra.

Fish

The following specimens, which were not included in Flower's catalogue, are numbered according to Owen's catalogue of 1853.

122   The upper and lower jaws of a big Parrot Wrass (*Scarus muricatus*) showing the formation of the 'beak' by the welding together of numerous separate denticles.

The surface of the 'beak' is chequered by small lozenge-shaped plates of an enamel-like substance, arranged in a quincuncial order. These are the apices of the teeth incorporated with the bone of the jaw. The upper specimen shows, by vertical section, the deeper embedded parts of the teeth. At the lower part of the section a denticle is exposed not yet fully welded to the bone of the jaw and below it can be seen a cavity common to the germs of many immature denticles, that form successively to gradually replace teeth destroyed and worn out at the cutting edge.

The Parrot Wrasses feed on seaweed.

218, 219   The jaws of a species of Sea Bream (*Sargus sp.*) showing a heterodont condition.

The teeth are separable into flat, chisel-shaped incisors in front, and hemi-spherical crushing molars behind.

In the upper jaw the molars are arranged in three parallel rows, in the lower in two.

305   The left ramus of the mandible of a Wolf Fish (*Anarrhichas lupus*).

The teeth are separable into prehensile fangs clustered at the anterior end of the jaw and a series of rounded, crushing molars behind.

A small part of the right ramus of the jaw has been kept to show in section the shallow implantation of the teeth and their imperfect fusion to the jaws by small, root-like processes.

The Wolf Fish feeds on Molluscs and Crustaceans.

328   The mandibular and maxillary bones of a File Fish (*Balistes forcipatus*), prepared to show the mode of attachment of the functional teeth, and the process of formation of their successors.

The teeth are loosely attached to the margins of the slight depression on which they rest. Each has a large but shallow pulp cavity upon its deep aspect within which projects a flat bony prominence of the alveolar wall—the relations of the tooth to the jaw being very similar to that between nail or claw and an ungual phalanx. In the lowest specimen part of the wall of the jaw has been removed to show a series of cavities in the bone, within which lie the well developed germs of the successional teeth.   In the middle specimens the phalanx-like sockets of the outer teeth are shown and the points of the inner row of teeth.   These teeth are smaller than those of the outer row and incline with their apices towards them, forming buttresses for their support.   The relation of inner and outer teeth is very similar to that between the two blades of a plane-iron.   At the side a tooth is mounted separately to show its shallow pulp cavity and the swollen edge by which it is attached to the margin of the alveolus.

517   The jaws of a Thornback Ray (*Raia clavata*) showing an uneven pavement of rounded denticles, suitable for crushing.

The following specimen was not included in Flower's catalogue of 1884.   The number refers to Owen's Catalogue of 1853.

Mammals

2445   The anterior extremity of the upper jaw of a young Piked Whale (*Balaenoptera acuto-rostrata*) showing the arrangement of the baleen plates in longitudinal series along each margin of the palate, at right angles to its long axis.

The apices of the plates have been removed to show their serpentine curve in the transverse plane and the hair fringing their mesial borders.   Each plate is broken up towards the mesial line of the palate into several platelets of diminishing size.

Fossil Reptiles

There were originally 351 Hunterian specimens of Fossil Reptiles and Fish; of these only three remain.   The numbers refer to the *Catalogue of Fossil Reptiles and Fish*, prepared by Richard Owen in 1854.

297   The cranium, with portions of the carapace and plastron, and some of the bones of the extremities, of the Long-headed Turtle (*Chelone longiceps*): (*Eachelys camperi*).

The skull of this extinct Turtle differs from those of existing Chelones by the regular tapering of its fore-part into a prolonged, pointed muzzle; but the proportions and relations of the cranial bones prove the marine character of the present fossil.

The orbits are large; the temporal fossae are covered principally by the posterior frontals; and the osseous shield completed by the parietals and mastoids overhangs the tympanic, exoccipital, and paraoccipital bones.   The compressed

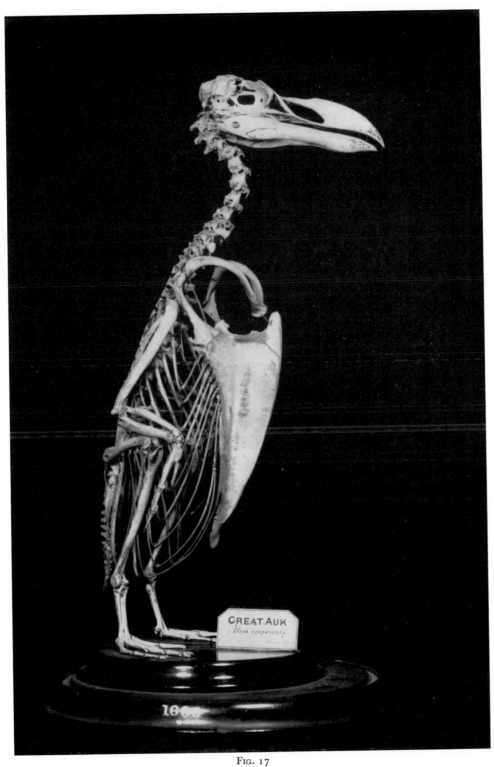

FIG. 17

The skeleton of the Great Auk (*Alca impennis*). *Comparative Osteology.*
Specimen No. 1605, p. 210.

spine of the occiput is the only part that projects further backwards. The palatal and nasal regions of the skull afford further evidence of the affinities of the present Sheppey Chelonite to the true turtles. The bony palate even presents, in a greater degree, the extent from the intermaxillary bones to the posterior nasal aperture which characterises the genus *Chelone*; and it is not perforated, as in the soft turtles (*Trionyae*), by an anterior palatal foramen. The extent of the bony palate is relatively greater than in the *Chelone mydas*, and the trenchant alveolar ridge is less deep; the groove for the reception of that of the lower jaw is shallower than in the *Chelone mydas* or the extinct *Chelone breviceps* (No. 299), arising from the absence of the internal alveolar ridge, in which respect the *Chelone longiceps* resembles the *Chelone caretta*.

The *Chelone longiceps* is distinguished from all known existing *Chelones* by the proximity of the palatal vomer to the basisphenoid, and by the depth of the groove of the pterygoid bones, and in both these characters in a still greater degree from the Trionyxes; to which, however, it approached in the elongated and pointed form of the muzzle, and the trenchant character of the alveolar margin of the jaws.

The parts of the same skeleton, preserved with the skull and cemented together by the petrified clay, are two of the middle neural plates, and the corresponding costal plates of the right side, portions of vertebrae, with the right xiphisternal piece, the humerus and femur.

The neural plates in this specimen are flat and smooth; the entire one measures one inch, two lines in length, and nine lines across its broad anterior part: this receives the convex posterior extremity of the preceding plate in a corresponding notch. A small proportion, about one-sixth, of the anterior part of the external margin joins the second costal plate; the remaining five-sixths of the outer margin form the suture for the vertebral end of the third costal plate. In this respect the *Chelone longiceps* resembles the existing Chelones. The length of the third costal plate, in the fragmentary example here preserved, is three inches; the impression of the commencement of the narrow portion, formed by the extremity of the coalesced rib, is preserved. The marginal indentations of the vertebral scutes are not half a line in breadth. The transverse impression between the first and second vertebral scutes crosses the first neural plate, nine lines from its posterior extremity; the second neural plate is free, as in other *Chelones*, from any impression, being wholly covered by the second vertebral scute.

The expanded ribs are convex at the under part, slightly concave at the upper part in the direction of the axis of the shell; they slope very gently from the plane of the neural plates, about half an inch, for example, in an extent of three inches;

thus indicating a very depressed form of carapace. The xiphisternal bone is relatively broader than in the existing turtles, and both the internal and external margins of its posterior half are slightly toothed. A part of the notch by which it was attached to the hyposternal remains upon the broken anterior extremity of the bone. It measures one inch, two lines across its broadest part; its length seems to have been three inches and a half.

The humerus presents the usual characters of that of the *Chelones*; its length is two inches, three lines; its breadth across the large tuberosities ten lines. The radius and ulna extend in this Chelonite from beneath the carapace into the right orbit; the radius is one inch and a half in length; the ulna one inch, three lines in length; portions of vertebrae adhere also to the mass, the state of which indicates that the animal had been buried in the clay before the parts of the skeleton had been wholly disarticulated by putrefaction.

From the eocene deposits of the Isle of Sheppey, Kent.

299   An almost entire skull of the Short-headed Turtle (*Chelone breviceps*): (*Argillochelys antiqua*).

In general form the skull of the present species of extinct turtle from Sheppey resembles that of the *Chelone mydas* more than the other fossil turtles do from the same locality. But the cranium of the *Chelone breviceps* is relatively broader: the prefrontals are less sloping, and the anterior part of the head is more vertically truncate. The orbits are relatively larger and extend nearer to the tympanic cavity. The frontals enter into the formation of the orbit in rather a larger proportion than in *Chelone mydas*. In the *Chelone caouanna* they are wholly excluded from the orbits. The trefoil shape of the occipital tubercle is well marked: the depression in the basi-occipital bounded by the angular pterygoid ridges is as deep as in most true turtles: the lateral borders of the expanded parietals are united by a straight suture along a great proportion of their extent to the large postfrontals.

These proportions are reversed in the *Podocnemys expansa*, in which the similarly expanded plate of the parietals is chiefly united laterally with the squamosal and tympanic bones. In other freshwater tortoises the parietal plate in question does not exist.

The same evidence of the affinity of the present Sheppey Chelonite in question to the marine turtles is afforded by the base of the skull: the basi-occipital is deeply excavated: the processes of the pterygoids, which extend to the tympanic pedicles, are hollowed out lengthwise: the palatal processes of the maxillary and palatine bones are continued backwards to the extent which characterises the existing *Chelones*; and the posterior or internal opening of the nasal passages is, in a proportional degree, carried further back in the mouth. The lower opening of the zygomatic spaces is wider in the present Sheppey Chelonite than in the *Podocnemys expansa*.

The external surface of the cranial bones in the fossil is roughened by irregular ridges, depressions, and vascular foramina, which give it a wrinkled or shagreen-like character. The lower jaw, which is preserved in the present fossil, likewise exhibits two characters of the marine turtles: the dentary piece, e.g. forms a larger proportion of the lower jaw than in the land or freshwater tortoises. The joint of the rami is completely obliterated at the symphysis, which is not longer or larger than in *Chelone mydas*.

From the eocene tertiary clay of the Isle of Sheppey, Kent.

308 A block of the Kupferschiefer, of the Zechstein formation, from the mines near Eisenach, Germany, containing part of the skeleton, and the impression of the skeleton of the *Protorosaurus speneri*.

The vertebral column is bent, so that the skull touches the base of the tail; the cervical vertebrae are remarkably large and powerful, and near them are preserved some slender intermuscular ossicles. The vertebrae at the base of the tail have long and simple compressed spines: these processes, after the tenth caudal vertebra, begin to expand at their summits, then to show a notch in the expanded summit, which deepens until it divides the spine into two distinct diverging processes.

This specimen has a very interesting history. The first mention of it appears in an article published in the year 1710 in a German journal, *Miscellanea Berolinensis* (Vol. 1, Part 2, Article 3, pp. 99-118). The author was Christian Maximilian Spener (1678-1714), a physician who had amassed a fine collection of curiosities. The specimen came into his possession through his brother, Professor of Mathematics and Physics at Halle, who had it from a friend, Mr Michaelis, Inspector of Mines in Thuringia, where the fossil was first discovered. When Spener died in 1714 his collection was sold and this item was purchased by John Woodward (1665-1728), geologist and physician, author of *The Natural History of the Earth*, a book which aroused much speculation and criticism. He too had a magnificent collection of minerals, fossils and shells, both English and foreign. The greater part of the English fossil collection was bequeathed by him to the University of Cambridge, together with a sum of money for the endowment of a Professorship in Geology. The foreign collection was sold. This particular item was bought by George Humphreys, a dealer in objects of Natural History, whose place of business was in St. Martin's Lane, just opposite to Old Slaughter's Coffee House, where John Hunter was a regular visitor.

Humphreys had a sale of some of his stock in 1779 and possibly Hunter bought this specimen then.

Spener himself thought that the animal was a crocodile; the title of his paper describing it is 'Disquisitio de Crocodilo in Lapide'. What puzzled him was that an animal native to the Nile valley should have been carried by the Flood all the way to Thuringia. John Woodward considered that water had played a very important part in the formation of the various strata of the earth's crust. Much of what is now dry land had formerly been submerged and this submersion he assumed to be the Flood of Noah. To account for the geological phenomena resulting from such a short immersion, he attributed to the waters of the Flood extraordinary powers of being able to dissolve rocks so that foreign bodies could be introduced, such as shells and the animals that had been overcome, which then became petrified.

Baron Cuvier (1769-1832), the great French naturalist, discussed this specimen in his *Ossemens Fossiles* (4th edition, 1836, Vol. X, p. 103) and was quite convinced that it is not a *crocodile* but a *monitor lizard*, many of which reach a length of three feet, the estimated size of this fossil animal.

More recently, in 1887, Harry Govier Seeley (1839-1909), geologist and palaeontologist, Professor of Geography at King's College, London, wrote a series of papers in the *Philosophical Transactions* on the subject of Fossil Reptiles. Of this fossil he states the opinion of Hermann von Meyer, who had decided that it was neither a crocodile nor a monitor lizard, but an extinct type differing from the Saurians. It was von Meyer who named it in 1832 *Protorosaurus Speneri* (*Palaeologica*, 1832, pp. 109, 208). He had never seen this specimen but drew his conclusions from illustrations. Richard Owen adopted the name in his *Odontography* (1840-1845, Text p. 268) but does not mention this Hunterian specimen. He suggested that the animal belonged to the Order Thecodontia (with teeth inserted into sockets) and was more nearly related to the Dinosaurs. Professor Seeley himself concluded that *Protorosaurus* had no close relationship with any living animals and that von Meyer was fully justified in regarding it as the type of a distinct Order of Reptiles. We do not know what John Hunter thought of it. The specimen was X-rayed in 1967 by the Department of Dental Science and the results show that what in Spener's illustration is indicated as the upper half of the jaw is in fact the cervical vertebrae bent back after a fracture of the backbone.

IV

Teeth and Jaws

THE ANATOMY OF THE HUMAN TEETH

Unless otherwise stated the plates mentioned are from Hunter's *Natural History of the Human Teeth.*

T27   The right superior maxillary bone of a Woman, injected, with some of the teeth, which have been deprived by means of acid of their earthy constituents, dried and afterwards preserved in oil of turpentine. (This specimen has since been preserved in alcohol. It is not described in the *Physiological Catalogue*, 1833.)

T28   A portion of the Human superior maxillary bone with the teeth, which, after having had their earthy constituents removed by an acid, have been dissected to show the pulp-cavities of the teeth, on the right side, and preserved in spirits. Illustrated in *John Hunter and Odontology*, Fig. 40, p. 57. (This specimen is not described in the *Physiological Catalogue*, 1833.)

T50   One side of the lower and of the upper jaw, of a foetus about three or four months old.   (*Osteological Catalogue* 5836)

T51   The left halves of the upper and lower jaws of a foetus of seven months, showing the development of the inner wall to an equality with the outer wall of the alveoli, and the more or less completed partitions of the sockets of the incisors and canines.   (5837)

T52   The left halves of the upper and lower jaws of a foetus of eight months, showing the more nearly completed sockets: a large vacuity still remains in the partition between those of the two molars.   (5838)

T53   The right ramus of the lower jaw of apparently the same foetus. The calcified germs of the two incisors and the canine are displayed *in situ*.   (5839)

T54   The lower jaw of a new-born infant, or foetus of nine months.
       The two mid-incisors have cut the gum; the crowns of the outer incisor,

canine, milk-molars, and first true molar, may be seen through the openings of the formative sockets, which openings are contracted above the molars. (5840)

T55   The left ramus of the lower jaw of a new-born infant, or foetus of nine months.
        The mid-incisor has cut the gum: the crowns of the outer incisor, canine, milk-molars and first true molar are exposed by the removal of the outer alveolar wall: the calcified summits of the permanent incisors and canine are exposed by the removal of the inner alveolar wall. The dried remains of the gum remain above the formative alveoli of the undeveloped teeth.   (5841)

T56   Part of the right upper jaw of a new-born infant. The mid-incisor is beginning to cut the gum: the crowns of the outer incisors, canine, two milk-molars and the calcified summit of the first true molar and of the permanent mid-incisor, are exposed by removal of the inner wall of the alveoli.   (5842)

T57   The maxillae of an infant probably about one year old.
        In the left upper jaw the mid-incisor, and apparently the second incisor, which is lost, have cut the gum: the crowns of the canine and milk-molars are seen in the formative sockets. The formative sockets of the permanent incisors are shown, and also that of a canine, or supernumary tooth, behind them, with the calcified germ of the tooth in an inverted position, the point being directed upwards against the bony palate, and the pulp-cavity opening towards the gum. The maxillo-premaxillary suture remains on the palate and on the inner surface of the nasal passage.
        In the right upper jaw the two incisors have cut the gum. The germ of a corresponding canine, or super-numerary tooth, is shown in a similar inverted position.

    Hunter refers to this specimen on page 115 of the *Natural History of the Human Teeth* as follows:

        'We often meet with supernumerary teeth, and this, as well as some other variations, happens oftener in the upper than in the lower jaw, and, I believe always in the incisores and cuspidati. I have only met with one instance of this sort, and it was in the upper jaw of a child about nine months old; there were the bodies of two teeth, in shape like the cuspidati, placed directly behind the bodies of the two first permanent incisores; so that there were three teeth in a row, placed behind one another, viz. the temporary incisor, the body of the permanent incisor, and that supernumerary tooth. The most remarkable circumstance was, that these supernumerary teeth were inverted, their points being turned upwards, and bended by the bone which was above them not giving way to their growth, as the alveolar process does.'

(5843 and 5844)
Works, vol. ii, p. 51.

T58   A section of the right upper jaw of a young infant. The two incisors have cut the gum: the crowns of the canine, milk-molars and first true molars are exposed by the removal of the outer alveolar wall, and the germs of the permanent incisors by the removal of the inner alveolar wall.   (5845)

T59   The left upper maxillary bone of a Child. The two milk-molars are in place; the canine has been removed from its socket, and the premaxillary part of the jaw removed to expose the germ of the permanent canine in the formative socket. The germs of the first bicuspid and first true molar are similarly exposed from the inner side. The crowns of an incisor and canine are separately displayed.

(5847)

T60   A section of the right upper maxillary bone of a Child.

The two milk-molars are in place. The deciduous incisors and canine have been removed: behind their sockets the calcified summits of the permanent incisors may be seen through the wide gubernacular openings. The crown of the first true molar may be seen in its formative socket.   (5848)

T61   The left maxillary and left ramus of the mandible of a Child, in which the deciduous teeth had been acquired and the first true molar was beginning to rise into place, being more advanced in the lower than the upper jaw.

The germs of the successional teeth and of the second true molars are exposed by the removal of the outer walls of their formative alveoli.

These preparations are figured (reversed) in Plate IX, Fig. 1 of Hunter's *Natural History of the Human Teeth*, with the following description:

'One side of the Upper and Lower-Jaw of a subject about eight or nine years of age, where the Incisores and Cuspidati of the Foetus were shed, and their successors rising in new sockets; shewing likewise the two Grinders of the child, with the Bicuspides forming underneath. The first adult Grinder was ready to cut the gum; and the Second Grinder in the Lower-Jaw is lodged in the root of the coronoid process, and in the Upper-Jaw it is in the tubercle.'

(5849)
Works, Plate VI, Fig. 11.

T62   The left maxilla and the mandible of a child about six years of age. In the maxilla, the second deciduous molar is in position; the outer wall of the alveolar process has been removed to expose the crypts containing the crowns of the permanent incisors, canine and first premolar. The first permanent molar is exposed in its socket, and posterior to this is the crypt of the second permanent molar. In the mandible, the deciduous molars on each side are in position; the crowns of the permanent incisors, canines, and the first premolars have been exposed by the removal of the outer wall of the alveolar process. The widely open sockets of the first permanent molars are well shown and the crypt of the developing second molar. This specimen is depicted in the collection of drawings but does not appear in the *Natural History of the Human Teeth*.   (5850 and 5851)

Drawing Book, vol. i, p. 190.

T63   The right half of the mandible of a child about six years of age. The deciduous series, viz. two incisors, a canine and two molars, are in place: the formative sockets of the successional teeth and of the first and second true molars are exposed from the inner side. The matrices of the second bicuspid and second true molar had not begun to be calcified.   (5852)

T64   Four lower jaws, at different periods of life, from the age when the five shedding teeth are completely formed, to that of a complete set.
          These specimens show:
    1.   The lengthening of the jaw backwards, which is seen by the oblique line made by the four condyles.
    2.   The gradual rise of the two processes above the line of the teeth.
    3.   The gradual increase of the teeth in proportion as the jaw lengthens.
    4.   The part formed, always keeping the same size.
                                                                    (5853)

          The following three specimens are mounted together:

T65   The calcified summits of the crowns of the deciduous teeth, viz., two incisors, canine, and two molars, 'from one side of both jaws, of a foetus of seven or eight months, showing the progress of ossification'. This is greatest in the first incisor and decreases to the last molar.   (5868)

T66   The calcified portions of the crowns of the deciduous teeth, from one side of both jaws, of a foetus of the ninth month.   (5869)

T67   The deciduous mid-incisors, canines, and molars, with the calcified summits of the

crowns of the permanent second incisors, and first molars, from one side of both
jaws, of a child eight or nine months old.   (5870)

These specimens are included in Fig. 6, Pl. IX, and described as 'the five temporary
teeth in a more advanced state, with the first adult grinder. The adult incisors and one
cuspidatus are also begun to be formed:' but by a printer's error "years" is given for
"months" in the description of the plate. In the text the specimens are rightly ascribed
to an infant of eight or nine months.

T68   The teeth of one side of both jaws, from a child of five or six years of age.
        The deciduous incisors are completed and the crowns of their successors
      formed. The fang of the deciduous canine is not quite complete, and the crown
      of the successor is about half-formed. The fangs of the first milk-molars are
      nearly completed, and the summit of the first upper premolar has begun to be
      calcified. The fangs of the second milk-molar are half-formed and widely open:
      the second premolar has not begun to be calcified. The crown of the first true
      molar is more than half-formed.   (5862)

T69   The teeth of one side of both jaws, from a child of seven years of age.
        The fang of the first deciduous incisor is partially absorbed, more in the upper
      than the lower tooth: part of the fang of the succeeding incisor is formed. Of
      the second incisor a smaller proportion of the fang of the deciduous tooth is
      absorbed, and that of the permanent one is developed. The whole of the
      deciduous canine, and of the crown of the permanent one, are completed. The
      fangs of the upper milk-molars are more absorbed than those of the lower ones,
      and the crowns of the upper premolars are proportionally more advanced. The
      whole of the crown with the beginning of the root of the first true molar is now
      formed.
        In the description of Fig. 2, Pl. X, Hunter remarks: 'This is an age in which
      there are more teeth formed and forming than at any other time of life:—forty-
      four in whole.'   (5863)

T70   The teeth from one side of both jaws of a Child eight or nine years old, principally
      to show the progress of the second set and the beginning and decay of the first
      set.
        The first deciduous incisor of the lower jaw has been shed, and the crowns of
      the second permanent molars have been formed. The fangs of the first true
      molars are more lengthened and those of the milk-molars more absorbed. (5864)

T71   The teeth from one side of both jaws of a youth about eleven or twelve years old, showing the further progress of the one set towards perfection, and of the other towards decay.

The deciduous incisors and canines have been shed, and the permanent ones have cut the gum. The fang of the canine is not yet complete. The second incisors have not been preserved in this series. The first upper pre-molar has come into place and has pushed out its predecessor: the first lower milk-molar and the second in both jaws remain, with their fangs much absorbed. Only the base of the fangs of the premolars is formed: the first true molars have the fangs nearly complete: the enamel seems to have been dissolved away from the summit of the crown by an acid. The crown of the second true molar is complete: that of the third, or 'dens sapientiae' is only beginning to be calcified.   (5865)

T72   The teeth from a child about eleven to twelve years of age. In this specimen the four deciduous molars have not been shed but the formation of the permanent molars is more advanced than in the preceding specimen. The canines, the mandibular second incisors and the first molars show slight hypoplasia of the enamel.   (5866)

T73   The teeth from one side of both jaws of a youth about eighteen years old.

The roots of all the teeth are fully formed, with the exception of the third molars.   (5867)

T74   A set of permanent teeth. The maxillary third molar has four roots.   (5857)

T75   Portion of a cranium and mandible containing a complete set of permanent teeth with the exception of the mandibular left third molar (lost post mortem). (5833)

T76   A section of the human skull, including the left halves of the upper and lower jaws, from which the outer walls of the alveoli have been removed.

The first molar above is implanted by three roots, the second molar above and the first below by two roots, one external to the other in the former, one behind the other in the latter: in the other molars the fangs are connate. A small osseous excrescence projects from the inner alveolar wall of the third molar of the upper jaw.   (5834)

T77   Eight specimens of permanent incisors at different stages of development. Some of these teeth form the subject of Fig. 3, Pl. XIII, where they are described as 'showing the gradual growth of a single tooth, from its first formation nearly, to its being almost complete'.

T78 A section of the lower jaw of a child.

It shows the mid-incisor and first milk-molar, and the sockets of the intervening outer incisor and canine, from which the teeth have been removed. The formative alveoli of the permanent mid-incisor and of the first bicuspid are also shown.

Two illustrations of this specimen (Figs. 2 and 3, Pl. IX) are given by Hunter. The descriptions are:

'Part of the Lower-Jaw cut through at the symphysis. The Incisor of the child is standing in its socket, and the adult Incisor forming in a distinct socket underneath.'

'Another view of the same piece of the Jaw, to show that the Bicuspides are formed in distinct sockets of their own, and not in the socket of the Grinder which stands above.' (5846)

T79 Six specimens of the first true molar of the lower jaw and five specimens of the first true molar of the upper jaw.

These teeth are shown in Hunter's Fig. 1, Pl. XIII. In the illustration there are drawings of thirteen teeth. The mandibular teeth are shown in the upper row: A is 'the common cavity in the body of the tooth'; B 'shows the cavity still deeper'; C 'shows the bony arch thrown over the mouth of the cavity, and dividing that into two openings, which give origin to the two fangs'; D, E, F 'show the progress of these fangs'.

The maxillary teeth are in the lower row: G 'shows the common cavity of the tooth'; H 'shows the slight tucking in of the mouth of the cavity, at three different points, from which three ossifications shoot'; I 'shows these ossifications, and the beginnings of three fangs'; H, L 'show the gradual growth of these fangs'. (5874, 5875)

T80 These specimens form the subject of Hunter's Fig. 2, Pl. XIII. The illustration is
T81 described as follows: 'Is a comparative view of the Incisors and Grinders of the child and adult; for the better understanding of which they are sawed down the middle, showing in a side view the gradual increase of these Teeth. The uppermost row is of the child, the lower of the adult.'

One of the teeth has been lost. (5871, 5872)

T82   Longitudinal and transverse sections of Human permanent teeth.

These specimens form the subject of Hunter's Plate XIV, Figs. I to XI. The descriptions are as follows:

'Figs. I, II, III, IV, V and VI. Shew the cavities of the Teeth in the Incisores, Cuspidatus, Bicuspidatus, and Molares.

'Fig. VII. A Molaris of the Lower-Jaw, with parts of its fangs sawed off, to show that the sides of the cavity or canal have grown together, and divided it into two small canals.

'Figs. VIII and IX. The cavity in the body of the Teeth seen in transverse sections.

'Figs. X and XI. Longitudinal sections of the Molares to expose the cavities.' (5860)

T83   Six of these teeth are shown in Hunter's Fig. 2, Pl. XV. The description is: 'A Series of Grinders of the Child, from their being complete to their utmost decay.'

T83a   Six of these specimens are shown in Hunter's Fig. 3, Pl. XV. The description is: 'A series of Incisores in the same state.' (5861)

T84   A series of specimens to show the fibrous structure of enamel, prepared by slitting the root and then fracturing the crown. The reference in the text on page 33 of *The Natural History of the Human Teeth* is: 'When it (the enamel) is broken it appears fibrous or striated; and all the fibres or striae are directed from the circumference to the centre of the Tooth.' (5859)

T85   Teeth prepared to show the relation of the enamel to the dentine. Several of the teeth have been subjected to heat to demonstrate the difference in composition of the enamel and the dentine.

Referring to the enamel, Hunter says:

'It would seem to be an earth united with a portion of animal substance, as it is not reducible to quick lime by fire, till it has first been dissolved in an acid. When a Tooth is put into a weak acid, the enamel, to appearance, is not hurt; but on touching it with the fingers, it crumbles down into a white pulp. The Enamel of Teeth, exposed to any degree of heat, does not turn to lime: it contains animal mucilaginous matter; for when exposed to the fire, it becomes very brittle, cracks, grows black, and separates from the inclosed bony part of the Tooth. It is capable, however, of bearing a greater degree of heat than the bony part, without becoming brittle and black.'

In a footnote he remarks:

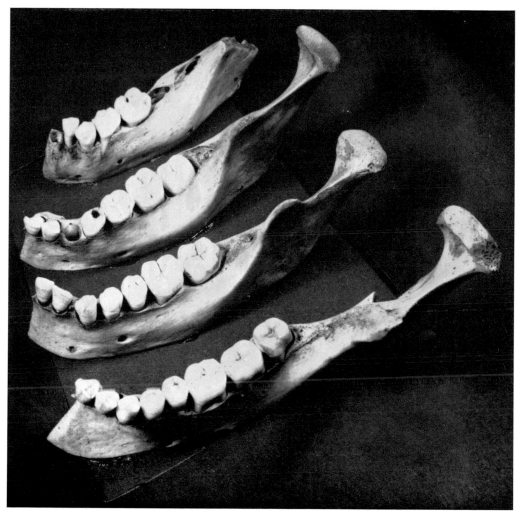

FIG. 18

Four lower jaws at different periods of life.   Specimen No. T 64.

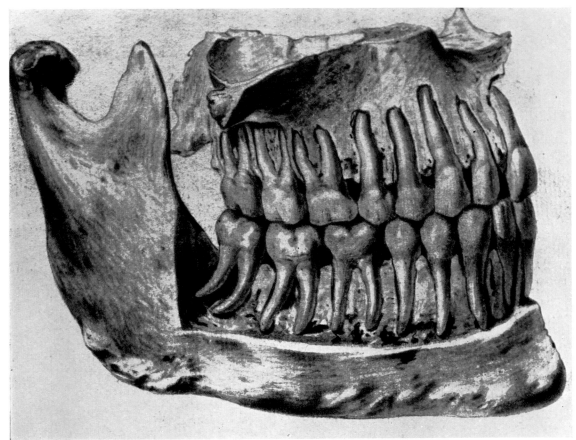

FIG. 19

Jan van Rymsdyck's illustration of Specimen No. T 76 which shows upper and lower jaws from which the outer walls of the alveoli have been removed. (Hunterian Drawing Book II, p. 188.)

'From this circumstance we can shew the Enamel better by burning a Tooth, as the bony part becomes black sooner than the Enamel. The method of burning, and shewing them after they are burnt, is as follows.—Let one half of a Tooth be filed away, from one end to the other, then burn gently in the fire; after this is done, wash the filed surface with an acid, or scrape with a knife. By this method you will clean the edge of the Enamel, which will remain white, and the bony part will be found black.'

This preparation was damaged by climatic conditions during the dispersal of the collection. The molar tooth of the Horse was split into several pieces.

(5858)

T86 The anterior part of a mandible containing the incisors, canines, and premolars. The teeth are much worn by attrition. Hunter's reference to this condition is as follows:

'A Tooth very often wears down so low, that its cavity would be exposed, if no other alteration were produced in it. To prevent this, nature has taken care that the bottom part of the cavity should be filled up by new matter, in proportion as the surface of the Teeth is worn down. This new matter may be easily known from the old; for when a Tooth has been worn down almost to the neck, a spot may always be seen in the middle, which is more transparent, and at the same time of a darker colour (occasioned, in some measure, by the dark cavity under it) and is generally softer than the other.'   (5856)

Natural History of the Human Teeth, p. 108.

T87 Three teeth showing the formation of secondary dentine:

A. A longitudinal section of a canine showing the formation of secondary dentine in the coronal portion.

B. 'An old Tooth, whose basis has been worn down below the original termination of the cavity in the body of the Tooth, and that end has been filled up, in the same proportion, with new matter, to prevent the cavity being exposed. This matter is of a darker colour, as represented in the figure.'

C. 'Another Tooth in the same state'. (Hunter's Figs. XXIV and XXV, Pl. XIV).

SPECIMENS ILLUSTRATING PATHOLOGICAL CONDITIONS OF THE TEETH IN MAN AND ANIMALS

Some of these specimens were included in the revised Pathology Catalogue of 1884. Similar specimens can be found in the *Catalogue of the Pathological Series* (1967) in the series P395-P401.

T90   This specimen is the subject of Fig. 8, Pl. VI and is described as 'A sketch of an Upper-Jaw where the Cuspidatus of that side had been formed high up in the Jaw, and, therefore, never would appear through the Gum.'   Illustrated in *John Hunter and Odontology*, Fig. 120, p. 132.   (5855)

T115 Section of the tusk of an Elephant, in which a leaden bullet is embedded.   The ivory around it has not a natural appearance but is closely united to the adjacent healthy ivory.   The section has cut through an abscess cavity; a portion of the bullet can be seen projecting into the cavity.   Illustrated in *John Hunter and Odontology*, Fig. 151, p. 199.

T116 Sections of the tusk of an Elephant, close by the surface of which an iron bullet is embedded.

T117 Section of the tusk of an Elephant in which an iron bullet is embedded.   Illustrated in *John Hunter and Odontology*, Fig. 152, p. 200.

T118 A portion of the tusk of an Elephant in which an iron bullet and a fragment of metal are embedded.

T119 A portion of the tusk of an Elephant in which an iron bullet is embedded.

T120 A portion of the tusk of an Elephant in which an iron bullet is embedded.

T120.1 A portion of the tusk of an Elephant which has been injured.   The position of the entry of the bullet is seen on the exterior of the tusk and the position the bullet occupied in the tusk by the rough depression on the cut transverse section. The vertical sections show that the pulp injured by the bullet has been replaced by an irregular osteo-dentine in which can be traced splinters of dentine from the original wall of the tusk.

    This is probably the specimen described in the MS. Catalogue and numbered 598.   The description is as follows: 'A portion of the Tusk of an Elephant in which an iron bullet has been received, and afterwards enclosed by new formed ivory, different Sections.'

T121 A section of the tusk of an Elephant, exhibiting a projection of imperfectly formed ivory at one part of the pulp cavity.

T122 A section of the tusk of an Elephant, wounded by a bullet which passed through one of the walls of that part of the tusk which was within the alveolar process, and was found in it nearly opposite the part at which the ball entered. The hole at which the ball entered the outer surface of the tusk is smoothly closed with new dentine; and on the interior of the pulp cavity, where the missile entered, there is a large irregularly knobbed projecting mass of new ivory. Illustrated in *John Hunter and Odontology*, Fig. 153, p. 200.

T123 Specimens of secondary dentine from the pulp cavity of an Elephant's tusk. These specimens are described in the MS. Catalogue as follows: 'Five various excrescences formed within the cavity for the Pulp, in the Tusk of an Elephant.' Illustrated in *John Hunter and Odontology*, Fig. 154, p. 201.

T124 A mass of secondary dentine found within the pulp cavity of the tusk of an Elephant. It has a nearly cylindrical form, pointed at its two extremities: it measures exactly five inches in length, and an inch and a half in diameter: on its surface there are several small nodules, irregularly scattered, but it is everywhere so smooth that it could not have been adherent to the walls of the pulp cavity. Illustrated in *John Hunter and Odontology*, Fig. 155, p. 202.

T125 A section from the base of the tusk of a Walrus, with nodules of secondary dentine in the pulp cavity.

T126 A section from the base of the tusk of a Walrus, in which the distal portion of the pulp cavity is filled with secondary dentine.

T135 The maxillae and mandible of a child about seven years of age; the deciduous dentition and the permanent first molars are in place.
      This specimen was prepared for John Hunter by his pupil William Lynn, afterwards President of the Royal College of Surgeons.   (5835)

T136 The left maxilla and left half of the mandible of an adult in which the roots of the teeth have been exposed by removing the outer alveolar plate. Brookes' Museum.   (5834)

T137 A Human molar longitudinally bisected. Presented by Everard Home.   (5876)

V

Dried Preparations

The only other printed catalogue of dried preparations was prepared in 1831 and consists of little more than a list of the specimens.   It was probably the work of William Home Clift.

33   The heart of a foetus, injected and dried, showing the ductus arteriosus.

94   The root of the aorta of a young Elephant, distended with air and dried to show the three semi-lunar valves that guard its exit from the heart and the sinus of Valsalva above each valve.

100   The mesenteric arteries and veins of a Boar (*Sus scrofa*), injected with wax and dried

113   The descending aorta of a Camel from the diaphragm to its division into the common iliac trunks, with its main branches, injected with wax and dried.
    A separate injection had been introduced into a longitudinally disposed plexus of lymphatic trunks lying upon the surface of the aorta and into some of the lacteals within the mesenteries, but the differentiation of the two systems is now difficult to see.

125   The heart of an Ox (*Bos taurus*), injected and dried.
    The ventricular mass is long and very acutely pointed, the apex being formed by the left ventricle alone.
    The auricula of the right atrium is a simple blunt lobe not superficially separated from the main chamber, the left auricula is very large.
    The aorta at a short distance from its origin divides into two equal trunks, one (the innominate) ascending to give off the carotid and subclavian arteries, the other forming the aortic arch; the vena azygos is double.

128   The aorta and great veins, with the right atrium, of a Bottle-nose Whale (*Tursiops tursio*) filled with wax and dried.
    This specimen shows that, as in many other Mammals, the left superior cava

is absent and the left jugular is connected by a transverse innominate anastomosis with the superior cava of the right side.

The abdominal segment of the vena cava inferior is of great capacity; anteriorly it receives large factors from the liver; posterior to the entry of the veins from the generative organs it is much reduced in size and is double.

129 The heart and lungs of a Porpoise (*Phocaena communis*) injected and dried.

The ventricular mass is wide and sharply pointed, in the centre of the apex is a small cleft indicating the division between the extremities of the two ventricles.

The left atrium is exceptionally large.

133 A portion of the aorta of a Porpoise (*Phocaena communis*) injected and dried, showing the thoracic rete in connection with the intercostal vessels.

134 The aorta, vena cava interior, and thoracic duct of a Porpoise (*Phocaena communis*) injected and dried.

143 The trunk and heart of an Ostrich (*Struthio camelus*), dried. The main blood vessels had been injected with wax of different colours, red in the arteries, yellow in the venae cavae, and green in the afferent renal and mesenteric veins but the colours can no longer be distinguished.

The afferent renal veins arise from factors in the tail region and at the hinder end of the pelvic cavity communicate by a wide channel with the mesenteric vein. Anterior to this anastomosis the veins run forward on the face of the kidneys as far as the femoral veins, connecting at irregular intervals with the factors of the inferior vena cava. Blood from the legs is conveyed directly to the heart by the vena cava inferior.

The arterial vessels shown present no features of particular interest.

144 The head and neck of an Ostrich (*Struthio camelus*), injected to show the arteries and veins.

147 A portion of a vein of an Ostrich, with a lymphatic vessel running upon its surface, injected with quick-silver.

173 The heart and part of the aorta of a Rattle-Snake (*Crotalus*), injected and dried.

177 The head, with the heart and some of the adjacent viscera of a Menopoma (*Menopoma alleghaniense*), injected and dried, showing the relative positions of the

atrium, ventricle, and conus of the heart, and the arterial arches springing from the swollen truncus.

182 The heart of a White Shark (*Squalus carcharias*), injected and dried, to show its form and the distribution upon the ventricle of the coronary arteries.

   At the back of the heart lies the sinus venosus which receives blood from two great venous trunks—the ducts of Cuvier. The chief mass of the heart consists of a large single auricle and a ventricle lying one behind the other, with the auriole cephalad. The anterior part of the ventricle is continued forward in a depression upon the ventral surface of the auricle as a tubular extension—the conus—which leads directly into the ventral aorta by which blood is conducted to the gills through paired lateral branches.

   The coronary arteries have been filled with a yellow injection.

203 The upper part of the trachea, with the larynx and laryngeal sacculus, of a Monkey.

204 A similar specimen.

205 The hyoides, larynx and a portion of the trachea of a Lion (*Felis leo*).

207 The os hyoides, larynx, and trachea, of an Elephant.

220 The bifurcation of the trachea of an Ostrich (*Struthio camelus*).

228 The bony larynx of the common Duck (*Anas boschas*), male.

242 The bony larynx of a Muscovy Duck, male.

250 The bony larynx of a Goosander.

257 The trachea and lungs of a small Crocodile, with the heart and aortae also injected and left attached.

259 The branchial vessels and gills of a Codfish (*Gadus morrhua*).

268 A Human Gall-bladder, with the lymphatic vessels, injected.

284 A portion of the Human ileum, minutely injected.

286   A portion of Human intestine, minutely injected, inflated, and dried. This is in
        very poor condition.

310   The stomach of a Seal (*Phoca vitulina*), inflated and dried.

325   The caecum and colon of a Beaver (*Castor fiber*), injected, inflated and dried.
        The caecum is of enormous proportions, voluminous at the base and gradually
        tapering to a pointed extremity; it is without sacculations.
        The ileum enters its base; and between this point and the head of the colon,
        the gut is sharply constricted.
        The colon is sacculated and gradually diminishes in calibre as it recedes from
        the caecum, increasing again slightly in girth after its second bend. This is in
        very poor condition.

340   Superficial lymphatic vessels of the liver of an Elephant, injected with red wax.

342   A portion of the jejunum of an Elephant, injected, inflated, and dried.

344   A portion of the small intestine of an Elephant, injected and dried; in longitudinal
        section.

348   A small portion of the small intestine of an Elephant, injected, distended, and dried.

351   A piece of the mesentery of an Elephant, injected and dried.

373   Part of the second cavity of the stomach of a Camel, inflated and dried to show the
        water cells.

387   The stomach of a Porpoise, distended with air, dried and varnished, and with its
        cavities opened to show their structure and method of communication.

388   The stomach of a Porpoise prepared in a similar way and with the blood vessels
        injected.

397   Part of the intestinal canal of a Bottle-nose Whale, including the passage of the
        ileum to the colon.
        At the point where these two segments meet, the gut is sharply flexed upon
        itself; there is no caecum.
                        Hunter, 'On the Structure and Oeconomy of Whales', *Works*, vol. iv, p. 360.

398   The bladder of a small Bottle-nose Whale, inflated and dried.

400   A segment of the small intestine and mesentery of a Whalebone Whale with the arteries and lacteals injected.

At some distance from the gut the larger blood vessels unite with one another to form an arcade from which branches are given off, which in turn anastomose before eventually breaking up to supply the intestine.

Between the meshes of this vascular network lie the main trunks of the lacteals.

402   A portion of the small intestine of a Bottle-nose Whale, injected, spread out and dried to show the sacculated structure of its lining membrane.

403   A portion of the intestine, similarly prepared, with the sacculi of the lining membrane widely opened.

407   The caecum of a Whalebone Whale, injected, inflated and dried.

416   A coil of the intestine of an Ostrich (*Struthio camelus*) injected, distended, and dried.

The portion of intestine describes a single spiral coil around its mesenterial border; its surface is marked by narrow transverse and fairly regular indentations.

441   The gall-bladder of a Goose (*Anser ferus*), inflated and dried.

450   Part of the stomach, the pylorus, duodenum, and gall bladder of a small Crocodile: the cystic and hepatic ducts are marked by bristles.

461   The gall-bladder of a Cod-fish (*Gadus morrhua*), inflated and dried.

466   The gall-bladder of a *Tetrodon*, inflated and dried.

471   The gall-bladder and bile duct of a Dog-fish (*Acanthias vulgaris*), injected.

532   The bladder and penis of a Bear, injected and dried. Note the tapering form of the penis, the position of the os penis, and the absence of accessory sexual glands.

540   The os pubis, with the bladder, urethra, penis, rectum, and anal glands of a large Canine animal, probably a Dog, injected and dried, showing the posterior bulb of the glans fully distended.

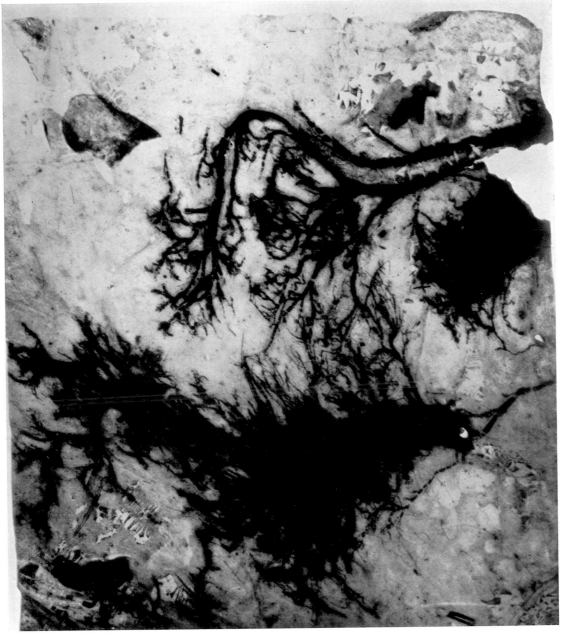

Fig. 20

The superficial lymphatic vessels of the liver of an Elephant.   Specimen No. 340.   Dried Preparations.

542   The penis of a similar animal, with the veins injected with mercury and a section removed from the glans and its posterior bulb and from the bulbus urethrae.

563   The female genitalia and bladder of an Opossum, injected, filled with wax and dried.

572   The distal half of the penis of a Boar, injected and dried.

573   The urethra and root of the penis of a Boar (*Sus scrofa*). The vesiculae seminales and Cowper's glands have been filled with mercury and the penile urethra with a red injection. One seminal vesicle and one Cowper's gland have been cut open to show their structure.

574   The penis of a Boar injected and dried, showing its slender form and great length. Near its base it is thrown into a strong sigmoid flexure, as is the case in many Artiodactyle Ungulates. The apex is spirally twisted and shows no development of spongy tissue to form a glans.
    This specimen and No. 572 are mounted together.

577   The epididymis of a Boar (*Sus scrofa*) injected with mercury, partly unravelled and mounted spirally in a circular frame.

591   The penis of a Bull (*Bos taurus*), injected and dried. The organ is in the position it assumes when withdrawn by the retractor muscles, and is bent by the action of these muscles behind their insertion into an extensive sigmoid curve. The retractor muscles have been retained.

592   The penis of a Bull, injected, dried, and cut across in the middle.
    Note its great length, slenderness, and acutely pointed free extremity, which seems to be without a true glans.

593   Part of the bladder with the urethra and root of the penis of a Bull with the vesicules seminales, and vasa deferentia injected with quick-silver: those of the left side are in section to show their structure.

594   Part of the bladder with the prostatic urethra, seminal vesicles, and ampullae vasa deferentia of a Bull, injected and dried.

599   The spermatic artery of a Bull, injected and corroded.

607   The bladder, urethra, and penis of a Porpoise (*Phocaena communis*), injected and dried.

613   A portion of the corpus spongiosum of a Whale, injected and corroded.

620   A small portion of a Human placenta, and the funis, injected.

623   A Human twin placenta with the vessels of the funis attached, injected.

626   A small portion of a Human placenta, with the umbilical cord, injected and dried. This preparation shows in a striking manner the spiral twist assumed by the blood vessels in the cord.

650   The urinary bladder of a foetal Foal, showing the internal iliac or hypogastric arteries passing forwards and upwards along the sides of the bladder to the funis.

691   The right half of the head of an Eagle dried and with the soft parts to a large extent removed to expose the orbit and show the eyeball and its muscles.

692   The left half of the head of an Eagle, dried. The eyelids have been stretched away from the eye, and the lower lid partly separated and turned down to show the large nictitating membrane extending backwards over the anterior parts of the cornea.

695   The cornea and bony sclerotic ring of the eye of a Great Horned Owl (*Bubo maximus*), dried and varnished.

696   The eye and eyelids of an Emu (*Dromaeus novae-hollandiae*) dried, showing the membrana nictitans with its muscles, the bristle-like feathers that fringe the upper and lower eyelids and the muscles of the eyeball.

701   The eye and a portion of the eyelids of a Ray, dried, showing the six muscles of the eyeball and two muscles attached to the upper eyelid, one to its dorsal part and the other to its outer angle.

703   Part of the left half of the skull of a small Shark with the orbit opened from above to expose the eyeball and its muscles.

VI

Microscope Slides

WILLIAM HEWSON'S PREPARATIONS

This collection of microscopic objects prepared by William Hewson, is stated by William Clift to have been purchased by Hunter at a sale of Hewson's Museum in 1778; the following letters copied from the life of Hunter (*Works*, vol. i, pp. 70, 71) tend to confirm this statement.

August 30th, 1778

'Dear Jenner,

I hope this winter to be able to get you some preparations of the eye and lymphatics; but Hewson's preparations are to be sold this month, now perhaps for four or five pounds some preparations may be picked up. If you have no objection to throw away so much money let me know and what subjects you would like best. I shall give you some commissions about heat, cold &c.

Yours JOHN HUNTER'

Jenner's reply is not preserved but in another letter of Hunter's, bearing the date September 25th, 1778, the following passage occurs:

'If Hewson's things go cheap I will purchase some that I think proper for you; those you mention will, I am afraid, be everybody's money and go dear.

Ever yours. J. HUNTER'

It also appears that these preparations passed after Hewson's death into the hands of his brother-in-law and successor, Magnus Falconar, surgeon and Professor of Anatomy who, like Hewson himself, died at an early age as the result of a wound received in dissection. The Museum formed by these two eminent anatomists was offered for sale in October 1778 and in the Preface to the Sale Catalogue the following passages occur:

'It is well known that the late ingenious Mr. Hewson prepared and collected a great number of anatomical articles; to which his successor Mr. Falconar added everything curious, useful or necessary that came in his way. By the joint labour and ingenuity of these two young anatomists, the Museum, now offered to public sale, was formed, enlarged and extended to its present state.

'It consists of upwards of a thousand articles in Anatomy, Zoology and Natural History; besides which it contains above three hundred choice preparations adapted to the microscope so ingeniously contrived that with little trouble they may be viewed to the greatest advantage; and so effectually preserved that they cannot easily lose their appearance, the wet ones being sealed hermetically.

'Except a small descriptive catalogue of a great part of the microscopical objects by Mr. Hewson, we could find none other; we therefore confess ourselves at a loss to determine what some of the preparations really are; yet we doubt not but that may be easily ascertained upon a closer examination than we could give them.

'It was the wish, and indeed the hope of the administrator that this valuable and useful Museum would have been purchased entire as a national benefit. That it might have been honoured with an apartment in some University Academy or Public School, where anatomy may be in want of such powerful assistance; but failing in his expectation it is now submitted to that Public who will, no doubt, pay due attention to the indefatigable labours of those men who in the pursuit of that invaluable Knowledge by which so many lives have been spared—lost their own.'

The microscopical preparations formed Lot 87 in the tenth evening's sale, thus:

Lot 87. 'An elegant mahogany inlaid cabinet with sixteen drawers, containing about three hundred microscopical objects from curious anatomical preparations, spread upon glasses and enclosed in glass tubes hermetically sealed.'

Probably Hunter may have transferred to Jenner the cabinet and some of the preparations as no such cabinet was ever known by any of the existing officers of the Museum to be present with the Hunterian collection.

William Hewson

b. Hexham, Northumberland, November 14th, 1739
d. Craven Street, London, May 1st, 1774

At the age of 20 Hewson came to London to complete his medical studies and attended classes at Guy's and St Thomas's Hospitals. He was also a pupil of William Hunter and lodged with John Hunter in Covent Garden. At the conclusion of his studies, he became William Hunter's assistant and later his partner, sharing the profits from the Windmill Street School. The association was dissolved in 1772 and Hewson then opened his own Anatomy School in Craven Street, attracting to it a large proportion of Hunter's pupils. His death two years later resulted from a wound received in the dissecting room. The school and museum then passed to his brother-in-law, Magnus Falconar, then only twenty years old, who in turn died four years later. Hewson's collection was then sold.

The preparations are now in a poor condition but are of great historical interest.

Preparations in spirit

2. A portion of the under lip, the internal surface of which displays numerous papillae and the openings of the labial glands, this preparation like the last has been injected slightly with blue injection.

3. A portion of the anterior part of the tongue showing the papillae which are partially injected with blue material; the papillae themselves have their free extremities split up or divided into a number of smaller papillae.

4. A portion of the upper part of the oesophagus showing a few scattered filiform papillae, the vessels of which are likewise filled with blue injection.

5. A portion of the human stomach from near the pylorus; the vessels have been filled with red injection; it exhibits the mucous membrane thrown up into hexagonal folds between which are to be seen the openings of the follicles of Lieberkuhn.

6. The internal surface of the upper part of the ileum showing the wavy divided folds of the mucous membrane, which are hardly enough divided to constitute distinct villi; the vessels have been filled in some parts with red injection, in others there are patches of extravasation.

7. A similar preparation in which the villi are better shown and the vessels more successfully filled with red injection.

8. A similar preparation from the lower part of the ileum in which the villi are few but the openings of the follicles of Lieberkuhn are very evident.

9. A similar preparation from about the middle portion of the ileum showing the villi, the vessels of which have been injected with size and vermilion.

10. The lower part of the ileum of the human subject exhibiting the wavy folds of the mucous membrane, which are not sufficiently divided to constitute villi; the vessels have been partially filled with red injection.

11. A similar preparation.

12. A portion of small intestine showing the villi, the vessels of which have been filled with red injection.

13.
14.
15. } Similar preparations.
16.
17.

18. A portion of the small intestine of a dog displaying the villi; the vessels have been partially filled with red injection.

19. A similar preparation.

20. A portion of the small intestine of an ass showing the villi; the vessels have been partially filled with red injection.

21. A similar preparation displaying part of a patch of Peyer's glands.

22. A portion of the ileum of a Lion showing the long filiform villi peculiar to the small intestine of the carnivora; the vessels have been partially filled with red injection.

23. A portion of the small intestine of a Goose showing the villi, the vessels of which have been partially filled with red injection.

24. Two portions of intestine, apparently of the human subject, placed side by side. One specimen exhibits the villi which are peculiar to the small intestine, the other the abundance of the follicles of Lieberkuhn and the hexagonal arrangement of the vessels around the follicles which is peculiar to the large intestine. This preparation was stated to have been the best of the Hewson collection; it has now deteriorated.

25.   A portion of the human colon, injected with red; it displays numerous follicles of Lieberkuhn around the openings of which the vessels are arranged in a hexagonal manner, which is peculiar to the stomach and large intestine.

26.   A similar preparation, the red injection has become black with age.

27.   A portion of the trachea partially injected red; some of the mucous follicles are to be seen in various parts of the preparation, the vessels present a peculiarly wavy arrangement.

29.   A portion of the upper eyelid of the human subject (probably a foetus). The vessels have been partially filled with red injection. Between the eyelashes and the vascular conjunctival surface may be seen six resinous-looking globules which are situated each in the opening of a Meibomian gland; they are composed of the secretion of the glands, which has become hardened by the spirit in which the preparation is preserved and has been squeezed out of the duct by the contraction of the tissues by the spirit.

30.   A portion of Schneiderian membrane taken from the posterior part of the septum, exhibiting the openings of numerous mucous follicles; the vessels have been sparingly filled with red injection.

31.   A portion of Schneiderian membrane from the anterior part of the nose, the vessels of which have been partially filled with red injection; there are one or two openings of the mucous follicles to be seen and there is a distinct appearance of villi on the surface of the mucous membranes at that end of the preparation which is nearest the number.

32.   A portion of Schneiderian membrane from the septum nasi exhibiting in some parts the openings of the mucous follicles, whilst at the end of the preparation the farthest from the number a few villi are to be seen; the vessels have, as in the preceding preparations, been partially filled with red injection.

34.   A portion of the kidney of a Lion injected red by the arteries; it shows very well the convoluted capillaries which form the so-called Malpighian bodies.

35.   A similar preparation.

42, 43, 44, 46, 47.   Preparations of Kidney.

49. A portion of kidney which has been injected with red by the artery; it shows the Malpighian bodies and the capillary plexus around the tubes.

50. A portion of liver which appears to have been injected with red; it exhibits but a faint trace of lobules.

51. A similar preparation but the injection has been more successful.

52. A similar preparation.

53. A similar preparation; the injection has been very successful.

Mounted Preparations

BRAIN

B1. A portion of the cortical substance of the brain injected red by the arteries, displaying the wavy vessels of the cortical substance.

B2-4. Similar preparations.

B5. A section of the brain showing the straight vessels of the medullary substance.

B6 and 7. Similar preparations.

B8. Section of brain displaying the vessels of both tissues, cortical and medullary.

INTESTINE

I1. A vertical section of small intestine injected red by the arteries, displaying the vessels of the filiform villi.

I2-6. Similar preparations.

I7. A portion of large intestine injected red, showing the characteristic hexagonal form of the vessels.

I8. A similar preparation, the arteries injected red, the veins yellow.

I9. A similar preparation.

KIDNEY

K1.   A horizontal section of the cortical surface of the kidney; vessels are injected red by the arteries. The Malpighian bodies and the capillary plexus around the tubes are well displayed in this preparation.

K2 and 3.   Similar preparations.

K4.   A similar preparation displaying straight vessels between the uriniferous tubes.

K5 and 6.   Similar preparations.

K7.   A portion of the cortical substance of a kidney injected red showing the Malpighian bodies.

K8.   A similar preparation, from an animal in which the capillaries are smaller than the preceding.

K9.   A similar preparation, the arteries injected yellow.

LUNG

L1.   Two of the gill laminae of a fish, injected red; a trace of the arrangement of capillaries peculiar to respiratory membranes is to be seen in one part of the preparation.

L2.   A portion of the lung of a reptile showing the cellular character and the characteristic arrangement of the vessels which have been filled with red injection.

EYE

E1.   Portion of the choroid of a Turkey very well injected; it shows the vasa vorticosa and the capillary arrangement on the inner surface.

MUSCLE

M1.   Two longitudinal sections of a muscle, placed diagonally on the glass. The vessel have been filled with red injection. The smallest section is probably one of the voluntary muscular tissues, whilst the larger from the characteristic vessels of fat upon its surface would appear to have been taken from the heart or from some other division of the involuntary class.

M2-8. Portions of voluntary muscles, the vessels filled with red injection.

M9 and M10. Horizontal sections of a Heart showing the ordinary arrangement of the
          vessels of this organ.

M11. Three sections of muscle with tendon attached, showing the difference in the
        arrangement of the vessels supplying these structures.

FOETAL MEMBRANES

G1. A portion of cho ion of a foetal in which both arteries and veins have been filled
      with red injection.

G2 and 3. Similar preparations.

G4. A similar preparation; the vessels have been filled with yellow injection.

G6. A portion of the chorion of some foetal pachydermal animal injected red by the
      arteries; the little circular spots in which Dr. E. described a venous plexus are
      to be seen in different parts of the preparation.

G7. Four villi from one of the placental tufts of the chorion probably of one of the above
      preparations.

G8. Portion of the lining membrane of the uterus of a pachydermal animal showing the
      circular spots analogous to those described in G6. The vessels have been filled
      with red injection.

JOHN THOMAS QUEKETT'S PREPARATIONS

Professor Quekett (1815-1861), the distinguished microscopist, Conservator of the
Hunterian Museum from 1856 in succession to Richard Owen, collected and catalogued
about fifteen thousand histological slides, many of which were prepared from specimens
in the main collections. About half of these have survived time and enemy action and
some can be regarded possibly as Hunterian preparations, in particular those of the bones
of the *Pterodactyl*. In his catalogue, Hunter had included these creatures among the Fossil
Birds: it was not until the early nineteenth century that they were named and recognised
as being Fossil Reptiles.

VII

Miscellaneous Items

Z1 Two chairs of Yorkshire type made for John Hunter with wood brought from Australia by Captain Cook. Circa 1775. These were part of a set of dining-room furniture in the Leicester Square house. They were bought for £40 in 1945 from the widow of Mr. J. H. Watson, F.R.C.S., of Burnley, who had acquired them from Thomas Madden Stone, Clerk to the College from 1853.

Z10 A leather-covered pocket instrument case, stamped 'John Hunter. London' in gold lettering on the flap, containing four instruments, one marked 'J. H.' and the other three 'J. H. London'. The instruments are as follows:
1 fleam, the blade covered by tortoiseshell shields, made by Savigny.
2 curved knives, also from Savigny.
1 small pocket knife (no maker's name).

Z11 A tortoiseshell and silver pocket instrument case bearing an engraved plate on the lid, inscribed 'John Hunter, St. George's, London'. It contains a fleam made by Wood (possibly of Spurrier Gate, York) one of the blades of which is engraved 'John Hunter, Surgeon.'

These two cases were presented to the Hunterian Museum in August 1961 by Mrs. Frances Hunter of Eastbourne. The gift helps to replace the instruments of John Hunter, formerly in the College but destroyed during the bombing of 1941.

Biographical Notes

ALDROVANDI, Ulysses (1522-1605)
Professor of Botany and Natural History at Bologna. In view of his great services to science, his salary was doubled and in return he bequeathed to the city his collections and library. Page 97.

ARISTOTLE (384-322 B.C.)
Philosopher and biologist, a pupil of Plato in the Academy at Athens where he remained for twenty years. For three years he was tutor to Alexander the Great under whose protection he gained a great reputation as a teacher. Page 58.

COLYER, Sir Frank (1866-1954)
Dentist; Honorary Curator of the Odontological Museum at the Royal College of Surgeons; author of *John Hunter and Odontology* and many other works on dental subjects. Pages 217, 226, 227.

CLIFT, William Home (1803-1832)
Son of William Clift; Assistant Conservator of the Hunterian Museum. Page 207.

DE BEER, Sir Gavin R. (1899-   )
Professor of Embryology in University College, London; Director of the British Museum (Natural History); President of the Linnean Society; writer on Comparative Anatomy, Evolution, History of Science etc. Page 96.

GARTHSHORE, Maxwell (1732-1812)
Accoucheur. From 1764 practised with great success in London; generous in friendship and practical assistance to Mrs. Hunter after her husband's death. Page 156.

GRAAF, Regnier de (1641-1673)
Anatomist and Physician of Delft. Pages 112, 113.

GRASSI, Giovanni Battista (1854-1925)
Professor of Zoology in Rome. Page 58.

HALLER, Albrecht von (1708-1777)
First Professor of Anatomy, Physiology, Surgery and Botany in the University of Gottingen. Page 160.

HILL, James Peter (1873-1954)
Professor of Zoology and Embryology in University College, London. Page 96.

HIS, Wilhelm (1831-1904)
Anatomist and Embryologist; Professor of Anatomy and Physiology in Basle and Leipzig. Page 154.

JENNER, Edward (1749-1823) of Berkeley, Gloucestershire
Close friend of John Hunter for more than twenty years; one of the greatest benefactors of mankind, who proved the efficacy of vaccination for protection against smallpox. Pages 173, 174.

KEITH, Sir Arthur (1866-1954)
Conservator of the Hunterian Museum and Master of the Buckston Browne Farm. Page 96.

LANKESTER, Sir Edwin Ray (1847-1929)
Professor of Zoology at University College, London; Linacre Chair of Comparative Anatomy in Oxford; Director of the British Museum (Natural History). Page 58.

LYNN, William (1753-1835)
Assisted John Hunter for twelve years in preparing specimens for the museum; later surgeon at the Westminster Hospital; President of the College in 1825. Page 227.

PATERSON, William (1755-1810)
Traveller; Lieutenant-Governor of New South Wales; made a number of expeditions in the Hottentot country; the one to Caffraria was made in 1778. Page 208.

REDI, Francesco (1626-1698)
Italian physician, naturalist and poet; author of the pioneer work on animal parasites (1684). Page 58.

RETZIUS, Gustav (1842-1919)
Anatomist and neurologist; Professor of Anatomy at the Carolin Institute in Stockholm. Page 154.

WALTON, Isaac (1593-1683)
Traded as an ironmonger; owned part of a shop in Fleet Street, two doors west of Chancery Lane; Royalist during the Civil War and after the Restoration found permanent asylum in the Bishop's Palace in Winchester. *The Compleat Angler* was published in 1653. Page 58.

WHITE, John
Surgeon General to the Settlement of New South Wales. The 'Journal' was published in 1790, edited by Thomas Wilson who acknowledged his debt to those who had assisted in the work, including John Hunter who 'to a sublime and inventive genius happily unites a disinterested and generous zeal for the promotion of natural science'. Pages 16, 177.

Index

246

	Page No.	Specimen No.
Armadillo	101, 166	3479, 3720
Arvicola amphibia	97	3462-5
Arvicola arvensis	183	3790
Ascidia conglomerata	194	X65
Ass	121-4, 161, 238	3546, 3547, 3553, 3554, 3701. Microscope slides: 20, 21
Astacus fluviatilis	52, 182	3185-7, 3782, 3783
Asterias rubens	24	2927
Auk, Great	210	Comparative Osteology: 1605
Babirussa	209	Comparative Osteology: 1820
Babirussa alfurus	209	Comparative Osteology: 1820
Balaena boops	174, 175	3743, 3744
Balaenoptera acuto-rostrata	212, 232	Comparative Osteology: 2445; Dry Preparations: 400, 407
Balistes forcipatus	211	Comparative Osteology (Fish): 328
Barbel	59	3205
Barnacle, Common	24	2929
Barnacle, Vitreous	25	2930
Bat, Fruit	129, 130, 176	3578-81, 3754, 3755
Bean	21, 23	2912-16, 2919-24
Bear	232	Dry Preparations: 532
Beaver	231	Dry Preparations: 325
Bee, Broad-legged Carpenter	191	X38
Bee, Hive	1, 47	3139-42
Bee, Honey	44	3125-42
Bee, Humble	1, 43, 44, 191	3117-23; X39
Bee, Leaf-cutter	42, 43	3110-16
Beetle	37, 192	3065; X42-X45
Beetle, Dung	38	3078, 3079
Beetle, Palm	38, 39	3080-3
Beetle, Rose	37	3070
Beetle, Stag	38, 192	3074-6; X42
Beetle, Water	192	X44
Belostoma grande	49	3161
Blatta americana	49	3162
Blatta dilatata	190	X31
Blatta orientalis	49, 50	3163, 3163A, 3164
Boar	228, 233	Dry Preparations: 100, 572-4, 577
Boltenia reniformis	193	X57
Bombex	40	3092
Bombus terrestris	43, 44, 191	3117-23; X39
Bombyx mori	30-4	2978-3036
Bombyx regalis	192	X47
Bombyx sp.	35, 36	3044, 3047, 3054
Bopyrid	188	X21
Bos taurus	106-9, 112, 158, 159, 165, 166, 176, 207, 228, 233	3499-515, 3528, 3687-91, 3718, 3721, 3751. Comparative Osteology: 1121, 1122, 1144; Dry Preparations: 125, 591, 594, 599

248 INDEX

	Page No.	Specimen No.
Chick	8-16	
Chigoe	51	3173
Cicada	193	X54, X55
Cicada australis	48, 49	3155-9
Cicada septendecim	193	X54
Clupea alosa	59	3212
Cockroach, American	49	3162
Cockroach, Australian	190	X31
Cockroach, Common	49, 50	3163, 3163A, 3164
Cod	59, 230, 232	3210. Dry Preparations: 259, 461
Columba aenas	172	3737-41
Colutaea arborescens	18	2876
Comatula solaris	24	2928
Connochaetes gnu	208	Comparative Osteology: 1411
Coralline, Lobster's Horn	184	X1
Coronula diadema	188	X17, X18
Cotoneaster vulgaris	20	2900
Cottus bubalis	60	3217
Cow	107-9, 112, 158, 159, 176	3502-14, 3528 3687-91, 3751
Crab	53	3190-5
Crab, Hermit	53	3190
Crab, Spider	53	3192
Crangon	52	3184
Crayfish	52, 182	3185-7, 3782, 3783
Cricket, Mole	190	X35
Crocodile	2, 81-3, 230, 232	3364-73. Dry Preparations: 257, 450
Crotalus horridus	75, 229	3314-16. Dry Preparations: 173
Cuckoo	83, 84	3376A, 3376B, 3377
Cuculus canorus	83, 84	3376A, 3376B, 3377
Cucumis melo	20	2901
Culex sp.	29	2967, 2968
Cuttle-fish	27, 28	2953-62
Cyanaea aurita	24	2926
Cymothoë lichtenaultii	52	3183
Cynips rosae	30, 48	2975, 3152
Cyprinus auratus	59	3207, 3208
Cyprinus barbus	59	3205
Cyprinus carpio	59	3206
Dace	59	3209
Dasyprocta agouti	100	3474
Datura stramonium	19	2885
Deer, Fallow	109, 110	3516, 3517
Deer, Red	208	Comparative Osteology: 1498
Deilephila euphorbiae	192	X48
Delphinium pictum	18	2873
Delphinus delphis	168	3728
Delphinus tursio	173, 174	3742
Dichelestium sturionis	188	X19
Dictamnus fraxinella	19	2881

	Page No.	*Specimen No.*
Felis leo	230, 238, 239	Dry Preparations: 205; Microscope Slides: 22, 34, 35
File Fish	211	Comparative Osteology: Fish: 328
Fir, Scotch	20	2902
Fistularia maxima	186	X8
Fly, Breeze-	29	2970, 2971
Fly, Caddis	48	3154
Fly, Flesh-	28, 29	2963-6
Fly, 'Lantern'	193	X56
Fly, Saw-	40	3091
Foal	122, 123, 234	3551, 3552; Dry Preparations: 650
Fowl, Domestic	84-6, 88-90, 93, 94, 96, 97	3378-82, 3389, 3410-20, 2439-44 3459, 3460
Fowl, Polish	210	Comparative Osteology: Birds: 1978
Fraxinella	19	2881
Frog	2, 55, 68-71	3270-3, 3279-85
Frog, Bull-	72	3291, 3292
Frog, Fish-	71, 72	3286-90
Fulgora lanternaria	193	X56
Gadus morrhua	59, 230, 232	3210. Dry Preparations: 259, 461
Gallus domesticus	84-6, 88-90, 93, 94, 96, 97	3378-3382, 3389, 3410-20, 3439-3444, 3459, 3460
Gallus ferrugineus	210	Comparative Osteology: Birds: 1978, 2888
Garlic	20	2888
Gastropacha quercifolia	193	X49
Gecko	77	3332, 3333
Geophilus electricus	190	X30
Geotrupes stercorarius	38	3078, 3079
Giraffa camelopardalis	208	Comparative Osteology: 1438
Giraffe	208	Comparative Osteology: 1438
Gnat	29	2967, 2968
Gnu	208	Comparative Osteology: 1411
Gobias sp.	59	3211
Goby	59	3211
Gold-fish	59	3207, 3208
Goosander	230	Dry Preparations: 250
Goose	7, 8, 85-8, 90-6, 232, 238	3388, 3390-405, 3421-8, 3433, 3438, 3445, 3446, 3449, 3450, 3456-8. Dry Preparations: 441; Microscope Slides: 23
Gorgonia pennata	185	X2
Grapsus sp.	53	3194
Grasshopper, Green	50	3166
Gryllotalpa	190	X35
Gryllus monstrosus	190	X33
Guinea-pig	100	3475
Gymnotus electricus	60	3220-2

	Page No.	Specimen No.
Vespa vulgaris	41, 191	3102, X40
Viper	75	3309-11
Vulture, Pondicherry	210	Comparative Osteology: Birds: 2375
Vulture, Royal	210	Comparative Osteology: Birds: 2375
Wag-tail	183	3788
Walrus	124, 125, 168, 227	3559-61, 3729, T125, T126
Wasp	41, 42, 191	3102, 3108, 3109, X40
Wasp, Mason	42	3107
Whale	174, 175, 212, 228, 231, 232, 234	3743, 3744. Comparative Osteology: 2445; Dry Preparations: 398, 400, 402, 403, 407, 613
Whale, Bottle-nose	228, 231, 232	Dry Preparations: 128, 397, 398, 402, 403
Whale, Piked	174, 175, 212	3743, 3744. Comparative Osteology: 2445
Whale, Whalebone	232	Dry Preparations: 400, 407
Whelk	26	2948
Willow	18, 30, 48	2859, 2974, 3152
Wolf-fish	60, 211	3219. Comparative Osteology: Fish: 305
Worm, Earth-	25	2931
Worm, Lug-	186	XII
Worm, Silk-	30-4	2978-3036
Wrass, Parrot	211	Comparative Osteology: Fish: 122
Xylocopa latipes	191	X38
Zea mays	19	2879
Zoanthus ellisii	185	X4
Zoanthus sociatus	185	X4

R. & R. Clark Ltd., Edinburgh